The Silent Millions

THE
SILENT MILLIONS

A History of the Jews
in the Soviet Union

JOEL CANG

TAPLINGER PUBLISHING COMPANY
NEW YORK

FIRST PUBLISHED IN THE UNITED STATES IN 1970 BY
TAPLINGER PUBLISHING CO., INC.
NEW YORK

COPYRIGHT © 1969 JOEL CANG

LIBRARY OF CONGRESS CATALOG CARD NUMBER 78-107013
SBN 8008-7184-7

PRINTED IN THE UNITED STATES OF AMERICA

CONTENTS

48127

INTRODUCTION

The decision to write on the position of the Jewish minority in the Soviet Union was taken in unusual circumstances and under the impact of a deeply felt experience. It was the result of a unique meeting with a group of Russian Jews on the very rim of Babi Yar', the ravine on the outskirts of Kiev, where in the autumn of 1941 the Germans carried out the biggest single massacre of Jews. During the Khrushchev era my wife and I made a tour of Russia on our own, and the trip included a three-day visit to Kiev, the capital of the Ukrainian Republic. As soon as we arrived in Kiev I asked to be taken to see Babi Yar'. News of the Babi Yar' massacre had reached the world outside while the war was still in progress. It figured prominently on the list of indictments against the Nazi leaders at the Nuremburg trials. Its chief perpetrator Colonel Blobel, head of the Nazi Extermination Commando, was sentenced to death and hanged.

It was natural that on touring the Soviet Union I should wish to visit the place. But when I asked for transport, the official guide from Intourist—the Russian travel agency—gave me a courteous but evasive reply. Repeated requests produced nothing. This only made me more determined in my efforts. Curiosity was further sharpened by the fact that when asked about Babi Yar' several people in the city, including Jews, were reluctant to give me any information. A number of Jews I approached merely shrugged their shoulders, shook their heads and sighed. Some kept silent.

Eventually I came across a Ukrainian taxi-driver who said, 'I'll take you there. Ukrainians and Jews have often suffered together!'

It was a warm autumnal afternoon. Kiev, a beautiful city with majestic views across the Dnieper, looked impressively peaceful. In dismaying contrast Babi Yar' was forsaken and desolate. A melancholy emptiness spread over the grassy ravine cut and

bruised by bare valleys with a few gnarled and twisted shrubs.
Clusters of windswept trees stood brooding over the history of
the place. There was nothing to mark the spot or commemorate
the victims. In my post-war travels I visited several localities
where the Nazis perpetrated atrocities on Jews. In Majdanek, the
camp near Lublin where some of my own relatives and many
friends perished, in Auschwitz, Treblinka and Dachau there were
some marks or monuments, some visible signs to remind posterity.
In Babi Yar' I found nothing. There was not even a flower. A
deadly silence reigned over the whole ravine.

Separated from the spot by a wide ditch about half a mile
long was the old Jewish cemetery of Kiev known as the 'Lukyanovska burial grounds'. (This has since been cleared in accordance
with a new development plan of the city. About ten thousand
bodies were removed to a new burial place further away). I was
still brooding over the scene when I saw a group of people
coming out of the Jewish cemetery. They walked slowly in my
direction and seemed to be led by a tall man leaning heavily
on a stick. He was limping. As they came near I greeted them
in Yiddish, and we all shook hands. It appeared that they had
been visiting the graves of relatives in the cemetery as is usual
during the autumn months before the Jewish New Year. Even in
Communist Russia this custom is still observed.

On learning that I had come from England, they began ques-
tioning me about the position of the Jewish people in Great
Britain. Were they treated in the same way as other citizens?
Was it really true, they asked, that there were some Nazis active
in England? Were the Jews safe, and were they able to practise
their religion undisturbed? Could Jews go to Israel? There was
a moment of silence when I mentioned that I had come specially
to see Babi Yar'. It appeared that some of them too had come
for the purpose of offering a prayer for their dead relatives who
had perished in the massacre. 'Did you know where to pray?'
I asked, 'There is no monument or gravestone.' 'The whole place
is sacred', one of them replied. In the group there were several
Jews whose relatives had been killed in Babi Yar'. One of them
was in the Red Army when the Germans entered Kiev.

The German armies invaded Soviet Russia on 22 June 1941, and Kiev was among the first Russian cities to be bombed by the Nazis. Although German patrols reached the city outskirts early in August, Kiev itself was not occupied until 21 September. The Red Army's resistance delayed the enemy's entrance into the city for forty-four days, giving the Russians an opportunity to evacuate important industrial establishments, and thousands of people including some Jews. But having signed a pact with Hitler, Stalin ordered the Soviet Press not to publish reports of Nazi atrocities against the Jews. As a result the Jews were unaware of the fate that was awaiting them, and did not make any special effort to escape. 'I never thought', said a former Red Army officer, 'that my wife and children were in danger.' They had perished in the massacre. Another Jew who also served in the Soviet Army lost his parents and four sisters. He himself had just returned from a concentration camp in Siberia where he spent eight years. Although he won four medals for bravery in the war he was arrested in 1949 by the MVD, as the secret police was then known,[1] on charges of 'carrying on illegal Zionist activities' and sentenced to ten years.

Each of the group had their own tragic story to tell. They had all come on that afternoon to mourn their relatives and friends who had died as victims of Nazism. They themselves had managed to escape death at Babi Yar' but had suffered cruelly as victims of Stalinism.

Although Jews in Kiev were not, as I found out, inclined to talk much about the event, the group I met that day showed a readiness to unburden themselves of their thoughts and feelings. Here in the field with no strangers around and with their own sad memories refreshed they tried to recapture for me much of what they knew about Babi Yar'. As our conversation continued a fuller account of the massacre emerged. Reports I had read earlier had differed over the number of victims. They varied between 33,000, the figure first given at the Nuremberg trials, and 100,000, quoted by worshippers in a Kiev synagogue. In the opinion of the group the true figure was nearer 100,000.

At the outbreak of the Second World War the Jewish population of Kiev registered in the official records was 180,000. 20,000 or more came into Kiev as refugees from Eastern Poland, which was occupied in 1939 by Russian troops as part of the agreement between Berlin and Moscow after Hitler's invasion of Poland. Only half of that total, I was told, managed to leave the city with the Russian forces. These consisted mostly of the younger people, the men in the forces, those in the factories, and specialists needed for the war. The older men, women and children were left behind—some because they could not leave in time, others because they refused to part with their parents who were too old to undertake a journey to remoter parts of Russia. All who were left behind perished.

Preparations for the massacre began a few days after the Germans entered Kiev. On 26 September official notices were posted all over the city ordering all Jews to report 'with all their valuables, clothing and food sufficient for three days' journey' for resettlement. Failure to comply with the order, the posters warned, would be punished by death. The reason for the deportation was, the Ukrainian population was told, a bomb explosion which had occurred a few days earlier at the Hotel Continental, the headquarters of the German Sixth Army. The hotel had been completely wrecked and many Germans killed. The Jews were blamed. According to the Nuremberg testimony of General Alfred Jodl, Chief of Operations of the German High Command, a Russian chart captured by the German High Command showed that the explosion was caused by a delayed action bomb, one of some fifty the Russians planted before leaving the city. But for the Nazis this was a chance to blame the Jews and to justify the Babi Yar' massacre to the Ukrainians.

On the appointed day, all the Jews in the city gathered in the half dozen streets surrounding the Jewish cemetery in the Lukyanovska area, not far from Babi Yar', in fact not far from the very place where we were standing that afternoon.

M. S. Lutsenko, a Ukrainian woman known as Auntie Masha, who was the warder of the Old Jewish Cemetery, has since supplied many details of what happened later that day. She was on duty in the cemetery at the time and saw all that happened from a hiding place. Years later she described it to Anatoly Kuznetsov, a Ukrainian writer. When all the Jews had been collected, the Nazi guards ordered them to deposit their parcels and form into columns of about a hundred. From her observation post Lutsenko saw how each column was marched up towards the edge of the Babi Yar' ravine. There they were ordered to undress and their clothing was collected and stacked up in heaps. The column of naked Jews was then forced to move towards the very rim of the ravine and the machine-guns opened fire killing them on the spot. As the fire was aimed at the heads of the victims many of the children, Lutsenko said, were thrown in alive. 'How they screamed! Oh Mother of God! And they were hit with shovels, hit and hit!'[2] The shooting went on for two days from early morning until dark.

A report which the German Extermination Units submitted to the higher authorities in Berlin, and which has since been found in the archives, stated that the total number of Jews shot during the massacre of 29 and 30 September 1941, was 33,771.[3] The action was taken, the report stated, 'as a measure of retaliation for the arson in Kiev.' But from information collected since by Soviet officials and the local Jewish community leaders, it was established that tens of thousands more were killed by the Nazis in subsequent executions carried out in Babi Yar' during the years of the German occupation. Among the victims were entire Jewish communities from the smaller towns around Kiev who were rounded up and brought to Babi Yar' and executed. The executions, the same Lutsenko told one of the Jews I met, went on for months after the first massacre.

The sun was beginning to set and it was time for us to part. Isolated and silenced for a quarter of a century under Stalin's rule, several of the group found relief in being able to talk freely of their sufferings. The emotion aroused by the place made them unusually anxious to unburden themselves of their tales of misery and humiliation. I was greatly affected. Understanding sprang up between us.

As I was taking leave of the group the tall man whom I had first seen limping out of the cemetery gates and who had remained silent throughout, came up close to me and said: 'Can I ask you a question?' He spoke in a very halting Yiddish of which he obviously had only a limited knowledge, and which must have accounted for his silence until then. What he wanted to know, and this he said in Russian, was whether it was true that an appeal had been made by Jews abroad to Khrushchev, who was then Premier, to permit Russian Jews to leave the country for Israel? I replied that it was true. There had been, I said, numerous appeals by Jews in Great Britain and in the United States. But no one as yet had received any response from the Kremlin. At this moment he leaned forward, embraced me and said, 'I would walk to Israel even if I had to lean not on one but on two sticks.' He was crying, and tears appeared in the eyes of the other Jews in the group.

On my way back into Kiev I passed by the Ukrainian cemetery situated in the vicinity of Babi Yar'. There I saw that everything was carefully tended and kept in order. There was a wall round the outside with specially painted, well-made wrought iron gates. Inside many of the clearly lettered tombstones had flowers around them. How sharply all this contrasted with the neglect and desolation of Babi Yar'!

The dead of Babi Yar' are remembered by the Jewish community in Kiev, if not by the Soviet authorities. On the Day of Atonement the 'Kaddish' prayer for the dead is said collectively on behalf of the Babi Yar' victims. The 'Kaddish' is normally said on the anniversary of someone's death, by his relatives and often his friends as well. The custom is called *Yahrzeit*. When I paid a visit to the central synagogue in Moscow, I saw a row of candles lit in memory of the dead. I was interested and asked who paid for them, and, in particular, why there were so many. Several of the candles, it appeared, had been lit that morning by members of the Communist Party in memory of their religious parents. No longer religious themselves, some of them still felt it their duty to carry out the small traditional ceremony. Three of the candles, it was explained, were from a father who had lost three sons in the war, all on the same day. But the majority were lit by the sons and daughters of Jews who had perished at the hands of the Nazis and whose remains are in the mass graves of which there are so many in the Ukraine, White Russia and other parts of Eastern Europe.

Synagogue attendance on that morning was very small and it was puzzling to hear nearly all the worshippers present joining in the 'Kaddish' in Hebrew. In answer to my inquiry, I was told that these prayers were not actually offered by relatives of the persons in whose memory the candles had been lit. Those reciting the prayer were hired 'Kaddish sayers'. As there are no Jewish schools in Russia today to carry on the teaching of Hebrew, few among those who bring their candles to the synagogue can pray in Hebrew. Under the circumstances the best they can do, the guide said, is to pay someone else to perform this duty for them. 'Kaddish sayers' are to be seen in synagogues all over Russia. By hiring themselves out for this task, still considered a sacred one, some of the old pensioners who remember Hebrew earn a few extra roubles and perform a *Mitzvah* (good deed) at the same time.

Having learned the history of nearly all the candles burning in the synagogue that morning I was puzzled by the reluctance of the same guide—not from Intourist—to disclose the name of the donor of one particular candle. But on leaving the synagogue one of the worshippers, who obviously had overheard my conversation, came close to me and whispered 'That candle you saw is burning in the memory of Colonel Itzik Fefer'. He was, of course, referring to the famous Yiddish poet who was executed in the Stalinist era (See pp. 104-6).

A day before our visit to Babi Yar' my wife and I had been taken on a tour of Kiev and been shown the city's many impressive monuments. For the capital of the Ukraine is a place crowded with monuments of all kinds recording Ukrainian history from its earliest days up to the Revolution and after. Together with monuments to Bogdan Khmel'nitsky, in commemoration of his revolt against Polish rule in the seventeenth century, to Shevchenko, the national poet, and to Lenin, we were shown a monument to a group of Ukrainians who fought in the Underground movement during the war. Our guide explained that this had been erected by the people and authorities of the Ukrainian capital who wished to honour the memory of those who fell as the victims of Fascism.

Were not the Jews who died in Babi Yar' victims of the same enemy? Why is their memory neglected? If the Jewish dead are dishonoured, how do the living fare? What is the position of the Jews in the Soviet Union today?

Albert Einstein who was himself a victim of Nazi persecution has described the position of Soviet Jews as follows:

A people, a nation, is like a tree which is born with its own shadow. The higher the tree the longer its shadow. If you like you may call it not shadow but fate. The shadow of the Jewish people is prophecy—vision of the end of the days. The shadow of the Romans was fame, domination of foreign lands. The shadow of the Russians is anti-Semitism.

Einstein made this comment in conversation with a Soviet Jew. He was among a group of leading Americans who welcomed Solomon Mikhoels the famous Soviet Jewish actor who, together with Colonel Itzik Fefer, came to enlist the sympathy of American Jewry in aid of the USSR in 1943.[4]

For those attempting to write a documented history of the Jewish people in Soviet Russia there are many problems. Very little of their history has been recorded. What has been published is the work of historians outside the USSR. As access to official documents is rigidly barred, these works are of necessity based on gleanings from the Press and on information gathered during visits to the USSR. They are thus limited in scope and incomplete. In Russia itself no comprehensive account of Jewish life since the Revolution is yet available. The last historical publications on the position of Jews in Soviet Russia appeared in the thirties, shortly before Stalin's great purges. Most notable among them were Yakov Kantor's essays.[5] There were a few other historical records, mainly propagandist. But since the purges and the liquidation of Jewish cultural institutions, hardly any records of Jewish life in the Soviet Union have been kept. One last effort was Lev Zinger's historical volume published in 1941.[6] While not as crowded with propaganda as some of the other volumes written by Jewish Communists, this cannot be considered a trustworthy record either.

Much of the history of the Jews in this period is to be found in the archives of the KGB (Commission for State Security). Naturally no foreign student has ever been given access to these records. All attempts to obtain from official Russian sources a fuller account of the 'Doctors' Plot' for instance, or of the execution of the twenty-four Jewish writers fail to bring any results (See page 108 ff). Not even the families of the victims themselves have been granted their requests for information. The same applies to cases involving non-Jewish victims. The official reason for such a refusal is that these matters are State secrets. Yet seen in relation to Jewish history in the Soviet Union this attitude reveals the pattern of official policy. It is designed to conceal the truth about Jewish life in present-day Russia. Its aim is to obliterate from memory the wrongs of Stalin's policy, and to conceal the reluctance of succeeding rulers to rectify them. More than this, the official records would reveal the role, if only a passive one, which Stalin's successors themselves played in perpetrating his crimes. Quite a number of those in authority in Russia today, including Brezhnev and Kosygin, held prominent positions under Stalin. By suppressing the memories of the sufferings of the Jews, they hope to create the fiction that there is no longer a Jewish problem in Soviet Russia.

The position is quite different for the students of the life and history of other national minorities in the USSR. On them there is plenty of documentation. They each have their own newspapers, their own schools, theatres, clubs, libraries and other cultural institutions in their native languages—all facilities which are rigidly denied to the Jewish minority. It is much easier for the research student of the minority problems in Russia to obtain details concerning the 60,000 Khakass living in South Central Siberia, who had no alphabet until after the Revolution, than to

establish a few reliable facts about the Jewish community of
200,000 in Kiev, or even about the Jewish community in Moscow,
estimated at twice that number.

Outside Russia it is not so difficult to find out information on
the position of the Jewish communities. Between the wars I was
writing frequently on the position of the national minorities in
Eastern Europe. The Treaty of Versailles contained a special
charter for the protection of national minorities. As Warsaw
correspondent of the *Manchester Guardian*, as it was then called,
it was my duty to keep what its editors defined as a watching
brief over the treatment of the Ukrainian, Jewish and German
minorities in Poland. National minorities then constituted about
one-third of the country's population, and the equality they enjoyed was regarded as the touchstone of justice in the country.

The obstacles to research facing the student of Jewish history
in contemporary Russia, however, are much more formidable
than they ever were before. Even in Tsarist days the facts about
Jewish life in Russia, however depressing, were known and made
available for research. The study of Jewish history was compara-
tively easy in those days. Despite all restrictions there existed
in Tsarist Russia numerous specifically Jewish organizations and
institutions. There were Jewish newspapers in Russian, Yiddish
and Hebrew; there was the work of individual historians; and,
most important, there were Jewish societies and journals devoted
to research and documentation. In particular there was the Jewish Historico-Ethnographic Commission which started as a
branch of the Society for the Dissemination of Education among
the Jews and finally became a centre for Jewish historical research.
It had a membership of over 400 of the most prominent Jewish
historians in Europe. Among them was Professor Simon Dubnov,
the author of many standard volumes on Jewish history, and
an acknowledged authority on the history of Jews in Russia.
With its headquarters in St Petersburg, the Commission gained
the co-operation and support of other Jewish historians of European and world fame, among them S. A. Bershadsky, the author
of three volumes of *Russo-Jewish Archives*, A. Ya. Harkavi,
V. O. Levanda and Yuri Hessen. The Commission published its

own journal, *Yevreyskaya Starina* (The Jewish Past), which soon became one of the leading Jewish historical periodicals in the world. Professor Simon Dubnov was its editor-in-chief and four prominent historians, M. M. Vinaver, Mikhail Kulisher, S. Goldstein and M. L. Vischnitzer, his assistants. Its main aim was the preservation of the Jewish heritage as an essential defensive weapon against assimilation. In the words of Professor Dubnov, the chief propagator of the study of Jewish history in Russia :

> the past of the Jewish people possesses a marvellous healing power for the suffering Jewish soul. Apart from solace, how much light, clarity and awareness is brought into our minds by the knowledge of our past! We no longer feel cut off and isolated, but know ourselves to be the successors of many generations, which lived for more than thought and suffering.[7]

After the Bolshevik Revolution the Historico-Ethnographic Society as it came to be known, was closed down along with other Jewish organizations and institutions. The years of its existence had marked a most productive period in Jewish historiography in Russia, in fact in Europe generally. Its journal— Dubnov was still able to publish a volume in 1918—counted 140 historians among its regular contributors. A bibliography, by A. G. Duker, of the twelve volumes of *Yevreyskaya Starina* showed the wealth of historical material it contained. There were nearly 600 items on Jewish sociology, language, archaeology, history, art, folklore and memoirs, which had all been written and published in Tsarist Russia. No society devoted to the study of Jewish history exists in Russia today.

Another important Jewish institution in Tsarist Russia which was forced to close after the October Revolution was the Jewish Library. Founded in the second half of the nineteenth century it became an important repository of books and documents on Jewish life and activities—economic, social, religious and artistic. It was the centre for historical records and archives on Jewish affairs in Russia. The final achievement of Jewish scholarship under the Tsars was the 16-volume *Jewish Encyclopaedia*, pub-

lished in 1914 in Russian. Its contributors included leading Jewish and non-Jewish historians of the day. It is interesting to note
too that up to 1914 a quarter of all the books ever published
in Hebrew had appeared in Russia.

Since the Revolution the study of Jewish history has ceased.
Anything that has appeared in this field during the fifty years
of Communist rule is a mixture of propaganda and deliberate
distortion. Only works which put forward the Communist point
of view have been published. Many of the authors have been
directly connected with the Soviet propaganda machine. One
such author is Solomon Rabinovich, a veteran Jewish Communist
engaged in the dissemination of official propaganda on the Jewish
issue, who has written two pamphlets, *Jews in the USSR*, published in 1965 and *Jews in the Soviet Union*, which appeared in
1967. These give a few statistics and correctly estimate the Jewish
population in the Soviet Union to be about three million, but are
on the whole misleading.

When in Russia I made many enquiries at bookshops for a
history of the Jews but everywhere I met with the same negative
reply. Even the few volumes published in this field in the early
years after the Revolution, and by Communist authors, were no
longer available. Jewish history seems to be a subject in which
the Government no longer wants the public to be interested.
There is not a single Chair of Jewish history in any of the universities or Russian institutions for higher education. In 1967
over four million students attended Russian universities. They
could attend lectures in English, French, or German history but
no student could follow a university course in Jewish history.

To ignore this subject, and the contribution made by Jews
to Russian history, are both features of a policy which attempts
to conceal the significance of the Jewish nation in the Soviet
Union. It is the same policy which, by neglecting Babi Yar',
attempts to destroy the memory of Jewish suffering, and pretends
there is no Jewish problem. In the official *History of the October
Revolution* published in Moscow on the eve of the fiftieth anniversary celebrations, the contribution of many of the Jews who
took part in the Revolution is underestimated, and the fact that

they were Jewish is omitted. The book was the collective effort of twenty prominent members of the Soviet Institute of History, and was published under the auspices of the USSR Academy of Sciences. In the introduction the editors stated that the purpose of publishing this volume was to tell the Russian reader of 'the manifold activities of Lenin and the other leaders of the Revolution in the period from 1917 to 1918.'

At no period in the history of the Bolshevik Revolution was there such a concentrated collective participation of Jewish revolutionaries as during those twelve months. But Jews figure very briefly in the official history. Of the leading Jewish personalities only Sverdlov is given his due. His role in the Revolution is emphasized, but the part played by Kamenev, Zinoviev and Trotsky is given brief and prejudiced treatment. Kamenev and Zinoviev are described as 'adventurers', 'opportunists' and 'traitors'. All three were elected on to the Central Committee at the 6th Party Congress in July 1917. (Out of 23 elected, 7 were Jewish, but this fact is not mentioned in the official history). Trotsky, who was already head of the Military Revolutionary Committee, was appointed People's Commissar for Foreign Affairs in Lenin's first government. But the outstanding contribution which he had made to the Revolution, and which had led up to this appointment, was practically ignored. Likewise his importance after the Revolution itself is passed over. The chapter on the Brest-Litovsk negotiations and the peace treaty with the Germans hardly mentions him, nor the other Jews—Adolf Yoffe, Karl Radek and Mikhail Lazarovich Pavlovich—who made such important contributions.

Jewish revolutionaries were active on many of the bodies which put the Revolution into effect. Twenty per cent of the delegates to the All Russia Conference of the Bolshevik Party in Petrograd on 20 April 1917 were Jewish. It was at this conference that Lenin's 'April Theses' were adopted. It took place a few days after Lenin's arrival from abroad, and Jewish revolutionaries were among the first to give him their support. This is glossed over in the official account of the Revolution.

Although small groups of Bolsheviks were active all over Russia the fountainhead of the Revolution was in Petrograd. This was particularly so after Lenin's return from exile. All important decisions were taken in the capital. To give them practical effect a committee of thirty-five persons known as the Enlarged Petrograd Soviet, or council, was elected. Eleven of its members were Jewish, including Axelrod, Ravich, Rozovsky, Vlodarsky, Spielman, Gorelik and Hessen. In the Executive Committee of the Russian Tade Union, elected in 1917, there were six Jews out of a membership of fourteen. At its 3rd Congress in July 1918 Solomon Abramovich Lozovsky was elected Chairman.[8] A leading role in the trade union movement in Petrograd at that time was played by Ezra Holzman. He was Chairman of the Transport Union, the most powerful branch in the movement, and responsible for the supply of war materials for the insurgent forces of the Bolshevik Party.

Among other Jewish revolutionaries active during the uprising were Riazonov, Larin, Bielensky, Raskol'nikov, Rosenholtz and Yanov. Raskol'nikov was Commander of the Kronstadt Sailors. The Peasants' Council which met in January elected Yanov as its Chairman. Another Jew called I. L. Gornstein but known as Burov, was elected a member of the Executive Council. Yakov Genzler was one of the leading figures in control of the pro-Bolshevik group of the famous Putilov Metal Works. To the same group also belonged Hanberg, known as Sergei Semionovich Zorin, an old Bolshevik who was Chairman of the Sestroretsk Works which organized the secret manufacture and supply of arms to the revolutionaries.[9]

A special role in organizing Russian Youth for the Bolshevik Movement was played by a young Jewish Revolutionary named Boris Rivkin. At the initial meeting of the Petrograd Revolutionary Youth, held in September 1917, Rivkin was elected Chairman. Five other Jews, Yashke Zeitlin, Lazar Shadsky, Bezimensky, Ger and Arsh, were elected to the Executive. Rivkin later became the First Secretary of the *Komsomol,* the youth organization which now has a membership of well over twenty million. Zlata Yonovna Lilina, a young Jewish revolutionary who returned with Lenin, became co-editor of the *Soldatskaya Pravda,* then one of the leading propaganda organs in Petrograd. Another Jewish woman who also played an important role as a propagandist was P. Y. Gusyev Drapkina. She was editorial secretary in 1917 to both *Izvestia* and *Pravda,* and was elected as the only woman member of the Military Revolutionary Committee in Petrograd. Only a couple of these are mentioned in the official history of the Revolution.

In the planning and execution of the Bolshevik insurrection which wrested power from the Provisional Government, Jewish revolutionaries played a prominent part. Plans were worked out towards the end of the summer of 1917. Of the seven people entrusted with the task of carrying them out, four were Jewish. Among the small Revolutionary Committee of Five, elected on 16 October 1917, two, Sverdlov and Uritsky, were of Jewish nationality. Once again these facts were omitted from the official *History of the October Revolution.* Grigory Chudnovsky shared with Vladimir Antonov-Ovseyenko the storming and the occupation of the Winter Palace, which had become the seat of the Kerensky government. It was Chudnovsky who directed the arrest of the Provisional Government, and it was through his efforts that the Cossacks who took part in the operation were prevented from taking revenge on the Kerensky ministers after victory. Chudnovsky was later appointed Commander of the Winter Palace. Another Jewish Bolshevik, Lashevich, led the famous Koksogolsk Regiment of the Red Guards which on the night of 7 November occupied the Ministry of Posts, the Russian State Bank, the Cossack Barracks and a number of other strategic points in the capital. Among other Jews who took part in the military operations of the Revolution itself were Semeon Grigorevich Rochal, Semeon (Samuil) Petrovich Voskov and Anton Slutsky, one of Lenin's closest supporters.[10] Rochal also played a part in the firing of the *Aurora* and was later nominated Chief Political Commissar to the Soviet-Rumanian front. Another Jew, Siva (Symcha) Mikhailovich Nachimson, was appointed Political Commissar of the Twelfth Army.

There were also about a dozen Jewish revolutionaries in the Bolshevik military forces in Moscow. Leading figures among them were K. Rozental who was in command of the arsenal of the Military Revolutionary Committee in Moscow, Yaroslavsky, Commander of the Kremlin arsenal as well as Chairman of the Revolutionary Committee, and Aaron Tiomkin, secretary and chief organizer of the Red Guards in Moscow.

Others who played an active role were Usnievich, Vyelanky, Rozenholtz, Myelnicharsky, Galperin, Kushnir, Rozental, and Alperovich.

The picture which emerges is one of evasion and distortion. It is a long way from Babi Yar' to the Academy of Sciences in Moscow, the sponsors of *The History of the October Revolution*. But the neglect of the ravine near Kiev, and the failure to give the Jewish revolutionaries their due, have the same intention behind them. The keynote of Soviet policy on the Jewish issue is silence. By forcing the Jews to remain silent, and by directing attention away from the Jewish problem, the authorities hope to deny its existence, and to create the impression that the Jews are happily assimilated into Russian society, unconcerned about their national identity.

The Silent Millions

I

THE BACKGROUND

The Jewish and the Russian people have been thrown together in a remarkable way across the path of history. Not since the Roman Empire has any single power controlled the destinies of so many Jews as Tsarist Russia. Half the Jewish population in the world lived, well into this century, under Tsarist Russian rule.

More than a thousand years ago, towards the end of the first millennium, the Russian princes and dukes destroyed the Jewish State of the Khazars on the Volga. In several attacks they shattered the nucleus of what might have become a Jewish State on the borders of Europe and Asia. As Tsarist aggressive power grew and Russia's conquering armies spread East and West, an ever larger number of Jews came under her oppressive dominion. Each century, each decade and each conquest made the Tsars the masters of more Jewish communities. Whether it was the partition of Poland towards the end of the eighteenth century, or the seizure of lands in the Far East, Jews who had enjoyed a comparative measure of tolerance, as was the case under the kings of Poland, found themselves at the mercy of Russian rulers.

Under the Tsars, restrictions on Jews—most frequently expressing the will and sentiment of the ruler himself—were introduced by a dual system practised throughout the centuries of Romanov rule and even earlier. First and foremost was the method of sending secret instructions to the police and advising them on the repressive measures they were to take against the Jewish population. Another method was to give them legal form by announcing them publicly as the decisions—*Ukases*—of the Tsar. As the absolute ruler the Tsar had no need to consult anyone about his decision concerning the Jews; nor was he responsible to any parliament.

In the 300 years of the Romanov dynasty two sets of anti-Jewish laws were issued. In 1834 Nicholas I issued the 'Charter of Disabilities' listing a whole series of anti-Jewish restrictions which had accumulated since the days of Peter the Great and before. The second series were the 'Ignatiev Laws' issued in 1882 by Alexander III. Both Tsars adhered to the maxim of 'Russia for the Russians' and both disliked the Jews. But Alexander III was regarded as the most anti-Semitic ruler that had ever sat on the Russian throne. He was the pupil of Konstantin Petrovich Pobyedonostsev, the Chief Procurator of the Holy Synod and one of the most reactionary figures in Tsarist Russia. With his encouragement Tsar Alexander III came to believe that international Jewry was plotting against the Russian Empire and had been involved in the assassination of his father. A year after his succession to the throne he published the 'Ignatiev Laws' bearing the name of his Minister but actually expressing his own sentiments. The laws affected hundreds of thousands of Jews who were to be driven out from the villages and small townships within the 'Pale of Settlement'.[1]

In the field of religion, the Tsars' policies were at first chiefly designed to bring about the conversion of the Jews. The openly declared aim was to turn the Jew away from his ancient faith and force him to accept Christianity. In these attempts the Tsars had the full support and co-operation of the Russian Orthodox Church. At the beginning of the nineteenth century conversion of the Jews in Russia was brought about through compulsory long-term service in the Tsarist army. Jewish boys of twelve or under, who were born to soldiers, were conscripted to serve periods of up to twenty-five years. Known as cantonists (from the word 'canton' applied in Prussia in the eighteenth century to a recruiting district), they were regarded as the property of the Tsar's military department. During that time the Church, working hand in hand with the army, undertook the conversion and 'salvation' of their Jewish souls. The percentage of converts was very high. In 1845 all the Jewish cantonists in the battalions of

Saratov were baptized and in the same year those in charge of the Perm battalions 'joyfully reported similar successes to the Holy Synod'.[2] Those who secretly returned to Judaism became known as the 'Siberian Marranos'.

When, by the middle of the nineteenth century, a more liberal atmosphere prevailed under Alexander II, emancipation of the Jew became the mainspring of official policy in Petrograd, or St Petersburg, as it was then still called. By lifting only a few of the oppressive laws, and especially by granting opportunities for the education of Jewish youth, the Tsar wanted to lure his Jewish subjects away from their old customs and traditions into accepting more progressive ideals. The main motive behind the official policy, however, was to try and make the Jew less Jewish, and by force or otherwise bring about his conversion and integration into the Russian population.

For centuries denationalization and assimilation were the twin features of Tsarist policy towards the national minorities. They were the two weapons employed in order to weaken and undermine the national cultures of the smaller ethnic groups in the multi-national Russian empire. In the case of the Jewish minority the measures taken were of a greater variety and often more crippling. Repressive Tsarist laws and crude, degrading police measures culminated in widespread pogroms. But as with other national minorities, assimilation was the ultimate goal. An admission to this effect was made by K. P. Pobyedonostsev, the spiritual adviser of Nicholas II who had likewise inspired the anti-Jewish policies of Alexander III, when he declared that he hoped to solve the Jewish problem by forcing one-third of the Jewish population to emigrate, one-third to be destroyed, and one-third to become assimilated.[3]

It was not only the Tsars themselves who encouraged the Jewish minority to assimilate. Jewish revolutionaries fighting against Tsarist tyranny held and proclaimed similar views. To them redemption of the Jew and non-Jew alike depended upon the downfall of Tsarism and the solution of economic issues.

There were two leading and active anti-Tsarist movements in

the 1870s, namely the *Narodniki*, (Populists) and the *Zemlya i Volya* (Land and Freedom). In both these organizations Jews were among the leading figures. Aaron Zundelevich and H. Magat played outstanding roles among the Populists. The most prominent Jewish personality in the *Zemlya i Volya* was Nicholas Utin, sometimes referred to as 'the first Russian Marxist'. Also active in the seventies were Paul Axelrod and Lev Deich. All of them were assimilationists. 'When I say that as *Narodniki* we must go to the people I mean to the Russian people' proclaimed Zundelevich.[4] It was not the fate of the disenfranchised Jewish tradesmen or even artisans, suffering from oppressive anti-Semitic Tsarist laws, that prompted these revolutionaries in their struggle against the Tsar. Their main concern was for the fate of the Russian *muzhik*—the peasant. Lev Deich openly proclaimed that 'For us there existed but one unhappy dispossessed people, consisting mainly of tillers of the soil and partly of factory workers whose speech was the dominant Russian language. The artisans we regarded as exploiters'. He went on to say that since most of the working elements among the Jews consisted of craftsmen who engaged in petty trade he considered them to be *geschäftmacher* (tradesmen).[5]

The attitude of the early Jewish revolutionaries in Russia towards religion, history and the whole traditional past of their own people was a negative one. Neither Jewish nationalism, nor indeed Jewry itself was worth preserving. Paul Axelrod anticipated that the era of equality and fraternity which was to follow victory over Tsarism would resolve the Jewish problem once and for all because it would bring about the 'enthronement of the poorest and most downtrodden'.[6]

While all of them considered religion an anachronism, at least one of the Jewish revolutionaries is on record as having accepted Christianity because he feared that the prevailing anti-Semitic atmosphere would prevent him from reaching the Russian peasantry as a Jew. Osher Aptekman, a leading member of the *Narodniki*, embraced the Russian Orthodox faith and was able to boast later that in this capacity he would have a greater chance of reaching the Russian masses. 'Now', he said, 'I am going to the Russian masses not as a Jew but a Christian. I am at one with the people'.[7]

Quite a number of these early Jewish revolutionaries in Russia came from religious Jewish homes and surroundings. Aaron Zundelevich, for example, was actually a pupil of the famous Rabbinic College and Seminary in Vilna. In the *Zemlya i Volya* he became a member of the executive, and the chief organizer. His masterly schemes for smuggling illegal anti-Tsarist literature from Western Europe into Russia actually gained him the nickname of 'Minister for Foreign Affairs of the Revolution'. He managed to organize and maintain regular contact and co-operation with Marxist organizations all over Europe. Another pupil of the same Rabbinic Seminary was Aaron Lieberman who towards the end of the nineteenth century had played a prominent role among the Russian revolutionaries. Like most of his associates in the fight against Tsarist oppression he too had a negative attitude towards the preservation of Judaism and Jewish nationalism. In his prolific writings in both Yiddish and Hebrew, as well as Russian, Lieberman advocated assimilation of the Jews with the people around them.

These early Jewish revolutionaries never, however, contemplated assimilation by force as a means of realizing their vision of a free Russian people and an emancipated Russian Jewry. To them assimilation meant a harmonious voluntary adaptation of the Jew's mode of life to his neighbour's. They strove for a Russia in which there would be liberty for all citizens and in which the Jews would enjoy the fullest equality. It was indeed their liberalizing ideals which held such an attraction for the younger generation of Jewish intellectuals and led them to join in ever increasing numbers the ranks of the anti-Tsarists. By their efforts they paved the way for the Bolsheviks, to whom liberty and freedom for all were among the principal redemptive ideas of the Revolution.

Despite all the oppressive laws emanating from the Crown and often supported whole-heartedly by the Russian Church, Jews in Tsarist Russia somehow succeeded in retaining facilities strictly denied to them today. Even in the darkest days of Tsarist persecution they could worship their God undisturbed and educate their children in the traditional manner. In spite of the restrictions of the 'Charter of Disabilities' and the 'Ignatiev Laws' and the great pressure for their Russification, the Jews in Tsarist Russia had at the beginning of this century some 7,000 schools and educational institutes. Within the very 'Pale of Settlement', which Trotsky described as 'one of the twin barbarisms of Tsarist Russia' there existed and flourished the most famous Jewish religious training colleges. These were the *Yeshivas* of Mir, Volozhin, Slobodka, Brest-Litovsk and many others which produced thousands of Rabbinical and Hebrew scholars.[8] Language, religion and culture are essential to the survival of a nation. Russian Jewry managed to preserve all three under the Tsar but each has been increasingly eroded under Communism.

In his religion the Jew found solace and a source of strength to sustain him throughout the ages in his struggle for survival. Although religious freedom is guaranteed by the Soviet constitution, orthodox Jews in the USSR—estimated to number about half a million—frequently meet with difficulties and obstacles, making it impossible for them to practise their faith. While other denominations are not exempted from official pressure, the Jewish religion is somehow regarded as the source of a more reactionary ideology and thus subjected to more restrictive treatment.

It would, of course, be ludicrous and grotesque to assume that the Jews feel any nostalgia for Tsarist days. No one greeted the downfall of Tsarism more wholeheartedly than they. At the same time it cannot be denied that under the Tsars the Jews managed to live as a community, retaining their collective and traditional pattern of life. Above all they could protest openly, often vigorously, against discrimination and restriction; they could voice their dissatisfaction and dismay, and demand justice. Today they have no opportunity to voice their protest; they must remain silent.

Comparisons may not always be convincing. But the position of the Jewish Press is a manifest example of the difference in Jewish life between the present day and the era before the Revolution. Under the liberalizing policies of Alexander II a process

of Jewish emancipation and progress began. Within a short period
a secular Jewish culture came into existence, the first and most
expressive upshot of which was a wide range of Jewish newspapers. They were all, or nearly all, in Russian, but they all
championed the Jewish right to equality and citizenship. Foremost among the Jewish journals in Tsarist Russia was the *Voskhod* (Sunrise) which for a quarter of a century was the organ
of Jewish liberalism in Russia. Towards the end of the nineteenth
century and in some cases well up to the October Revolution
there were the following newspapers serving the Jewish minority
in the Tsarist empire : *Den'* (Day); *Vestnik Russkikh Yevreyev*
(Herald of Russian Jews); *Rassvet* (Dawn); *Budushchnost'* (The
Future); *Yevreyskaya Zhizn'* (Jewish Life); *Yevreyskaya Mysl'*
(Jewish Thought); *Sion* (Zion); *Yevreyskii Mir* (Jewish World);
Yevreyskoye Obozreniy (Jewish Survey); *Novyi Put'* (New Road);
Yevreyskiye Vesti (Jewish News).[9]

With a censorship as strict as was that of the Russian Tsars,
the Jewish newspapers were not always able to print what they
desired. But they managed to overcome all difficulties and did
a magnificent job in defending the Russian Jews. Thanks to the
Voskhod, in particular, there sprang up a whole generation of
Russo-Jewish writers and poets, eminent historians, talented pub-
licists, economists, sociologists and literary critics who made a
valuable contribution to Russian literature generally.

Side by side with the newspapers in Russian there were also
journals in Hebrew and Yiddish. There was the *Hamagid* (The
Preacher) which began publishing in 1857, and two other weekly
newspapers—the *Hakarmel* (Mount Carmel) in Vilna and the
Hamelits (First Star) in Odessa. In 1862 a fourth Hebrew newspaper, the *Hazefira*, began to appear in Warsaw under the editor-
ship of Nahum Sokolov. In addition there were numerous other
Jewish Russian journals of a specialized nature, some political,
others literary or devoted to social and historical writings. The
Bund, the Jewish Socialist party, which had no legal status under
the Tsars, used to publish regular journals in London and Paris,
and smuggle them to St Petersburg, Odessa, Moscow and all
parts of Russia. There were also journals published in Geneva

and smuggled into Russia. These included the *Vestnik Bunda* (*Bund* Herald) and the *Otkliki Bunda* (Echoes of the *Bund*). A notable contribution to Jewish Russian history was made by the journal *Perezhitoye* (Our Past) and *Yevreyskaya Starina* (The Jewish Past) which was directed and edited by the Jewish historian Simon Dubnov, who published ten of its thirteen volumes (See p. 17). Jewish economic affairs and the Jewish role in the Russian economy was dealt with in a special journal called the *Yevreyskii Ekonomicheskii Vestnik* (Jewish Economic Herald). There was the *Vestnik Yevreyskovo Prosveshcheniya* (Jewish Education Herald). There were many Jewish libraries in Russia and they had their own journal called the *Yevreyskaya Biblioteka* (The Jewish Library). A very important role was played in the Jewish community by the *Vestnik Yevreyskoy Obshchiny* (Community Herald); it acted as a constructive link between the hundreds of Jewish communal organizations and bodies which existed throughout Russia. It recorded their decisions and activities and was a valuable manifestation of the vitality and wide ramification of Jewish life in Tsarist Russia. Because it was published in St Petersburg, the Tsar's capital, it carried in its columns information concerning the legal status of Jews, and was avidly read by Jews active in community affairs. The influence of these Jewish newspapers in the struggle for Jewish rights cannot be over-estimated. In the very year of the Revolution, when most of the papers had been forced to close down, the Hebrew *Ha'am* (The People) made its appearance in Moscow. Within a short time it had a subscription list of some 15,000, but it too had to close down on orders from the *Yevsektsiya*, the Jewish Section of the People's Commissariat for National Affairs.

But even in Tsarist days Jews in Russia were treated differently from those elsewhere. In Tsarist Russia the Jews' response to emancipation was different from that in Germany, France or England. In Germany the emancipated Jew of the middle nineteenth century aspired to become more German than the Germans. In England Jews blended increasingly into the national pattern. But in Russia only a small section of the Jewish population adopted the mode of life and the culture of the majority when, under Tsar Alexander II, the Jews were given a better opportunity and a greater degree of freedom.

Even on the road towards assimilation Russian Jews under the Tsars did not become as estranged from the Jewish community and Jewish way of life as they did in Germany. The so-called upper classes—lawyers, doctors, engineers and intellectuals—who because of their professions were granted permission to live and work outside the 'Pale of Settlement', maintained a close attachment to their people, as did the rich industrialists and bankers.[10] Although a privileged group, they remained within the community. There were many Jews playing a growing role in the industrialization and modernization of Tsarist Russia. They built railways, and opened and exploited coal mines, oil wells, sugar refineries and other enterprises.[11]

Faced with the dilemma of a return to the ghetto or assimilation the Russian Jews evolved a new formula, a kind of national self-assertion which compromised between the past and the present. In practical terms this meant becoming involved in the fight against discrimination, against Jewish disabilities, and for equality.

A decree passed at the end of the nineteenth century, issued in St Petersburg over the Tsar's signature, placed the following minorities in a class lower than the Russians: (i) non-Russian Siberians (ii) the Samoyeds in the province of Archangelsk (iii) the Nomads in the province of Stavropol' (iv) the Kalmuks or Kalmyks, living as nomads in the provinces of Stavropol' and Astrakhan, (v) the Kirghiz (vi) all non-Russians in the Akmolinsk, Semipalatinsk, Semirechesk, Ural and Turgai regions (vii) the non-Russian population of the Trans Caspian areas and (viii) the Jews.[12]

Although last on the list of this Tsarist decree, the Jews managed to enjoy one privilege denied to some of the other minorities. The electoral law of 1907 stated that peoples living 'in the peripheral regions of the Tsarist empire . . . which had not yet achieved the required level of civic development' were not to enjoy the right of participating in the elections to the first State Duma—the Russian Parliament. For them, it was declared, 'elections to the Duma must be temporarily held over'.[13] The Jewish minority, however, had electoral rights and could vote. As a result the Jews managed to have 12 representatives in the first Duma, 4 in the second, and 2 in the third.

The presence of Jewish representatives in the State Duma marked a definite chapter in the struggle for the political rights of Russian Jewry. From their appearance in the First State Duma on 27 April 1906, to the promulgation of the Equal Rights Decree by the Provisional Government of 1917, the fight against restrictions on Jews gained increasing support from liberal deputies. Quite a number of the deputies leaned towards the left and openly so, which gave the First Duma the nickname of 'Duma of the people's wrath'.

The twelve Jewish elected deputies were: L. M. Bramson, Dr G. Ya. Bruk, Dr M. Chervonenkis, Dr Frenkel, G. B. Iollos, Nisan Katsenelson, Shmarya Levin, M. Ya. Ostrogorsky, S. Ya. Rosenbaum, M. I. Sheftel, M. M. Vinaver, and B. P. Yakubson. The leader of the Jewish parliamentarians was Vinaver who was a prominent member of the Cadets, otherwise known as the Constitutional Democrats, to which several of the other Jewish members also belonged. Three of them were members of the *Trudoviki* (Labour Group) with a programme resembling somewhat that of the Social Revolutionaries. At the same time, however, five of the Jewish deputies were Zionists the most outstanding of whom was Dr Shmarya Levin, a stirring orator whose eloquence won many supporters to the Jewish cause and fight for equality. Significantly, a resolution to grant full rights to Jews won 100 votes for, 10 against with 3 abstentions.[14] They were, however, deprived of representation in municipal councils; Article 804 of the Law on Personal Status stated that they were 'ineligible for the exercise of any functions in towns which are either exclusively reserved for Christians, or are of such a nature that they cannot conveniently and decently be entrusted to Jews'.

The Jewish Defence Bureau, formed in St Petersburg in 1900, also played an important role in the battle for Jewish rights. It counted among its members the most prominent Jewish lawyers in Russia as well as some members of the Duma. Its main purpose was to defend Jews prosecuted for political offences. Such prosecutions often had a religious and racial background, and were part of the repressive measures taken against the Jewish population. Another very important organization founded and active in the Russian capital was the Jewish Democratic Group which included such well-known personalities as Simon Dubnov the historian, Baron Alfred Ginsburg, and a number of other influential and wealthy citizens. Baron Ginsburg also headed the Society for the Dissemination of Education among Jews which aimed to spread modern ideas especially among the young, to make them more adaptable to the new conditions of life in a modern State. A number of other organizations managed to survive the October Revolution. Driven out of Russia some are still active in Jewish life today. They are the ORT (*Obshchevstvo Remyeslennovo Truda*), a society for the teaching of crafts to Jews, which survived in Poland until the Arab-Israeli war of 1967 when the Polish régime adopted a much stronger anti-Jewish line. Another was the TOZ (*Towarzystwo Ochrony Zdrowia*), a society for the care and health of Jews, now known as the OSE (*Obchestvo Zdravoochroneniya Evreyov*).

It was in Tsarist Russia too that the Zionist Movement which had such a tremendous influence on Jewish life all over the world was born and gained momentum. The first groups of Jewish immigrants to settle in Palestine came from Russia. They founded Kibbutzim and were among the first to lay the foundations of the Jewish State. *Poale Zion* (Labour Zionism) originated in Poltava, a city in the Ukraine. Under Ber Borochov's leadership it became the headquarters for 'Proletarian Palestinism', the Marxist-Zionist movement, which was both an ideological and a political force, and which played such an important role in the building of Israel. The first and second Presidents of Israel, Dr Chaim Weizmann and Itzchak Ben-Zvi, were Russian Jews, as are Shazar and Golda Meir, the President and the Prime Minister at the time of writing. It was in Poltava that the first Labour-Zionist journal, *Yevreyskaya Rabochaya Khronika* (Jewish Labour Chronicle) made its appearance as the leading organ of Zionist socialism. Another journal propagating the same ideology

B

was the *Molot* (Hammer) published in Simferopol. *Poale Zion* also published the Yiddish paper *Forverts* (Forward) in Vilna.[15]

But Zionism in Russia ran into trouble soon after the Communists came to power. At the 2nd Conference of the Jewish Communist Sections—the *Yevsektsiyas*—held in Moscow in June 1919, Zionism was denounced as a 'counter-revolutionary' force which was 'strengthening the influence of clericalism among the Jewish masses'. Owing to its policy towards Palestine, the statement ran, the Zionist Party 'serves as an instrument of united imperialism which combats the proletarian revolution'. The full force of Zionism in Jewish life had become manifest when the movement came into the open after the Tsar's abdication. Figures available a few months later showed that it had over 1,000 branches scattered throughout the Russian empire with some 300,000 shekel-buying members.[16]

The outlawing of the Zionist movement was followed by the arrest of several thousand Zionist leaders, many of whom were deported to Siberia.[17] *Poale Zion* was able to carry on for a little longer but then it too came under the ban and had to close down along with all other Jewish national organizations. Soon Zionism was being denounced in the Soviet Press as hostile to the Soviet Union. This hostility on the part of the Soviet Union towards the Zionist movement still persists to the present-day as was shown in the Soviet representatives' speeches at the United Nations in 1967 when they compared Zionism with Nazism.

Under the Tsars Jewish life was active in another sphere. The General Union of Jewish workers in Lithuania, Poland and Russia was founded in Vilna in 1897, a year earlier than Lenin's own political movement in Russia. Later known as the Bund, it had great influence among the Jewish workers in Eastern Europe. In 1904 it had a membership of 23,000 while Lenin's Russian Social Democratic Workers' Party had less than half that number. Julius Martov and several other of Lenin's closest collaborators in the struggle against the Tsar started their political activities in its ranks.

An encouragement to the Jews in their struggle for greater

freedom in Tsarist Russia was the warm sympathy often shown
to them by Russian intellectuals. In 1890 Vladimir Solovyov, the
Russian philosopher, decided to publish an open protest against
anti-Semitism in Russia, and succeeded in collecting over a hundred signatures from leading intellectuals including Leo Tolstoy
and Vladimir Korolenko. But despite its mild tone it was barred
from publication.[18] Leo Tolstoy and a group of other prominent
writers and thinkers were also vocal during the pogroms and
vehemently protested against them. Berdyayev, the famous Russian thinker and a deeply religious man, condemned Tsarist persecution of 'the people of the prophets'.[19] In the Duma, Professor
Kokoshkin called Tsarist anti-Jewish restrictions 'a relic of barbarism'. Most bitter in his denunciation of Tsarist anti-Jewish
measures was the famous revolutionary and democratic writer,
Vladimir Korolenko, whose essay condemning the Kishinev
pogrom caused a deep stir in the civilized world. Prohibited in
Russia it was printed illegally by the Bund in London and smuggled for distribution throughout Russia.

Under the Tsars, Jewish life survived, but the personal prejudice of the ruler survived too—culminating at the beginning
of the twentieth century in events which foreshadowed Stalin's
anti-Jewish moves. It has been established that the Tsar spent
about 3,000,000 roubles—£300,000—on the printing and publication of the 'Secret Protocols of the Elders of Zion', an anti-
Jewish document which appeared in 1903. The Tsar and his
ministers had become more sensitive towards the many protests
abroad against his repressive anti-Jewish measures. The 'Secret
Protocols' were not only another attempt to discredit the Jew,
but at the same time designed to justify the pogroms which had
become a characteristic feature of Tsarist Russia in the late nineteenth and early twentieth centuries.

A further such effort was made on the eve of the First World
War when Nicholas II used his secret police to fabricate a ritual
murder case. Mendel Beilis, a Jewish official in a Kiev brick
factory was arrested and charged with murdering a Christian boy
found dead in the neighbourhood. Reactionary Russian newspapers opened a wild anti-Jewish campaign. A pogrom atmos-

phere once again swept Russia threatening the lives of six million
Jews in the Tsarist empire. (It was during this campaign that
Stolypin, the Tsarist Premier, was assassinated by a young anar-
chist by the name of Bogrov, the son of a lawyer of Jewish
origin). The Beilis trial went on for two years from 1911 to 1913,
when, contrary to the Tsar's expectations, he was acquitted,
although the Tsar himself continued to believe that the Jews
used Christian blood for ritual purposes.

The Tsars were not, however, alone in their anti-Jewish thinking. Socialist and Communist theoreticians of the nineteenth century, led by Karl Marx, propagated ideas of assimilation and
denationalization, which prejudiced them against the survival of
minorities. The Jews in particular suffered from Marx's antagonism. Rationalized, this antagonism was merely part of his overall
assimilation theory; but seen in its true light, it can only appear
as a highly emotional bias.

It has been suggested that Marx's rabbinical origin—he was
born a Jew and baptized—was in part the cause of his hostility
towards the Jew. Whether or not this is the case, he indulged in
ostentatious Judophobia; he made sweeping condemnatory statements on Judaism and the Jews, some of which still persist and
are repeated in Soviet propagandist literature. When Marx entered the political scene as a social reformer the position of the
Jews in Europe was still, despite the emancipatory ideals of the
French Revolution, that of an oppressed minority. Even if he
wished, Marx could not have avoided taking note of the miser-
able lot of millions of Jews, of the political, economic and social
restrictions from which they suffered almost everywhere. In
championing the causes of the downtrodden and voteless, Marx
naturally also devoted his time and attention to the fate of the
Jews who in Europe and beyond, especially in Russia, were still
categorized as second- or third-class citizens.

But even though he championed their cause, he was not their
friend. Karl Marx took up the Jewish question more in an
attempt to refute the theories of another Socialist theoretician,
Bruno Bauer, than from a desire to defend the Jews themselves.
Bauer argued that for the Jews to deserve full emancipation and

equality they should renounce their religion and accept Christianity[20]—a truly medieval concept which was in strange harmony with the ideas often expressed by the Tsars. Karl Marx took strong exception to such views. In an essay entitled *A World Without Jews* written in reply to Bauer, he argued that political freedom could not be made conditional on the renunciation of religious tenets. Emancipation and the granting of civil rights should be carried out without any conditions whatsoever. But while disagreeing with his friend on the question of religion, Marx shared Bauer's other antagonistic theories about the Jews. Like Bauer, he did not consider the Jewish people a nation. He regarded them merely as a caste, or a 'chimerical nationality'.

In his critical views on the Jewish people and Judaism in particular, Karl Marx went even further than Bauer. To Bauer, Judaism was merely a lower form of religion than Christianity; to qualify for full citizenship the Jew had to be lifted to a higher level of religious belief. But to Marx Judaism was an evil in itself, 'an anti-social element' from which the Jew himself must be purified before he became fully emancipated. Marx adopted the theories promulgated by Ludwig Feuerbach, the German philosopher to whom 'Judaism was *utilismus* and nothing else'. Elaborating on this theory Marx presented a truly vicious image of the Jewish people and their God.

> What was the essential foundation of the Jewish religion? [he wrote] Practical needs, egotism . . . The god of practical needs and private interest is money. Money is the zealous one God of Israel . . . The bill of exchange is the Jew's real God. His God is the illusory bill of exchange.

Unable to free himself from an emotional prejudice against the Jewish people, Marx expressed himself repeatedly in derisive, even insulting, terms :

> What is the object of the Jew's worship in this world? Usury. What is his worldly god? Money.
> Very well then; emancipation from usury and money, that is from practical, real Judaism, would constitute the emancipation of our time.

He finally explained how this emancipation would come about :
through the assimilation of the Jew in society :

> As soon as society [he wrote] can abolish the empirical
> nature of the Jew, that is, usury and its preconditions,
> being a Jew will become impossible because his conviction
> will no longer have any object, since the subjective basis
> of Judaism (practical necessity) will have become human-
> ized, and the conflict between man as a sensual individual
> and as a species will have been abolished.
> The social emancipation of Jewry is the emancipation of
> society from Jewry.[21]

It is now generally admitted that Marx had no real knowledge of the Jewish problem as a whole. His essay on the Jewish
question was published in 1844 when he was only twenty-five.
Professor Isaiah Berlin maintained that it was 'a dull and shallow
composition'.[22] Besides, Marx was a thinker of many phobias. He
often used harsh language about other people too. He had a deep
dislike for the Slavs, for instance. 'I have no trust', he once wrote
to Engels, 'in the Russians. There is no such thing as honour
in the Russian language.' He had no sympathy for the Scandi-
navians; he regarded the Danes, for instance, as being 'a people
endowed with enthusiasm for brutal, piratical old Norse nationalism'. Nevertheless, it cannot be denied that his dislike of the
Jews—which Thomas Masaryk, the late President of Czechoslovakia, called 'really anti-Semitic'—had a definite effect on the
anti-Jewish policies in Soviet Russia, and the Marxist world generally. For Marx the term 'Jew' did not always have the overtones it sometimes has today. He employed it more as an economic symbol than a term of invective. Yet the condemnatory
force of his remarks made them stick in the minds of many a
Marxist, as I discovered in the USSR as well as in other Communist countries. The condemnatory phraseology Marx used to
describe Judaism has found its way into a sizeable number of
books and articles in Russia denouncing Judaism. Its anti-Judaic
expressions have a sharpness and stigmatizing quality which made
them appeal to many a Russian writer and propagandist with
a deeply-rooted prejudice against the Jews.

Karl Marx seems to have derived strange satisfaction from stigmatizing the Jews. In his correspondence he occasionally used such expressions as *der verfluchte Jude* (damn Jews, or *Juedchen* (little Jew). Writing about the French Stock Exchange to American newspapers, Marx spoke of the 'Bourse Synagogue,' and always referred to European bankers as Jewish bankers. Commenting on the loan to the Russian Tsar, he remarked that 'every tyrant is backed by a Jew, as is every Pole by a Jesuit'.

A remarkable illustration of how this animosity to the people of his origin accompanied him all his life was the attitude Marx showed to Tsarist persecution of the Jews. Among the sharpest and most observant commentators on contemporary events and always quick to react, Marx maintained an unbroken silence on the humiliating mistreatment of millions of Jews in Tsarist Russia. He commented frequently on the Tsar's policies but avoided the Jewish problem. At the time of his writings and sojourn in London, leading intellectuals, writers, scholars, and poets, from all over the world including Russia herself, openly protested against the anti-Jewish outrages. They expressed sympathy with the Jewish victims of Tsarist persecution. But Marx, although he wrote profusely on the maltreatment of the Irish by the British, never sympathized with Russian Jewry.

In a way Marx's personal troubles almost symbolized the fate of the Jews. He suffered many expulsions and was compelled to wander from country to country as a stateless refugee. He left his native Germany to seek greater freedom in France. Expelled from France he settled in Belgium. In 1848, the year after the *Communist Manifesto*, Marx was expelled from Belgium and returned for a while to Germany, but again he was forced to leave and seek refuge abroad. Having renounced his Prussian citizenship in a moment of anger, he was a stateless person. He applied for British citizenship, but his application was rejected on the grounds that 'this man was not loyal to his King'. How strange that a great social thinker whose personal life in many ways reflected the vicissitudes suffered by the Jewish people, should have remained so cold and unmoved by their misfortunes. His assimilationist views and his anti-Jewish prejudices, albeit in a less direct way than his other teachings and ideas, have undoubtedly influenced Communist attitudes today. Fifty years after the Revolution many of these ideas continue to be echoed in the writings of Communist propagandists, and to contribute to the shaping of Communist policy towards the Jewish question.

LENIN AND STALIN: EARLY ATTITUDES

Unlike Karl Marx, his devoted pupil Vladimir Lenin was more friendly towards the Jews. In his copious writings on the nationalities question he showed sympathy, and occasionally warmth for the oppressed Jewish subjects under the Tsar. As a Russian engaged from his early years in the planning of a revolution in a country with six million Jews, Lenin was bound to be concerned with the Jewish problem. This arose naturally from his preoccupation with the fate of all the oppressed national minorities in the Tsar's empire suffering under Russian domination. 'Can a nation be free', Lenin asked, 'if it oppresses other nations?' His answer was that only through granting the fullest equality to all nationalities, including the Jews, could the Russian people themselves become really free and civilized.

In a political sense Lenin's preoccupation with the Jewish question dates back to the early years of this century. He came into direct contact with the Jewish labour movement through the Bund, the first Jewish workers' organization in Eastern Europe to have a Socialist programme. Although illegal, as were all such movements under the Tsar, it quickly won support among the poor workers in the cities, in the ghettos of Warsaw, Lodz, Bialystok, Vilna and Kovno. Poverty-stricken Jewish artisans and small traders were soon stirred by the ideas of change and revolution. Lenin's own Russian Revolutionary Movement was not formed until a year later in 1898. But it quickly gained sympathy within the Jewish masses who were drawn into the maelstrom of Lenin's party. In fact, within a very short period a number of the most prominent leaders of the Bund became Lenin's associates and friends.

Lenin valued the support and co-operation given to him by

the Jewish workers for two reasons. Firstly, the Bund already had a well-organized following with a membership of between 30,000 and 40,000, whereas the Social Democratic Party, of which Lenin was the most prominent figure, had only some 8,000 registered members at the beginning of the century. Secondly, he had a high regard for the intellectual qualities of its leaders, no less than for its membership. The Bund consisted largely of urban elements with a higher standard of education. Revolutionary aspirations and a desire for progress were more advanced among the politically conscious Jewish workers. In this respect they contrasted favourably with the Russian peasants whose attitude Lenin himself often referred to as 'sluggish'.

But while inspired by the same Marxist theories of social advancement and revolution, the Bund, as Lenin was soon to find out, was not prepared to go with him all the way. There were many bridges linking the two revolutionary movements the Jewish and the Russian. There was also a gulf between them.

There was complete agreement between the two parties on the kind of joint action needed to bring about the overthrow of the Tsar. Both parties were sincerely convinced that only a revolution could solve the problems of the millions of workers and peasants for whose emancipation they struggled. Like Lenin's Russian followers, the majority of the members in the Jewish Socialist Movement opposed religion, clericalism, and Zionism. They believed that Jewish backwardness, like that of other national minorities, should be eradicated, and that in the fight for equal rights in the country of his birth the Jew should abandon his hopes for a Messiah and a return to Zion. On all these subjects the Bundists were willing to follow the road towards revolution in close allegiance with Lenin. But they would go no further. In the first place, the Bund categorically denied the Marxist theories to which Lenin subscribed i.e. that the Jews were not a nation, and therefore could not claim full national rights. This was a bitterly fought issue between the two movements. On no account would the Jewish socialists agree to submerge their national identity, in particular their culture, in the battle for the Russian revolution. A resolution adopted by the 4th Convention of the Bund held in 1901, demanded explicitly that 'the concept of a nation must also be applied to the Jewish people'. It further stipulated that 'a State such as Russia which is made up of a great number of nationalities, must be transformed into a federation of nationalities with complete national autonomy for each without consideration of the territory they inhabit'.[1]

Among the demands which the Bund put down as basic for co-operation with the Russian revolutionary movement were:

(i) A guarantee of cultural autonomy for the Jewish minority. This meant the right to conduct their education and all other cutural activities—the Press, the theatre, publishing houses—in the Yiddish language, with the support of the State.

(ii) The right of the Bund to have a separate Central Committee within the Russian revolutionary movement, and to be recognized as the sole representative and spokesman for all the Jewish labouring masses in Russia, Poland and Lithuania.

As Lenin opposed these demands, a bitter struggle ensued which led to a final split. Lenin was prepared to grant a certain form of cultural autonomy by which Jewish schools would be maintained, but on a purely secular basis. But as he denied that the Jews were a nation, he opposed their demand for a separate political organization. He admitted that the Jews spoke a distinct language as did the Ukrainians, the Poles and other minorities, but maintained that Yiddish was not the language of every Jew. In some countries, and especially in Western Europe where Lenin spent much of his time in exile, the Jews were adopting increasingly the language of the country they lived in. Coupled with the absence of territorial unity. This deprived them in his opinion of any just claim to full nationhood. He further argued that Jewish workers who agreed to co-operate with the Russians in the battle against the Tsar constituted only a very small section of the Jewish people. The vast majority, he maintained, were bourgeois-minded and opposed the Revolution. It was they who insisted on nationhood and nationality. But to agree to the preservation of Jewish nationalism of the bourgeois type was dangerous, and at the same time incompatible with the tenets of true Socialism. To Lenin, as to Marx his master, the true solution of the Jewish problem was 'internationalism'—the fusion of all nations into one society. For the Jews, including the members of the Bund, this should be the only goal. However forcibly put, Lenin's arguments were of no avail. Submission to Lenin's views would mean assimilation, and this the Bund refused to accept.

Lenin's opposition to the Bund was not, as has been suggested, due to any personal animosity, still less to any anti-Jewish prejudices. Although he conducted the fight with determination, sometimes with bitterness, there seems to be no reason to believe that he was at any time imbued with hostile feelings. The conditions Lenin laid down to the Bund were primarily dictated by a desire to form and lead a centralized, closely-knit revolutionary movement. He opposed any deviation from this principle, and to the end of his life insisted that authority within the Party must always rest in the hands of a central body. He would not agree to any splintering off into separate independent parties. He admitted that national groups had a distinct role to play within the movement, but only as part of it. They could never become independent movements on the lines the Bund suggested. To Lenin the respective national languages were merely instrumental in the dissemination of Communist ideology among the various national groups.

While opposing Jewish demands, Lenin made a concession to other national minorities. He agreed to the formation of labour groups of the Ukrainians, White Russians and Georgians. But even in their case he insisted that sub-divisions could only be tolerated as agencies for the transmission, in their respective national languages, of the programme, the decisions and the slogans of a centralized revolutionary party. Yet the concessions he granted for the transitional period immediately after the Revolution became a fixed feature of the Soviet system. The Ukrainian, White Russian, Georgian, and several other national minorities whose leaders, with those of the Jewish minority, had fought alongside Lenin for the overthrow of Tsarism, retained Communist Parties of their own. This the Jews were rigidly denied.

The arguments and counter-arguments between Lenin and the Bund went on for several years until the final clash at the London Conference of the Russian Democratic Party in 1903. Here a full-dress debate of the Bund's demands took place for the first time in the open. It was an historic occasion. For it was soon revealed that while united in a common fight for freedom, the two movements differed over the methods to be employed and, in particular, over the position the Jewish minority was to be given within the framework of Communist Russia. Was it to remain a Jewish movement, or abandon its national identity and assimilate?

The open battle between Lenin and the Bund actually started in Brussels where the Conference, the 2nd Party Congress, had begun in July. Transferred to London the debate became charged with emotion. Animosity finally led to complete rupture. Significantly—and this may be a pointer to the assimilationist policies of later days—it was neither Lenin nor any of the Russian delegates present, who were in the forefront of the attack against the Bund and its Jewish cultural demands but Lenin's Jewish associates. The attack was opened by Leon Trotsky who accused the Bund of 'splitting the revolutionary forces'. Trotsky insisted on Lenin's idea of a strong central executive. To grant the Jewish Socialists' demands as formulated by the Bund would mean, he argued, endangering the cohesion of the forces arrayed against the Tsar. He, too, distrusted nationalism, and in particular Jewish nationalism. He feared that the granting of cultural autonomy to the Jewish workers' movement would lead to some form of Zionism. In an article he published after the London Conference in *Iskra* (the Spark)—the organ of the Russian revolutionaries—Trotsky described the Bund's principles as the 'hysterical sobbings of the romanticists of Zion'. He called Theodor Herzl, the founder of political Zionism, a 'shameless adventurer'.[2]

Another of the Jewish delegates to enter the battle against the Bund was Julius Martov-Zederbaum. A former founder-member of the Bund, Martov defected to Lenin's group. He was soon joined there by another Jewish revolutionary, Paul Axelrod. Born into Jewish families and brought up in a Jewish environment, these future Communists were alien to Jewish traditions and especially to the Jewish religion. Sometimes referred to as 'un-Jewish Jews' they advocated assimilation as the ultimate aim of socialism and internationalism, and as the best possible solution to the Jewish problem.

Lenin had gone to a great deal of trouble to organize opposition to the Bund in correspondence with his supporters months before the Conference. The leader of the Bund, Vladimir Medem,[3] who appeared under the assumed name of Goldblat, had done likewise. Both leaders were fully aware that any decision taken at this gathering would influence the whole future of the Jewish issue. Attempts to postpone a final resolution failed. The Bund demanded a vote of no confidence and lost.

The London Conference, it soon appeared, was of further historic import. It determined the Communist attitude towards the Jewish problem, and laid the basis for future policy. In addition it saw the emergence of the Bolsheviks as the majority power in the movement. The Bund delegates left the Conference in anger, and Lenin had the opportunity to gain a majority over the Mensheviks. Thus the Bolshevik Party was born and Bolshevism appeared as a distinct political movement.[4]

Victorious though he was at the London Conference, Lenin carried on a determined fight against the Bund long afterwards. The question of national minorities loomed ever larger on the international scene and demanded clarification. So did the issue of national cultures. Basically Lenin's views on the Jewish question were in harmony with those of his master. Like Karl Marx he refused to regard the Jewish people as constituting a nation, and therefore opposed the demands for Jewish cultural autonomy. In common with other Socialist thinkers at the beginning of this century, Lenin maintained that through abolishing the discriminatory laws against the Jews and the Ghetto, the whole Jewish question would be solved. What the Bund asked for was in a way a direct challenge to such theories, and Lenin while offering opposition displayed some uneasiness. Perhaps he regretted finding himself in the role of one of the organization's chief opponents. Some such feeling was reflected in the essay which he wrote soon after the London Conference entitled 'The Position of the Bund in the Party'. The essay was first published in *Iskra*, of which Lenin became the sole editor, and was a kind of afterthought, or even an apology.[5]

In justification of his views Lenin repeated some of the theories on Jewish nationhood formulated by Karl Kautsky, then a recognized authority on the nationality question, and the chief interpreter of Marxist doctrine. He quoted Kautsky's statement that : 'The Jews have ceased to be a nation, for a nation without a territory is unthinkable'. The possession of territory was the chief element in the definition of a nationality to Kautsky and other Socialist thinkers of that period. Altogether Kautsky wrote disapprovingly of the Jews in the ghettos, regarding them as a nefarious and undesirable element.[6]

It would be wrong to maintain that Lenin was burdened by any of the prejudices towards the Jews which clouded Marx's judgment. Nevertheless Lenin, too, considered the idea of a separate and distinct Jewish people as utterly inappropriate, unattainable in practice, and scientifically unjustifiable. The whole idea seemed to him to have a reactionary political implication. 'All over Europe,' he wrote 'the decline of medievalism and the development of political liberty went hand in hand with the political emancipation of the Jews, their abandonment of Yiddish for the language of the people among whom they lived, and, in general, their undeniable progressive assimilation with the surrounding population.' This conclusion anticipated fundamental Communist policy.

Returning to his London battle with the Bund Lenin explained that :

> . . . the idea of a Jewish 'nationality' is definitely reactionary not only when expounded by its consistent advocates (the Zionists) but likewise on the lips of those who try to combine it with the ideas of Social-Democracy (the Bundists). The idea of a Jewish nationality runs counter to the interests of the Jewish proletariat, for it fosters among them, directly or indirectly, a spirit hostile to assimilation, the spirit of the 'ghetto'.

What Lenin feared most was nationalist separatism. He feared that it created barriers between nationalities, and advocated a complete abandonment of nationalism, including what he called 'Great Russian chauvinism'. Elaborating on the Jewish issue, Lenin pointed out that at the time of his writing there were ten and a half million Jews in the world. Nearly half of them lived in civilized conditions in Germany, France and England, where all circumstances favoured maximum assimilation. The other half, those in Russia and Galicia, lived in wretched and oppressed conditions, in circumstances favouring maximum separation and minimum assimilation. 'That is precisely what the Jewish problem *amounts to* : assimilation or isolation',[7] he wrote. What Lenin wanted to achieve was maximum assimilation. This has become the focal point of Communist policy on the minorities' issue.

More than a decade elapsed between Lenin's open clash with the Bund and his confrontation of the Jewish problem as a practical isue immediately after the October Revolution. During that period the whole problem of national minorities became a dominant feature in all political discussions in Europe and especially in those of the revolutionary groups, of which Lenin was a leading figure. The Jewish problem, and the search for its solution was also raised at many conferences. And it was during this period that Lenin came in much closer contact with Jews than ever before, a contact which resulted in some revision of his attitude, if not of his theories.

Nine years after the battle with the Bund at the London Conference, Lenin transferred his Party headquarters from Paris to Cracow. He chose Cracow for two reasons. Firstly because this ancient capital of Poland, then in the Austrian Empire, was close to the frontiers of Russia and Germany. This made contact with the Tsar's secret opponents in Russia much easier. They could come and go more often and without any particular difficulties or great expense of funds. Secondly, Cracow had by that time become the centre of the revolutionary activities of the Polish socialists. It was here that Marshal Josef Pilsudski, the future ruler of Poland, and at that time a leading figure in the

Polish Socialist Party, had his headquarters. While differing from Lenin in many ways the Poles were also working for the overthrow of Russian domination and the independence of Poland. Contemporary Polish statistics which have recently come to light showed that there were no less than 4,000 political refugees in Cracow at that time. This has been revealed from official documents giving the names of revolutionaries under police supervision, among whom Lenin, listed as 'Wlodzimierz Uljanow', was, as the police register remarked, 'a new and dangerous number.'

Lenin was forty-two years of age—the Austrian police made a mistake of ten years—when he and, his wife, Nadezhda Krupskaya, took up residence, together with his mother-in-law, at 41 Queen Hedwig Street, on 2 July 1912. Until then Lenin's contact with Jews had been limited. The Jews he had known had always been thoroughly assimilated; many of them had long opted out of the Jewish community. But in Cracow, which in those days had a large Jewish community, he found a different kind of Jewry steeped in Jewish traditions and in the orthodox way of life. Under the benevolent reign of Franz Joseph I, Jews enjoyed full rights of citizenship. Many of them, especially those who belonged to the professional classes, played an important role in the political affairs of the country. As a leader of a political movement Lenin sought to establish relations with local political groups and the numerous Poles engaged in plotting against the Tsar. Among the leading Polish Socialists were two Austrian-Jewish leaders, Herman Diamand and Victor Adler. There were many others including Stanislaw Mendelson, Nahum Sokolov's son-in-law, who was a leading member, in fact co-founder, of the Polish Socialist Party and editor of the journal *Class Struggle*. Lenin was in frequent contact with all of them and was often invited to lecture on the nationalities issue, among others, at specially arranged gatherings of Polish intellectuals and revolutionaries.

Nadezhda Krupskaya has left an absorbing account of those early days in Cracow with her husband. Her book, *Reminiscences of Lenin*, offers an instructive glimpse into the relationship which the Communist leader and his wife developed with the local population. She also wrote warmly of the Jews in Cracow, who 'lived in a separate quarter of the city and dressed differently.' 'You could buy everything at the Jewish shops at half price, but you had to haggle there, pretend to go away, then come back again, and so on'. There is also a passage in her *Reminiscences* about the prevailing attitude of some Poles towards the Jews: 'In the waiting room at the out-patient hospital, the patients would seriously discuss whether a Jewish child was the same as a Polish child or not, whether it was cursed or not. And a little Jewish boy sat there listening to it all'.[8]

A veteran Polish Socialist, S. Drobner, himself a Jew who had come in contact with Lenin during his stay in Cracow, recalled how he had heard Lenin cracking Jewish jokes to some of his friends. Lenin told him the story of a Russian policeman who, on hearing two Jews denouncing someone as 'a big idiot' arrested them on charges 'of insulting the Tsar'. When the Jews protested the policeman declared angrily, 'Oh I know very well who you called an idiot, you meant the Tsar!'

Because of his wife's illness—Nadezhda suffered from thyroid trouble—Lenin had to move to Poronin, a village in the Carpathian Mountains. It was there that one of the two Party Conferences held in Poland before the First World War took place. At both these conferences the national aspirations of the minorities were discussed along with other major issues concerning the independence and freedom of the subjected peoples both in Russia and in the Austro-Hungarian empire, the second multi-national empire in Europe. The conferences were attended by numerous revolutionary leaders from Russia, Stalin among them. Zinoviev and Kamenev, who in fact had been in Poland with their families some time before Lenin's arrival, were also present. The years preceding the First World War were aflame with controversy on the nationalities issue, and Krupskaya testified in her memoirs how 'Vladimir Ilyich devoted a great deal of attention to the national question. Ever since his youth he had hated national oppression in every form. Marx's saying that there could be no greater misfortune for a nation than to subjugate another nation, was near and comprehensible to him'.[9]

It is on record that from Cracow Lenin used to maintain regular contact with the Bolshevik deputies in the Duma, the Russian parliament. He used to send them instructions on how to carry on the battle for the rights of national minorities in the Tsarist empire. In fact he often wrote the text for their speeches, which were smuggled to St Petersburg by special couriers. Some of these couriers crossed the Russian frontier not far from my native village. A leading figure in arranging the illegal trips of Lenin's messengers across the frontier was Nicolas Krylenko, who served as a link between St Petersburg and Cracow. He was a teacher of Russian in a High School in Lublin where his mother earned a livelihood by making dresses for the well-to-do middle-class Jewish families. A secret member of the Bolshevik Party, Krylenko turned his mother's humble home into a meeting place for Russian revolutionaries on their way to and from Cracow. He later became Minister of Justice in Bolshevik Russia, afterwards Chief Prosecutor, and played an infamous role in some of Stalin's purges.

Lenin's principal essay on the minorities issue was entitled 'Critical Remarks on the National Question'. As a practical politician, he appreciated the contribution which Jews in Russia had made to the fight against the Tsar, and for the Revolution. He was aware that, because of their humble position and political oppression, the Jews in Russia were particularly sympathetic to revolutionary ideas. Nevertheless, he considered the Jewish mode of life, Jewish traditions, and in particular their religious practices as a reactionary force which barred their way towards real progress. Like so many other Communist leaders, Jews among them, Lenin considered these traditional forces to be remnants of feudalism, which prevented the Jews from enjoying complete emancipation.

While adopting a milder attitude towards Judaism and the Jews than Karl Marx, Lenin nevertheless used strong language against the demands for a Jewish national culture. On this point he was adamant; such claims he considered petit bourgeois and un-Marxist. He conceded that the Jews were the most oppressed and persecuted nation. But :

. . . Jewish national culture is the slogan of the rabbis and the bourgeoisie, the slogan of our enemies.

Whoever, directly or indirectly, puts forward the slogan of Jewish 'national culture' is . . . an enemy of the proletariat, a supporter of all that is *outmoded* and connected with *caste* among the Jewish people; he is an accomplice of the rabbis and the bourgeoisie. On the other hand, those Jewish Marxists who mingle with the Russian, Lithuanian, Ukrainian and other workers in international Marxist organizations, and make their contribution (both in Russian and in Yiddish) toward creating the international culture of the working-class movement—those Jews, despite the separatism of the Bund, uphold the best traditions of Jewry by fighting the slogan of 'national culture'.[10]

Formulated in this categorical manner, Lenin's theories later became the basis of Soviet policy. Yet Lenin never denied the existence of a Jewish question in Russia. When, after the Revolution, he had to deal with the problem in a practical way he called for a solution on humane principles. Despite his opposition to the Bund's demands for a national Jewish culture, Lenin insisted that the Jewish minority be given facilities to set up Jewish cultural instructions in which Yiddish was to be the language of instruction. Had he lived longer and allowed this process to continue, it might have proved a valuable force in Jewish life in Communist Russia, as it has done with the other major national groups which have not suffered so acutely since Lenin's death.

Lenin remained in Poland until the outbreak of the First World War. The day war was declared he was arrested on suspicion of being a Tsarist agent and imprisoned in Nowy-Targ gaol. But his friends, including the Jewish deputy to the Austrian Parliament, Herman Diamand, intervened, and he was released. On 26 August 1914, Lenin was allowed to leave for Switzerland where he remained until the downfall of the Tsar,[11] when he was transported into Russia by the Germans in the famous sealed wagon.

How far the two years in Cracow influenced Lenin's views on

the Jewish problem is difficult to ascertain. As a keen observer of social conditions, he could not have been unimpressed by the tenacity with which the large Jewish communities in Cracow, and in the surrounding townships, clung to their traditional way of life. They were all Yiddish-speaking Jews, loyal to their country and government, but making progressive efforts towards emancipation. From all accounts collected in Poland afterwards it emerged that in discussions with Polish Socialists Lenin frequently dwelt on the Jewish issue. He was anxious to elucidate in discussions with other Marxists a proper course of action. It was partly because of this—Polish Socialists maintained—that he asked Stalin to undertake the task of writing a separate treatise on the subject. Lenin himself has left a record of his meeting with Stalin in Cracow. In a letter to Maxim Gorky dated February 1913 about the problem of national minorities Lenin wrote, 'we have here a wonderful Georgian who is writing a long article for *Prosveshcheniye*, for which he has gathered all the Austrian and other material'.[12] Lenin is believed to have handed Stalin some of the notes he had himself made on the nationalities issue, which were incorporated into his lectures on the subject, and in the speeches he had written for the Bolshevik representatives in the Duma.

Stalin was not present at the London Conference. In August 1903 he was serving a term of imprisonment in Tsarist Siberia. But he was fully informed of what took place from articles in *Iskra*, having been one of its chief distributors in Russia and in regular contact with the Party. Encouraged by Lenin, Stalin, who until then was known as Koba-Djugashvili, went to Austria in order to study the complex minority issue in the Austro-Hungarian Empire. If on a smaller scale than Tsarist Russia, Franz Joseph also ruled over Germans, Magyars, Czechs, Poles, Jews, and numerous other smaller ethnic groups. The situation in Austria-Hungary thus offered a good opportunity to become acquainted with a progressive European state peopled by a mosaic of nationalities. Even before he came to Cracow to meet Lenin— Stalin too crossed the frontier from Russia into Austrian Poland via my native village—he had won some fame as a specialist on the minorities' issue. The population of Georgia also consisted of a number of national groups, and Stalin frequently referred to them in political discussions. Lenin therefore considered him the right person to be entrusted with the mission of studying the issue for the benefit and guidance of the Party.

It is still a matter of some controversy whether what Stalin produced in his essay actually met with Lenin's approval. Views differ.[18] Stalin's thesis on the nationalities issue, written and published in Vienna in 1913, generally took a harsher line than Lenin, especially in regard to the Bund and the Jewish problem. 'Marxism and the National Question', as Stalin's essay was called, was largely devoted to the Jewish question, and contained a much more violent indictment of the Bund than had been made by any one of its opponents at the London Conference. Written by the future Commissar of Nationalities in post-revolutionary Russia this essay became an ominous handbook of Communist policy, and a guide to the treatment of the Jewish minority. Almost half of its contents is clouded by denunciations of the Bund and its demands for Jewish national cultural autonomy. All this centres around Stalin's refusal to consider the Jews a nation.

Stalin asked, 'What is a nation?' He replied that 'A nation is primarily a community, a definite community of people . . . a nation is not a racial or tribal, but a historically constituted community of people'. He then went on to develop the idea that a nation is not conceivable without a common language and a common territory. As the Jews had no common territory Stalin categorically denied them the right of nationhood.

He questioned their very unity.

> . . . but what . . . national cohesion can there be . . .
> between the Georgian, Daghestanian, Russian and American
> Jews, who are completely disunited, inhabit different terri-
> tories and speak different languages? . . . if there is any-
> thing common to them left it is their religion . . . But how
> [he asked] can it be seriously maintained that petrified reli-
> gious rites and fading psychological relics affect the 'fate'
> of these Jews more powerfully than the living social, eco-
> nomic and cultural environment that surrounds them? And

it is only on this assumption that it is generally possible to speak of the Jews as a single nation.

In consequence Stalin put forward the view that the Jewish people were on the road towards complete assimilation. In this he fully agreed with other Socialist thinkers and Marxist theoreticians. He pointed out that Marx, referring mainly to the German Jews, had expressed the same opinion in his essay *A World Without Jews*, as early as the 1840s; further that Kautsky had repeated the idea in respect of the Russian Jews in *Das Kischinjewer Blutbad* (The Kishinev Bloodbath) in 1906; and finally that Bauer, writing at the same time as himself, described the situation of the Austrian Jews in similar terms.

Stalin maintained a particularly venomous line towards the Bund and its demand for cultural autonomy for the Jewish working masses. He accused them of propagating ideas which would separate the Jewish worker from others, ideas which did not differ from those cherished by 'bourgeois nationalists'. He accused them of demanding the preservation of the Sabbath, and separate hospitals where dietary laws would be observed, and thus misinterpreted some of the resolutions adopted at conferences of the Bund held during the first decade of this century. He was even sarcastic over the principal demand for the Jewish language as stipulated in the resolutions submitted by the Bund at the London Conference. He referred to Yiddish as jargon and made fun of those Jewish workers' leaders who would like to preserve '*all* the national peculiarities of the Jews, even those that are patently noxious to the proletariat, the isolation of the Jews from everything non-Jewish', and wound up, '. . . that is the level to which the Bund has sunk!'

Still only a novitiate in Marxist ideology, Stalin leaned heavily on the views of others, rather than producing any new philosophy of his own. There are several passages in this treatise in which Stalin comes out clearly on the side of the minorities and their right to use their native language in schools and cultural institutions. '. . . *national equality in all forms*', he wrote, '. . . *is an essential element* in the solution of the national problem.' He called for the prohibition of 'all national privileges without exception and all kinds of disabilities and restrictions on the rights of national minorities. That, and that alone, is the real, not a paper guarantee of the rights of a minority.[14] Yet towards the Bund and Jewish national aspirations, his language is hostile.

The essay, it is now agreed, already contained some of the seeds which later brought forth an anti-Semitic policy, and the destruction of many of the nobler ideas of Jewish freedom and Jewish equality. It is pointed out in support of this view, that the essay dates from the period of Stalin's first meeting with Trotsky, and the beginning of their mutual antagonism. Trotsky was at that time hovering between the Bolsheviks and the Mensheviks, each fighting for supremacy in the revolutionary movement, and had crossed swords with Lenin on several occasions. Stalin, as Lenin's supporter, became Trotsky's chief opponent. At a later encounter with Stalin in Petrograd Trotsky noticed 'in his yellow eyes . . . the same glint of animosity' that he had noticed at that first meeting in Vienna.[15]

At the time of Lenin's death, in 1924, when Stalin became the ruler of the Soviet Union, the Jewish minority in Russia had already reached the stage where a Communist policy of assimilation could have been put into operation without causing terror. In their loyal support of the October Revolution Jewish Communists of the *Yevsektsiya* had worked zealously to spread the new ideology among Russian Jewry. They had laboured to detach the Russian Jew from his past, from his traditional attachments to religion and Zion. They had managed to isolate him from the Jewish community abroad. All this was more or less in accordance with the assimilationist theories of Marx, formulated by Lenin, and elaborated by Stalin himself before he came to power. Had it not been for Stalin's impatience later, assimilation might have been achieved without bloodshed.

3

THE POST-REVOLUTIONARY DECADE

In the hands of Russian rulers anti-Semitism has always been an instrument of policy. A deeply-rooted prejudice of the Tsars and fostered widely by the Church it never became racial: its basis was economic and religious. The Tsars frequently exploited it to divert attention from administrative failures. For the leaders of the Russian Orthodox Church hostility towards the Jew was both a manifestation of loyalty to the Tsar and an expression of piety. Yet, although constantly plaguing the life of the Jew in Russia, anti-Semitism there has never taken the barbaric form it assumed in Nazi Germany. For when given a pseudo-scientific backing and a racial-nationalistic content, political anti-Semitism found its home in Germany and not in Russia. The anti-Semitic ideas of Marr, Dehring, Treitschke, Stoeker and others, including Nietzsche, struck root in Germany. Even the anti-Jewish teaching of Houston Stewart Chamberlain, the renegade Englishman and forerunner of Julius Streicher, found its only home in Germany because the English people would not accept his theories.

Similarly, the Russian people as a whole have never been predisposed towards anti-Semitism. The reaction of the Russian population to the anti-Jewish propaganda put out by the Nazis during the Second World War is a case in point. In the Ukraine and in certain areas of Lithuania and Latvia the German invaders found support for their anti-Jewish measures. But only a small percentage of the people co-operated with the Nazis in the mass executions. German documents published after the War revealed that in certain areas of Western Russia and Eastern Europe the local population had been horrified by the brutal treatment of the Jews by the Nazis. In a report to Himmler, sent in the Autumn of 1941, SS Brigade Commander Stahlecker stated that 'native anti-Semitic forces were induced to start pogroms against the Jews during the first hour after capture although this proved very difficult.' In Estonia, the local population refused to take part in the pogroms. True, a section of the local population in the Baltic countries is known to have taken an active part in the slaughter of Jews in Vilna, Kovno, Minsk, Riga and in some of the smaller localities. True, very few Jews were helped to escape liquidation at the hands of the Gestapo. Yet the majority of the people disapproved of the harsh methods.

It was only a section of the aristocracy in Tsarist Russia which persistently held anti-Jewish views, and which acted as the source of official discrimination. Such discrimination began early. Under Ivan the Terrible (1530-84), the aim of anti-Jewish measures was to drive the Jews to conversion. When his armies occupied new Polish territories Jews who refused to renounce their faith were thrown into the river and drowned.

Conversion remained an instrument of Government policy long after Ivan the Terrible had disappeared from the Russian throne. When, after the reign of Alexander II, conversion was no longer permitted as an alternative to death, Jews had to submit to all kinds of oppression, discrimination and maltreatment, culminating in the pogroms. But even in the worst days of anti-Jewish riots, Russian anti-Semitism was mainly a tool in the hands of the rulers in alliance with the Church. In fact, the Tsar and his police had to devise special measures to keep anti-Semitism alive among the hungry workers and long-suffering peasants. Even the pogroms had often to be organized by the police and prepared in advance by officials. Hundreds of pogroms occurred in Russia between the middle of the nineteenth and the beginning of the twentieth century. But few of them could have been described as truly spontaneous outbursts of violence springing from an in-grained and uncontrollable racial hatred of the Jews. Perhaps the worst, most brutal pogrom was that at Kishinev in 1903. It exceeded in ferocity most other similar events on Russian soil. It has since been established that the Kishinev pogrom was insti-gated and organized by the Tsar's Minister of the Interior, Plehve.[1] When it finally broke, only the dregs of the city's population actually took part in the plunder and killing. The vast majority of the people stayed away. After the pogrom Russian intellectuals led by Tolstoy were among the first to protest and condemn the riots.

The Romanov dynasty found anti-Semitism useful though often expensive to propagate. It was a political weapon with which the Tsars aimed, often successfully, to beguile the uneducated Russian worker and peasant into thinking that the Jew, and not the despot in St Petersburg, was the cause of all his troubles. Once the Tsarist rule had come to an end and the Orthodox Church had been deprived of its powers and influence, hostility towards the Jews rapidly declined. In fact, shortly after the downfall of the old régime anti-Semitism disappeared almost completely. Russia was then in a state of great turmoil and insecurity. The people were suffering from all kinds of shortages. In Petrograd thousands were unable to buy bread. In a telegram to the Tsar which Rodzianko, the chairman of the Duma, sent on 27 February 1917, urging Nicholas II to reconvene Parliament, he said : 'The last bulwark of order has been eliminated. The Government is absolutely powerless to suppress disorders . . . The reserve battalions of the guard regiments are in rebellion. Officers are being killed . . . Civil war has started and is waxing hotter and hotter.'[2] Unrest was spreading all over the country. Yet the Jews were left in peace. Not even in the urban areas which used to be affected by reactionary Tsarist propaganda did any anti-Jewish disturbances occur. It is a fact that during the eight months' rule of the Provisional Government, between the Tsar's abdication and the Bolshevik Revolution, no anti-Jewish activities of any kind were reported. Once again it was demonstrated that anti-Jewish prejudices and activity in Russia always emanated from the centre of power.

As the Bolsheviks took over power they found that the majority of the Russian people were against them. Lenin and his associates had of necessity to avail themselves of the support, sympathy and co-operation of the national minorities. Although their theories about the Jewish people were vague and uncrystallized—Lenin and Stalin as we know refused to recognize the Jews as a nationality in their own right—they found that a fair section of Russian Jewry was willing to co-operate. The majority of Jews, like other Russians, held back. There were two reasons. First, they were scared by the Communists' battle against religion, which threatened the religious traditions which, despite all difficulties, the majority of Russian Jews had maintained for centuries. Secondly, they were made apprehensive by the Bolsheviks' ruthless methods of undermining the Jewish traditional occupations of business and trade and their determination to subject such a middle-class way of life to forceful change.

Soon, however, the civil war broke out in Russia. Former Tsarist Generals managed to mobilize considerable armies to fight the Bolsheviks. In the Ukraine, White Russia, and in several other regions their battles against the new régime were accompanied by savage attacks and pogroms on Jews. As a result hundreds of Jewish communities in the Ukraine and White Russia were destroyed. Nearly a quarter of a million Jews were killed or maimed in pogroms reminiscent of the worst days of Tsarist rule. Almost all of them had been organized by the anti-Communist military group under the command of Petlura, Denikin, Machno and some of the other generals fighting against the Bolsheviks. In their predicament many more Jews turned to the Bolsheviks for protection. They found an amicable welcome and a desire to co-operate. Anti-Semitism on the part of the Communists sank to its lowest ever level.

Immediately after the Revolution, anti-Semitism was declared 'a counter-Revolutionary activity'. Both Lenin and, for a long time afterwards, Stalin took a strong stand against anti-Semitism. Although Lenin regarded Judaism as an anachronism he condemned anti-Semitism as 'barbarism'. Stalin denounced all national and racial chauvinism as 'a survival of the barbarous practices of the cannibalistic period', and anti-Semitism as a tool serving 'the exploiters and as a lightning rod protecting capitalism from the attacks of the working people'. He appealed to Communists to fight against anti-Semitism because it was 'a phenomenon profoundly hostile to the Soviet régime'.[3]

At the outbreak of the First World War over 6,000,000 Jews

had been living under Tsarist rule, the majority of them in Poland, Lithuania and the Ukraine. When the Tsar abdicated, these territories were to a large extent still under German occupation. But there were still some 3,000,000 Jews who came under the administration of the Provisional Government. Nearly 700,000 more were in the Russian army. To those under the Russian sphere of influence the October Revolution brought emancipation and complete equality. Most of the restrictions to which the Jews had been subjected for centuries under the Tsars had already been removed from the Russian statute books by the Provisional Government after the February Revolution. A decree issued in Petrograd on 2 March 1917 over the signatures of the new Premier, Prince G. E. Lvov, and the Minister of Justice, A. F. Kerensky, had granted an amnesty to political prisoners, and freedom of speech and of assembly. It had abolished 'all restrictions based on class, religion and nationality'.[4]

After the October Revolution, Lenin's immediate task was to confirm these measures, and to grant full citizenship rights to the Jewish minority. No less than 500 anti-Jewish laws and restrictions had accumulated throughout the three hundred years of Romanov rule; Trotsky gave their number as 650.[5] All these were abolished with the undertaking that none of them would ever reappear.[6] Political equality followed; all offices in the Party and in the Government were opened to Jews. In fact the Jews being an urbanized and educated section of the population were encouraged to accept positions in the administration while many of the educated classes of Russian society refused to co-operate with the Bolsheviks. It is known, for instance, that Lenin once offered Trotsky the important post of Commissar for Home Affairs. Trotsky declined on the grounds that it might have added to the anti-Bolshevik and anti-Jewish propaganda which was raging at the time of the civil war. In the main, however, Jews willingly accepted the new opportunities to take an active part in the running of the country. Finding themselves at the beginning of a new era, large numbers of Jews accepted Lenin's policy and Bolshevik promises with hope and anticipation. Having been given the chance to enter Soviet society on the same basis as other nationalist minorities, Russian Jews set themselves energetically to the task of building the new system.

In January 1918, when the reins of power were more or less firmly in Lenin's hands, a special Commissariat for Jewish National Affairs was formed in Petrograd. The step was received with satisfaction by the Jewish public. Stalin had by then been appointed People's Commissar for National Affairs. His study of the minorities question in the pre-revolutionary years qualified him for this position in which he had full charge of the complex problem of the national minorities. On assuming his new responsibilities, Stalin made a number of pronouncements on the question of equality of citizenship. The views he expressed made a favourable impression in Jewish circles and there were quite a number who believed that he had their welfare in mind.

In their own sphere, Soviet Jewry managed within a few years of the Revolution to build up an imposing network of Jewish schools, with Yiddish as the language of instruction. They were also given facilities for the establishment of other Jewish cultural institutions. Collectively, these became a valuable asset for the development of Jewish culture in Soviet Russia after the Revolution, and especially for the preservation of Yiddish as a vehicle of literary expression. No less important, from the Jewish point of view, was the campaign against racial prejudice. Under Lenin's direction the Communist Party, the Government, the Trade Unions and especially the Press, each in its own sphere, conducted a vigorous campaign against anti-Semitism. Lenin, more than any other Soviet leader, realized that the new liberties would mean nothing unless the Russian people were educated out of the anti-Jewish prejudice which had been spread by the Tsar and the Church for so long.

Contrary to allegations by some anti-Semitic writers the new policy of emancipation was in no way due to the influence or pressure of the Jewish revolutionaries, many of whom had worked closely with Lenin. Neither Trotsky, nor Zinoviev, nor Kamenev, Lenin's close friends, were ever really interested in the Jewish question in Russia. When Medem asked him whether he fought against the Tsar as a Jew or as a Russian, Trotsky replied:

'Neither, I am a Social Democrat, and that is all'.[7] Trotsky maintained no ties with Jews and their traditions, religion and culture.

The son of a Jewish farmer—a rare species in Tsarist Russia—Lev, or Lyova, as young Bronstein was called in his childhood, knew neither Yiddish nor Hebrew. His parents also spoke no Yiddish and conversed in a mixture of Russian and Ukrainian. Nothing in Trotsky's upbringing or environment inspired him to take an interest in Jewish history. When later he was sent to a Jewish private school 'knowing no Yiddish' he could neither understand his teacher nor get along with his school mates. He was, in fact, much happier when he later went to a school in Odessa where the pupils were of German, Russian, Polish and Swiss origin, thus giving him 'his first taste of cosmopolitism'.[8] A convincing illustration of how complete was his mental detachment from the issues affecting the Jewish people was the slighting way with which he treated their existence in his *History of the Russian Revolution*. In this lengthy work Trotsky devoted about four sentences to the Jews. Likewise in his *Diary in Exile* written in Paris in 1935 after he had been expelled from the Party and forced to seek asylum abroad, there is not a line of commiseration nor any sign of interest in the gathering storm threatening the Jewish people. This despite the fact that Hitler was already in power and that the Jewish question was already the subject of much debate.[9]

The majority of Jewish Bolsheviks, in fact, were assimilated estranged Jews living in a different world from their fathers. Most of them came from assimilated families. They were ignorant of the ideas which for centuries had played a vital part in the national existence and survival of Russian and East European Jewry generally. They were convinced that the redemptive guarantees of the October Revolution were in themselves sufficient to bring about a solution of the Jewish problem, and that as a result Jews would assimilate and submerge. Under Lenin they were given the opportunity to put these theories to the test—not merely to preach assimilation, but to participate in making it a reality.

The main instruments used in the implementation of this policy of assimilation were the *Yevkom* (*Yevreyskii Komissariat*—Jew-

ish Commissariat) and the *Yevsektsiyas* (*Yevreyskaya Sektsiya*—
Jewish Sections), established with Lenin's support in January
1918. The *Yevkom* was a central body, the *Yevsektsiyas* local.
The function of these organizations was outlined in the Yiddish
daily *Die Wahrheit* in such a way as to give the Jews the impression that they would have some measure of direct control over
their own affairs. *Die Wahrheit* announced that Jewish offices
would be established side by side with the Workers' Councils, the
Soldiers' Councils and in the country with the Peasants' Councils.
The report stated that the Jewish sections would be organized
to join with the corresponding Soviet sections of other nationalities to form distinct local Soviets. The Commissariat had the task
of holding regional and national conferences of the Jewish organizations to settle the large-scale aspects of the Jewish problem.
This hopeful, rather than factual, statement was followed by a
special 'Manifesto' issued by the Jewish Commissariat, and an
appeal to the Jewish working masses in the Soviet Union.[10]

In reality neither of the two organizations had much power in
political matters. The Jews were soon disillusioned. Instead of
bringing about the regeneration of Jewish life in the new political
and economic circumstances, the organizations became the chief
proponents of assimilation. Their constitution changed rapidly,
reflecting the shifting attitude of the leaders of the Communist
Party to the Jewish problem. What began with the inspired idea
of building a new Jewish life ended with the annihilation of the
old.

Much has been written about the activities of the Jewish Commissariat, especially in the first few years after the Revolution.
It is only now, however, that fuller details of its activities are
being revealed and examined. When first established under the
control of the 'Commissariat for Nationalities'—under Stalin's
chairmanship—it had six separate departments. The most important of these dealt with the dissemination of political propaganda.
Until the Revolution there was practically no Communist literature in Yiddish. The Commissariat was therefore responsible for
the dissemination of Communist ideology among Jews in the
country. A first step in that direction was the translation of

pamphlets introducing the works of Marx, Engels and Lenin to the Jewish readership. These were published in tens of thousands in Moscow, Leningrad and in the many other Russian cities where the Commissariat established branches.

The task of another of its departments was to battle against anti-Semitism and pogroms.

Brought to life with great pomp and publicity the Jewish Commissariat was a body without a soul. It was not an independent organism. It took its orders from the Communist Party and was under its constant supervision and control. In fact all its officials, from Semen Dimanshtein, the first and only Commissar, down to the most junior official, were in the pay of the Party.

As the Commissariat for Jewish National Affairs, it existed for a short period only. In 1920 it was abolished and replaced by a Jewish department—known as the *Yevsektsiya*—of the People's Commissariat for National Affairs. There were constant changes in the construction, constitution and importance of the Jewish sections. By 1923 it had a staff of only five officials. This was shortly reduced to one. After Lenin's death, further changes were to take place. In 1926 the limited number of sections which still existed, especially those which survived in the larger towns like Moscow, Leningrad and Kiev, were reorganized. Some disappeared in the process. With the fulfilment of their role as the propagators of Communism, their existence was no longer deemed necessary. Their influence was narrowed down from week to week. This went hand-in-hand with the liquidation of Jewish cultural institutions. In 1930 the *Yevsektsiya* finally disappeared never to be resurrected.

It has never been really disclosed who in the Party, and particularly in the Central Committee, was responsible for these numerous changes in the *Yevsektsiya*. Was it Stalin himself, or some committee working under his direction? What was clear from the outset was that its main purpose was to assimilate the Jews.

The leaders of the *Yevsektsiya* were not wholly unconscious tools in the hands of the Party, as some students of the history of Soviet Jewry have suggested. They were fully aware of their mission and the service they were expected to render to the Party and Communism, fully aware that they had to accept the prospect of assimilation in silence. As early as 1922, Esther Frumkin, one of the leading Bolshevik Jewish figures in the movement, explained at a conference of the Jewish sections, that while anxious to attract the nationally-minded Jewish intelligentsia to Communism 'we never took an oath to promise eternal life to the Jewish people . . .' 'The source of our inspiration and our enthusiasm must not be the preservation of the nation, but the victory of the proletarian revolution, the building of socialism'.[11] Her views were shared by her colleagues in the organization. Alexander Chemerisky, another prominent figure in the *Yevsektsiya*, made it quite clear that assimilation of the Jewish minority had to be recognized as 'one of the conditions' of building socialism. The inevitability of large-scale Jewish assimilation was accepted as an unavoidable consequence of the economic development and industrialization of Russia. It was part of the national Russian reconstruction and modernization process in which the Jew had to play his full part. Assimilation was the price demanded of the Jew for his participation in the building of Soviet Russia.

It soon became clear, therefore, that in order to enjoy their newly won emancipation, Jews, as indeed all others, had to abandon increasingly most of their traditions, customs and beliefs. The teaching of Hebrew was forbidden and religious instruction to children under eighteen made a punishable offence. All Jewish communal organizations were suppressed and the central body of community life dissolved, never to be re-established. Most of the old patterns of Jewish life came to be regarded as 'bourgeois evils' with a 'counter-revolutionary' influence.

Never before had the Jews been subjected to pressure of this nature. As we have seen even in the most oppressive period of Tsarist rule, they had been allowed to retain their identity, worship their God in the language of their ancestors, and educate their children as they pleased. Under Communism, these traditional elements of Jewish life—the 'rock of Judaism'—were condemned to disappear. Only the Yiddish language was allowed to

remain. It soon became clear that this was not so much a privilege in the process of emancipation as a temporary concession of
a political nature. The majority of Jews in the Tsar's empire
spoke only Yiddish. In Russia proper, 90 per cent knew Yiddish.
In the Ukraine and White Russia, the percentage was even
higher. Only with the help of the Yiddish language could they be
made to grasp the full implications of the changes brought about
by the October Revolution. Yiddish was retained to perform
what Semen Dimanshtein, the Commissar for Jewish National
Affairs, described as a twofold task: to assure the flow of Party
propaganda to the Jewish masses, and to make the 'Dictatorship
of the Proletariat' prevail in the Jewish street.[12] Thus it was used
not to soften the effects of the Revolution but as a weapon
with which to attack the old system of life and introduce the
new.

The Spring of the Revolution was hardly over when a section
of Russian Jewry, including some who were Communists, began
to realize that language alone was not enough. Torn out of the
fabric of Jewish spiritual life and with all communal organizations in ruins, Yiddish was not sufficient to assert the Jews' distinctiveness. Soon it proved too weak to sustain the millions of
Russian Jews in their national identity. Transformed so rapidly
from a middle-class, closely-knit community, linked by history
and tradition into a working mass, they were pressed into a mould
in the process of integration with the majority. In addition, they
were deprived increasingly of all other means of Jewish self-
expression and of the possibilities of educating their children in
the traditional manner. Above all, they were forbidden to maintain the former, hitherto uninterrupted contact with relatives and
Jewish communities outside Russia. They were forced to remain
absolutely silent, to voice no protest or criticism of their rapidly
worsening position. As a result the Jewish minority became helpless, a mass of individuals each in constant dread of losing the
newly granted facilities to share in the building of the new Russia.
Reduced to this status the Jew could no longer resist the official
forces which planned to bring about his assimilation.

From the outset there had been differences between the treatment of the Jews and of other groups. Even in the early days of the Revolution Jewish supporters were not permitted to form a separate Communist Party, as were other minorities, especially those living in territories of their own, like the Ukrainians, White Russians and Georgians. Attempts by a group of Jewish party members to form their own Communist entity met with immediate hostility. At first, it was thought that opposition to the formation of a separate Jewish Communist Party emanated mainly from Trotsky and some of the other leading figures of Jewish origin, known for their complete assimilation. However, it soon transpired that objections came from a higher quarter, in fact from Lenin himself, and were prompted by his antagonism towards the Bund and its demands for an autonomous existence.

Lenin, who favoured a strong, centralized authority, was determined to prevent the birth of any independent Communist group. It was this same hostility to Jewish Socialist demands which led to the break with the Bund at the now famous London Conference of Russian revolutionaries in 1903.

Concurrently with the granting of concessions to the Jews immediately after the Revolution, the official policy was to counteract anti-Semitism at all levels of Russian society. But just as the newly-granted rights turned out to have been designed merely to ease the process of assimilation, so the measures against anti-Semitism proved half-hearted and ineffectual. Although outlawed and denounced, anti-Semitism never disappeared completely. One indication of this is the fact that so much was written about it. Between 1920 and 1930 some thirty pamphlets and books varying in size from 50 to 400 pages apeared, all drawing attention to, and complaining of, the growth of anti-Semitism. They expressed alarm at its ramifications and often criticized the inadequacy of official measures to eradicate it. Some of the titles alone testify to the nature and extent of prevailing anti-Jewish sentiments.[13] One such publication was S. K. Bezborodov's *Signals. On Anti-Semitism*. Another with an alarming title by the same author was *The Poison of Anti-Semitism in our Time*. Leonid Radishchev wrote another in the same series entitled *Against Anti-Semitism*.

A double effort in the campaign against Anti-Semitism in Russia was made by M. Y. Alexandrov, who wrote two books almost within the first decade of the Revolution. One was entitled *The Class Enemy Masked*; the second, *Hatred of the Jews— Where Does it Come From? Whom Does it Benefit?*

Today, no publications appear which point to anti-Semitism in Russia. But in the early days after the Revolution, there were no such restrictions. On the contrary, Lenin himself denounced anti-Semitism and described it as 'a weapon' in the hands of counter-revolutionaries. Mikhail Kalinin, then Chairman of the Central Executive Committee, and Anatoly Lunacharsky, the People's Commissar for Education, both wrote openly admitting the existence of anti-Semitism and advocating measures for its eradication. Lunacharsky's article was entitled *On Anti-Semitism* and was published in Moscow in 1929. He wrote that anti-Semitism was being exploited by those who wanted to see the new system overthrown. 'Anti-Semitism is the mask worn by every counter-revolutionary.'

There were numerous other Russian authors preoccupied with the same problem. G. L. Zhigalin published in 1927 a 104-page booklet called *The Accursed Heritage—On Anti-Semitism*. Other books on the same theme were—to mention only a few—Nikolai Semashko's *Who Persecutes the Jews and Why?*, Y. Kochetkov's *Are the Jews our Enemies?*, L. Liakov's *On the Hatred of the Jews*, M. Y. Maltsev's *Anti-Semitism on Trial*, and Yury Sandomirsky's *The Road of Anti-Semitism in Russia*.

The urgent need to combat anti-Semitism was best emphasized in G. Nagorny's *To War against Anti-Semitism*, and M. Ryutin's *Anti-Semitism and Party Activities*. This last one was published barely ten years after the Revolution. So was Kalinin's essay, *The Jewish Question and the Resettlement of Jews in the Crimea*, condemning attacks against Jews settling in the Crimea which also appeared in 1926.

As might have been expected, the response to the reappearance of anti-Semitism so swiftly in the wake of the Revolution was most bitter among Jewish Communists. Alexander Chemerisky, following Lenin's maxim, wrote a book entitled *Anti-Semitism, a Weapon of the Counter-Revolutionary.* Yury Larin, a writer with a wider horizon and an historian's approach to the Jewish minority issue in the USSR, left in *Jews and Anti-Semitism in the USSR*, a fuller record of numerous and alarming instances of anti-Semitic incidents in many parts of Communist Russia.

Mildly tolerated, even in the early days of the Revolution, anti-Semitism persisted in coming to the surface from time to time. Despite official lip-service to tolerance and the solemn pledges of the Soviet Constitution, restrictive measures were introduced, designed to suppress and destroy Jewish national distinctiveness. If no longer a constant element of official policy as under the Tsars, anti-Semitism has never been completely absent from Russian planning, and Communist policy. Varied in extent and intensity it has never been buried so deep that the men in the Kremlin could not revive it whenever opportune.

For more than a decade after the Revolution hostility towards the Jews emerged in places where it had not existed before. The Russian worker objected to the appearance of Jews in the factories. He resented their 'intrusion' into a section of economic life which under the Tsars had been completely barred to them. In the collective farms too, the participation of the Jews was not welcome. Forced out of their former occupations as middlemen in the towns, large numbers of Jews turned to the land, and this gave rise to a new wave of anti-Semitism among the peasants. Land-hungry for centuries, the peasants objected to the newcomers. In the Crimea the local peasants sent petitions to the Government protesting against the settlement of Jews on land in the area. Another charge, reminiscent of the pre-revolutionary years, and frequently made in the decade following, was that 'too many of them' had infiltrated into leading positions in the Party and the Government. They were accused of enjoying 'special privileges'. They were also often blamed for economic shortages and administrative failures. Incidents, especially in factories, were so numerous and widespread that the management in some State establishments, and Party officials, were compelled to turn a blind eye.[14] Toleration of anti-Semitism was considered a lubricant to keep the wheels of Soviet industry turning, especially during the early and difficult stages of the building up of the Soviet economy.

If the older generation found little protection from anti-Semitic insults, and frequent assaults in factories and offices, the younger Jews were in no better a position. To the surprise of Communist leaders themselves it was found that even in the *Komsomol*, the Young Communist League, many members were violently anti-Semitic. The Jewish Press in the Soviet Union carried frequent reports of anti-Semitic outbursts by young Russians. Cases were even recorded of members of the *Komsomol* imitating the reactionary anti-Semitic 'Black Hundred' of Tsarist days with their calls of 'kill the Jews and save Russia.' Such reports came from several localities in the Ukraine and White Russia where anti-Jewish prejudices have always been much more prominent than elsewhere. One of the main objectives of the Communist Party programme was to instruct the younger generation to respect 'the human values and fraternal feelings' of all citizens in the USSR. Soviet society was to be a brotherhood of equals. Yet a survey among the Pioneers—the youngest members of the Party—revealed that they were often the worst instigators of anti-Jewish activities. *Molodaya Gvardiya*, a periodical issued by the Central Committee of the *Komsomol* movement, reporting on 'anti-Semitism among the youth' admitted that conditions in the Pioneer groups were sometimes even worse as regards the treatment of Jews than in the ranks of older members of the movement.

Officially the Soviet authorities made several attempts to counteract anti-Semitism, but the very laws framed for this purpose carried within themselves the seeds of failure. Contrary to all assurances, anti-Semitism—as a manifestation of prejudice and hostility to the Jew—has never been made expressly illegal in the Soviet Union. What the criminal code in post-revolutionary Russia condemned, and still condemns, is 'agitation and propaganda arousing national enmity and dissension.' There is nothing in the code of laws specifically forbidding anti-Semitism and making it a crime. In a multi-national state like the Soviet Union 'national enmity' may mean anything from a call to dislike a Great Russian, a Ukrainian, a Georgian, an Uzbek, to an insult or defamation of any of the national minorities. But no one knows better than the Kremlin leaders themselves that hostility towards the Jew has been the most frequent and most widespread racial and national prejudice besetting Russian life for centuries. A law making anti-Semitism a punishable offence might have been an effective counter-measure—but no such law was ever enacted by the Soviet authorities.

With a surprising lack of realism, the battle against anti-Semitism after the October Revolution began with a declaration which took the form of official advice rather than a State law. Several months after the Bolsheviks came to power the Council of Peoples' Commissars condemned 'pogromist agitation and attacks on the working Jewish population.' This in itself suggested a differentiation in regard to the Jewish population. Only agitation and attack on the 'working' section was condemned as a 'counter-revolutionary weapon used by the Tsars.' In the Soviet Union, it was stated, 'there can be no place for national oppression.'

Following this directive the Council of Peoples' Commissars asked all revolutionary organizations to take 'such steps as will effectively destroy the anti-Semitic movement at its roots'.[15] Guarded and restrained as this first official Soviet condemnation of anti-Semitism was, the distinction between the Jewish bourgeoisie 'who is our enemy', and 'the Jewish worker who is our brother' was ominous. It was obviously left to the respective organizations to decide for themselves to which category an individual Jew or group of Jews belonged. The treatment of the Jews and the whole fight against anti-Semitism depended on this decision. In a country where anti-Jewish prejudices had been fostered and exploited for centuries by Crown and Church, an official denunciation hedged around with qualifications and differentiations between Jew and Jew was doomed to certain failure.

It was not until four years after this mild attempt to eradicate anti-Semitism that the Soviet Government thought it necessary to incorporate a measure of a sterner nature in a new collection of laws. The first Soviet Criminal Code published in 1921 contained a paragraph stating that 'agitation and propaganda arousing national enmities and dissensions, would be punishable by a minimum of one year's solitary confinement.' In time of war and if the offence was of a flagrant nature, the punishment stipulated was death. Yet here again, although the provisions of the new law could be applied to include anti-Jewish propaganda, the codifying authorities clearly avoided making any specific mention of anti-Semitism.

Nor was anti-Semitism specifically mentioned in the 'Statute on Crimes against the State' issued later and incorporated in the Soviet Criminal Code published in 1927. The crime of national enmity and incitement to hatred was this time extended to include agitation 'aimed at arousing national or religious enmities and dissension.' It was also made applicable to the 'dissemination, manufacture, or possession of literature of such a nature.' The punishment foreseen was loss of freedom for 'no less than two years.' In times of war or during popular disturbances, and if committed in 'aggravating circumstances' the offender could be punished by death.

Lenin was still alive when the first Criminal Code was published. It is reasonable to suppose that he also saw the draft of the subsequent issue. According to a record left by the Commissar for Jewish National Affairs, Semen Dimanshtein, published in Moscow in 1935, Lenin was always keenly interested in all measures against anti-Semitism. It was Lenin who, when the first condemnation of anti-Jewish activities was issued, added the warning that 'pogromists will be outlawed.'

Yet there was in all these efforts to root out anti-Jewish prejudices a curious vagueness. A reluctance to admit the existence of anti-Semitism, and to deal openly with it, is revealed in the attitude of the Soviet Press. Anti-Semitic events were reported regularly only in the Jewish newspapers—of which quite a few were still extant in the decade following the Revolution. Likewise, it was only they who drew attention to the inadequacy of Soviet laws against anti-Semitism. The official Russian newspapers, although they must have been aware of the widespread incidence of anti-Semitism, took only occasional notice of what was becoming a common feature of Communist rule. In response to pressure on the part of leading members of the Communist

Party, including some Jews, *Pravda* and *Izvestia* did from time to time draw attention to the need to fight anti-Semitism. As the tide of anti-Semitism rose, and the *Yevsektsiyas* declined, the fight against anti-Semitism became the responsibility, officially at least, of the propaganda department of the Communist Party's Central Committee. Here it was obviously inconvenient and embarrassing to draw attention to the re-emergence of anti-Semitism so soon after the Revolution. The equal treatment of minorities, the triumph of brotherhood among the Soviet people, was clearly a sensitive area where the Central Committee could not admit failure.

Such action as was taken against anti-Semitism was motivated by purely political reasons. It lacked the moral qualities, religious and social, which are so essential in the treatment of human prejudices. The Communist leaders themselves were evidently not completely free of anti-Jewish reservations. They were thus unable to approach and deal with the subject with an open mind. Burdened by such an attitude it was easy for Stalin to slip back into anti-Jewish hostility at the time of the purges; it was easy for Khrushchev to follow the same road when he was in power; as it is still easy for Khrushchev's successors today.

4

STALIN: ANTI-SEMITISM TO THE END OF THE WAR

As long as Lenin was in the seat of power Stalin did not oppose the official policy of granting the Jewish minority full equality. He co-operated in the establishment of Jewish cultural institutions; he paid lip-service to the rights of the minorities. But with Lenin's death, his power over the minorities—already considerable—increased. As soon as he came to full power his personal animosity towards the Jews began to infect the administration throughout the country. Jews became the main victims of police persecution. Tens of thousands were arrested on trumped-up charges of dealings in foreign currency and illegal possession of gold. They were imprisoned without trial. This was particularly so during the period of the New Economic Policy. Cases were known in which the Cheka, as the secret police were then called, actually forced numbers of Russian Jews who had relatives in America to write and ask for dollars with which to 'buy themselves out' of gaol. Alarmed, their relatives usually responded quickly. When the money arrived it was seized by the police because of Russia's urgent need for foreign currency, and more often than not the Jews remained in gaol.

The first decade of the Revolution was hardly over when Stalin began purging the Party machinery of his opponents— or those he suspected of disagreeing with him. Former Bolsheviks were expelled from the Party and preparations made for their trial. Ironically, among the first victims of Stalin's terror were Jewish Communists who had themselves played an important part in the dissemination of Communist ideology and the dissolution of Jewish organizations of a traditional character. The very leaders who had worked so hard to force the Jewish masses away from their old way of life were themselves arrested and accused of 'spreading' Jewish nationalism and separatism. The first to be purged and liquidated were the old Bolsheviks, Zinoviev, Kamenev and Radek, once Lenin's closest associates. Hundreds of others, many of them of Jewish origin, including nearly all the heads of the *Yevsektsiyas* were arrested and imprisoned. Trotsky was sent into exile. Among them also were Semen Dimanshtein and Professor Josef Lieberberg, Chairman of the Executive Committee of the Biro-Bidjan region, who was a former chief of the Yiddish section in the Ukrainian Academy of Sciences.

Stalin's purges were chiefly an act of vengeance on those who dared to contradict or oppose his policies. But the arrest of Jewish leaders, writers and poets, took place for quite other reasons. It was a purely anti-Jewish measure unconnected with any opposition to his authority and power. Jewish intellectuals, especially teachers and instructors in the training colleges and officials in cultural institutions, were arrested after the schools and libraries had been closed down, and were charged with 'carrying on Jewish nationalist activities.' Stalin interpreted this as constituting a crime although it was not defined as such by law. It was a political measure employed as a justification for anti-Jewish policies.

While this was taking place, Jewish cultural institutions—schools, theatres, training colleges and newspapers—were being suppressed throughout the Soviet Union. Between 1934 and 1939, the 750 Jewish schools which used Yiddish as the language of instruction were closed. 115,000 children were involved. Jewish intellectuals who had loyally served as the most devoted propagandists of Communism, were dismissed, and often arrested on charges of spreading 'bourgeois nationalism.' It was during this period, too, that the *Yevsektsiyas* lost all their influence and were finally abolished in 1930. With undiminished persistency anti-Semitism continued to manifest itself in all sectors. Yet, with their vast propaganda machinery at home and abroad, the Soviet authorities somehow managed to hide the injuries inflicted almost daily on the status of the Jewish minority. To preserve appearances Stalin retained a few Jews in his Government, in the Central Committee, and used the propaganda device of granting numerous prizes to Jewish authors and artists still in favour with the Kremlin. This was intended as a sop to Jewish protests abroad, especially to Jewish Communists in Europe and America whose activities as propaganda cells for Communism were still appreciated by their masters in the Kremlin.

But the ambivalence which had characterized the official attitude to anti-Semitism even under Lenin, persisted. Denunciations of anti-Semitism frequently went unrecorded. Stalin's equation of anti-Semitism with cannibalism was expressed in January 1931 in a statement to a representative of the Jewish Telegraphic Agency abroad. But it had to wait three years before it found its way into the columns of *Pravda*. It was not until 1936, at the time of the 8th Party Congress that Molotov recalled this unequivocal condemnation of anti-Semitism. He was addressing the Congress on the subject of the growing Nazi and Fascist forces, and contrasting these with the 'humanism' of the Communist ideal as expressed by the Stalin Constitution as it was then formulated. It was also Molotov who in his speech to the Congress referred to the 'Jewish origin' of Karl Marx—a fact never repeated in any Communist publication in Russia. This vacillating manner of coping with anti-Semitism was also reflected in the Soviet Courts. An examination of the Russian Press over a number of years failed to produce any record of a sentence passed against anti-Semitism.

The final blow came with the closure in 1937 of *Emes*, the last Yiddish newspaper in Moscow, and for many years the organ of the Communist Party and its link with the Jewish masses. The foundations of the Jewish Press had been laid with a Yiddish daily in the first days of the October Revolution. With the approval of the authorities a number of Jewish journalists met (oddly enough in the building which had been occupied by the Tsar's foreign ministry), and decided to issue a Yiddish daily. It was to be a sister publication of *Pravda*. But as the Hebrew language was already in disgrace the editors decided to give it a Germanic title, and thus it was called *Die Wahrheit* which, like *Pravda*, meant 'truth'.

As most of the Jewish revolutionaries, of whom there were many in Petrograd in those days, knew no Yiddish, and as the Jewish journalists who knew the language refused to serve on a Jewish Communist paper, the authorities had to fall back on the assistance of two journalists from London—the secretary of the Jewish Labour Fund, A. Kantor, and a member of the London Jewish Trade Union Society, A. Shapiro. Both were anarchists, and had returned early in 1918 to serve the Revolution. They were immediately accepted as the only two Yiddish-writing journalists willing to co-operate. Thus *Die Wahrheit* came into existence. When hostility to Hebrew diminished slightly the paper changed its name to *Emes*. The paper performed a vital function, for it was only within its pages that anti-Jewish manifestations were fully reported. Since the liquidation of *Emes* no Yiddish daily has appeared in Russia.

As Stalin's antagonism grew, so did his distrust, and the arrest of Jewish leaders became a daily occurrence. By 1937 the purges became so common a feature of his rule that not even the most servile among the Jewish Communists, some of whom had rendered great service to the Party, and were loud in their praise of its leader, could feel safe any longer. Most prominent among the Jews arrested at that period was Moshe Litvakov, a former head of the *Yevsektsiya* in Moscow, and one of the most prominent Communists in Jewish affairs in Russia.

With the approach of the Second World War, the anti-Jewish drive became more pronounced. While Stalin was secretly negotiating the pact with Hitler for the partition of Poland, signed a few weeks before Hitler's invasion of that country, large numbers of Jewish officials who held high positions in the Communist Party and Soviet Government were being dismissed. The most outstanding Jewish personality among them was Maxim Litvinov, the Soviet Foreign Minister. After nearly a decade in this high office he was abruptly sacked on 3 May 1939. Thousands of other Russian Jews in various security positions also lost their jobs. Large numbers who had been serving in Soviet Trade Missions abroad were recalled. A certain proportion of them received minor posts in the remoter areas of the USSR far away from the capital. But thousands were thrown out of what may be called white-collar jobs and forced to find employment in factories and mines.

The number of Jews in the Diplomatic Service abroad was also drastically reduced. Jews had been appointed to serve as Russian diplomats abroad as a matter of policy, partly because of their knowledge of languages, but also with another motive. As the result of the civil war which followed the Bolshevik Revolution, there was a great shortage of food and other necessities in Russia. The Soviet régime was in urgent need of assistance. A Jew sent abroad in the Soviet Diplomatic Service could more easily establish contact with relatives and make an appeal for aid to Russia more personally and often more effectively.

In addition to all this Stalin issued orders to the Soviet Press to refrain from mentioning the Nazi crimes and atrocities against the Jews. In contrast with the Press in every other country, which reported the daily German brutalities against Jews, the Soviet papers maintained an absolute silence. It was this deliberate silence which—as has since been established—was largely responsible for the death of tens of thousands of Russian Jews. Unaware of Nazi crimes many Jews remained in their homes in Western Russia, without taking adequate steps to seek refuge in the remoter parts of the country. This was particularly the case with the Jewish communities in the Ukraine and White Russia, who were later caught in a trap when the Germans invaded the USSR. Polish Jews, who escaped to Russia during the Second World War, told me when I met them (as foreign correspondent of the *Manchester Guardian* and *The Times*) in Warsaw, after their repatriation at the end of the war, that they had come across many Russian Jews who were so completely unaware of Hitler's atrocities that they even thought of seeking safety for themselves by crossing into Poland, which was by then already partly occupied by the Germans.

Hitler's attack on Russia forced Stalin to make a dramatic change in his foreign and home policy. As an ally of Great Britain and of the Western democracies he had adopted a more tolerant line towards the minorities including the Jews. So from

June 1941 there was a brief respite in his policy towards Soviet Jewry—but no change of heart. For not even then were the brutalities against Jews committed on Russian soil by the advancing German armies reported in the Soviet Press.

An incident regarded as symptomatic of Stalin's unbroken hostility towards the Jews was the shooting of two leaders of the Bund in Poland. Henryk Ehrlich and Victor Alter, who for years had been in the forefront of the Socialist movement in Poland, sought refuge in Russia after escaping from Warsaw before the advancing German army. On reaching Soviet territory they were immediately arrested and deported. After Hitler's invasion Stalin signed an agreement with the Polish Government, then in exile in London. As a result hundreds of thousands of Poles deported to Russia during the early part of the war were released. Ehrlich and Alter too were released from prison in September 1941 and brought to Moscow, where they co-operated with other leading Jewish personalities in the formation of a Jewish Anti-Fascist Committee. This was a Government sponsored and controlled agency for propaganda and for the enlisting of support among Jews abroad. But their freedom was short-lived. After two months, in December 1941, both were arrested, taken to Lubianka prison, and shot—it is believed without a trial.[1]

Professor Stanislaw Kot, who was Polish Ambassador in Moscow at the time, has left a detailed record of the endeavours he made to save these two Jewish leaders, both of whom were internationally known.[2] He had several interviews with Andrew Vyshinsky, then Deputy Foreign Minister, in a vain attempt to refute the false allegations the NKGB had made against them. Accusations that they had had contacts with Nazi leaders were repeated by Vyshinsky; the Polish Ambassador's vigorous denials had no effect. All efforts to obtain the details surrounding the re-arrest and death of the two Jewish Socialists have so far produced no result. Their death was kept secret for some years and was only disclosed after repeated appeals to the Soviet authorities and the direct intervention of Socialist leaders in the United States. In Jewish circles the whole tragic incident has been attributed both to Stalin's growing anti-Jewish sentiments and to the long-formed antagonism towards the Bund which he had harboured since Lenin's time. Old animosities die hard. Enmity towards the Bund persisted long after the causes for opposing their programme had disappeared. In the opinion of Jewish Socialists, Ehrlich and Alter were the innocent victims of an ideological war first proclaimed by the Bolsheviks against the Jewish Socialist Party at the London Conference of 1903.

Anti-Semitism did not cease to make itself felt. It was active both within the fighting forces, and among the Russian civilians, and not merely in those areas which came under German occupation, but even further afield in the remote regions of the USSR where hundreds of thousands of Jews sought refuge. More than two decades had already passed since the October Revolution had supposedly ushered in equality and brotherhood between the peoples of the Soviet Union. It was only reasonable for the Jews in Russia to expect that they would find help from their neighbours when faced with death at the hands of the Nazi invader. More often than not no help was forthcoming. Those Jews who were not evacuated—and in fairness to the Soviet authorities it should be stated that a considerable percentage had been—perished. In the Ukraine and White Russia, where the Germans were sometimes welcomed as liberators by the anti-Bolshevik elements, the participation of a part of the local population in the Nazi liquidation of the Jewish communities was frequent and brutal. The local police who served the Nazi invaders, sometimes outdid their German masters in the slaughter of Jews. The tragic result was that when the Russian Jews returned they found that the number of Jews saved with the help of the local population was minimal. Ilya Ehrenburg, who as War Correspondent of the Russian Armies accompanied the Soviet Forces throughout the war, and into the areas liberated from the Germans, testified in his diaries that in the Ukraine and White Russia he found very few Jews who had been saved 'by their noble neighbours'.[3] The passivity of the population of Communist Russia towards the Jews during the Nazi occupation was more discreditable than in any other country. Admittedly, the German invasion and the German 'final solution' of the

Jewish question put to a severe test the character and the humanity of nations, individually and collectively. Only very few passed the test with honour. Comparisons have been drawn between the manner in which the King and people of Denmark saved their Jewish community, and the attitude shown by the rulers and populations of other countries, both in Western and Eastern Europe. Statistics have been collected of the number of Jews saved with the aid of the local population in Poland and Hungary, and those in Belgium, Holland and France. In Poland anti-Semitism was perhaps no less entrenched than in the Ukraine or White Russia. Yet when all the figures are put together, it becomes evident that proportionately more Jews were rescued by Poles than by the population of Communist Russia.

Tens of thousands of Polish Jews—many were forcibly deported—sought refuge in the USSR. When the war was over and many of them were given the opportunity of returning to Poland, I interviewed some of them about their experiences in the Soviet Union. Most frequently they were only allowed to pass through Warsaw—then almost completely in ruins—and ordered to seek new homes in Western Poland, especially in those parts which before the war were part of Western Germany. Many of them maintained that their experiences in Russia had been clouded by anti-Semitism, and that frequently this was stimulated by Moscow.

There were, of course, many among them who found help and friendship among the native people of Uzbekistan, Kazakhstan, Kirghizia, Georgia and other places in Central Russia and Asia where they spent their war years. Some of the repatriated Polish Jews spoke with warmth of the humanity of the people in those remote areas. Yet even as they were trying to find a temporary home and shelter, and to survive the war in the direst conditions, they often found that anti-Semitism had, as many of them put it 'reached our new homes well in advance of our arrival.' For the most part, they said, the people were friendly but the authorities rarely so.

Whole volumes have been written, many of them of an autobiographical nature, describing the experiences of Polish Jews in the Soviet Union during the war. Among the latest is a record of the bitter anti-Jewish atmosphere prevailing in the midst of the war in Ferghana, one of the main cities in the Ferghana valley—an area divided between the republics Uzbekistan, Tadjikistan and Kirghizia. For years before the ten million inhabitants had practically no knowledge of the existence of Jews or a Jewish problem. But suddenly assaults on Jews became frequent. In the local market place Polish Jews were called *yevreyskaya morda*—literally Jewish nozzle or cow-face. Frequently they were also attacked and beaten.

The experience of one Polish Jew is a case in point. A Russian, who had been invalided out of the army assaulted him and called him *Zhid*. This particular insult entitles the victim in certain cases to prosecute. Leon Leneman in *In an Anderer Wolt*[4] describes how the accused was brought before the court where, undeterred, and accompanied by some of his friends, he continued his anti-Jewish insults. In fact, the judge, himself a Jew, was also insulted in a similar way, as was the Jewish lawyer who was defending. The accused and his colleagues kept shouting that 'whilst we fought for Russia the Jews were hiding in areas far away, many of them here in Ferghana.' The judge then pointed out that the defending lawyer had two sons who had been killed fighting in the Red Army. But this failed to still the anti-Jewish catcalls, in which some of the public joined in. The anti-Jewish atmosphere in the court was such that the judge felt compelled to break off the proceedings without giving any verdict.

For the Polish Jews who spent the war years in Russia this experience of anti-Semitism even in the far-distant regions of the Soviet Union was a most surprising and disappointing experience. It was also a new chapter in the history of Jewish wanderings. They had come from Capitalist Poland into Communist Russia. In their native Poland they had frequently been subjected to discrimination, and suffered the effects of a traditional anti-Semitism which had become especially severe in the years immediately preceding the Second World War. In addition to being treated as Polish refugees, they found that they were also made to feel unwelcome because of their Jewish nationality.

Among the most disillusioned repatriates were, I found, the Jewish Communists. For years before the war they had cherished warm sympathy for Communist Russia. Quite a number of them had suffered imprisonment, having been sentenced by Polish courts for their pro-Communist activities as members of the Communist Party in Poland. They went to Russia as comrades, to a land which they believed held great opportunities for them freedom above all. It did not take them long to realize that Communist ideals were one thing, and reality as it was unfolded to them in Russia quite another. Despite their adherence to Marxism they could not reconcile themselves to the reality which they found in the Soviet Union, and they returned to Poland broken in spirit. They went to Russia as Communists full of hope and anticipation; they came back to Poland depressed and disenchanted Jews.

That anti-Semitism should have persisted, even in war-time conditions, has come as a startling revelation to many. To those who hoped that Communism would eradicate anti-Semitism, it is a particular shock to find that the people of Russia were less inclined to help the threatened Jews than were, for example, the Poles. Why should the populations of Communist Ukraine and Communist Russia have reacted less humanely to the Jews' peril than the people of non-Communist Poland? The reason can only be that the Soviet authorities made no effort to counteract anti-Jewish propaganda put out by the Germans, or to discourage the public from co-operating with the Germans in the extermination of the Jews. Research on this point has failed to produce a single document or proclamation which warns the Ukrainians and White Russians of any punishment for helping in the German mistreatment of Jews. The result was that in White Russia and the Ukraine the Gestapo Extermination Unit found people among the local population who were most willing to collaborate in the liquidation of Jews. Ukrainians were even mobilized for similar mass atrocities against Jews in Poland. The Soviet authorities must have been fully aware of the facts but took no action. The same negative policy was followed by the Communist organizations acting clandestinely in Lithuania and in White Russia. While denouncing German atrocities and appealing to the local population to fight the enemy they never referred specifically to the victimization of the Jews.

The Soviets have been very selective in the release of war documents. There is reason to believe that a good many which might throw more light on that period of the war are still locked up in the archives. The fact that nearly thirty years after the war Russian Courts are still only occasionally trying people for co-operating with the Nazis, indicates that the process of examining and dealing with war-time records of this nature is not complete. But in none which have so far been made public is there any evidence that the authorities took any definite steps to counteract the violence of German anti-Semitic propaganda and its horrific effects upon the Jewish population.

This contrasts sharply with the numerous warnings which the Polish Underground authorities issued during the war, appealing to the local population to assist the Jews in search of safety and to refrain from participating in the Nazi exterminations. A significant document was issued after the German liquidation of the ghetto of Siedlec, and published by the Underground bi-weekly, *Gwardzista*. After describing the massacre in gruesome detail and how 'little Jewish children were shot in the arms of their mothers', it appealed to Poles to 'render shelter and help' to Jewish survivors. It further exhorted the Poles to accept Jews into the partisan units. A short while earlier another of the Polish clandestine publications exploded the German lie that 'Jews were being transferred to the Lublin area for resettlement only'. It told the Jews that they were all destined to suffer 'mass execution and complete destruction'.[5]

Large numbers of Poles in fact failed to heed these warnings and appeals. Co-operation with the Nazis was fairly common. Yet some Poles at least, horror-stricken by the Nazi brutalities against the Jews, managed to bury their traditional hostility. Some were encouraged by pecuniary offers; but some were prompted purely by feelings of humanity. By 1942 the Polish Underground authorities established in Warsaw a special Council for Aid to Jews—*Rada Pomocy Zydom*. All democratic Polish

groups active in the fight against the Germans were members
of the Council including a representative of the Catholic Church.[6]
There was also a locally organized Committee to help the Jews
in Vilna which included several professors of the local university,
the director of the archives and several nuns.[7]

But Stalin, it appears, could neither free himself nor his administration from anti-Jewish prejudices. Not even in the war period
would he permit a real change in policy. As a result the twenty-
five years the Russian Jew had lived under the Communist flag
of international solidarity gave him little protection when faced
with death at the hands of the Nazi invader.

Long before the war started, but especially after the dismissal
of Maxim Litvinov from the Soviet Foreign Ministry and the
negotiation for a pact with Hitler, Stalin had ordered steps to
be taken to hide the true nature of Nazi atrocities against the
Jews. Even after the German invasion of Russia the Soviet Press,
when reporting Nazi savageries on the local population, fore-
bore to mention that the majority of the victims were Jewish.
Pravda and *Izvestia*, as indeed the Soviet Press generally, merely
described them as 'crimes against Soviet people.' Only rarely was
it admitted that the majority of the sufferers were Jews.

For instance, Molotov, the Soviet Foreign Minister, issued two
official statements early in 1942 about German atrocities in
Russian-occupied areas. The first (on the massacre in Kiev of
52,000 men, women and children, stated that the victims were
Ukrainians, Russians and Jews. He must have known that this
took place at Babi Yar' where the majority of the victims were
Jews. In the second statement he spoke of the extermination of
Russians, Ukrainians, White Russians and other peoples of the
Soviet Union. Again, the fact that the majority of the victims
were Jews was ignored. The statements were widely circulated
abroad, but not mentioned in the Russian Press.

Soviet propaganda was peculiarly two-faced over the Jewish
question. In the reports for circulation abroad, in their releases
to foreign correspondents, and in Moscow broadcasts in foreign
languages, German atrocities against the Jews in Russia were
described in their full, grim detail. This was done through two

distinct channels. One was the Press Department of the Soviet Foreign Ministry under Solomon Lozovsky, Deputy-Chief of the Soviet Information Bureau. The other was the Jewish anti-Fascist Committee formed in Moscow during the war with the participation of prominent Jewish personalities. Lazar Kaganovich, a Deputy Premier, was regarded as its patron-in-chief, Solomon Mikhoels, the famous actor, its chairman. The Committee was specially founded for the dissemination of news about the fate of Jews in the areas under Nazi occupation, and for mobilizing the sympathy of Jews in the free world for Russia's struggle against Hitler. From both these sources the public abroad was fed with regular and detailed information about German barbarities against the Jews. Yet the Russians were kept in ignorance. In the Press and on the radio, the Jewish issue was ignored.

News of the valour and patriotism of Russian Jews on the battlefield suffered the same fate.

When Hitler invaded Russia, nearly half a million Soviet Jews were already serving in the Red Army, Navy and Air Force. Even in the early stages of the war and especially in the heroic defence of Moscow, an increasing number of Jewish fighting men displayed great courage on the battlefield. Since the trial and execution in 1937 of Marshal Tukhachevsky on charges of treason, thousands of other high-ranking Russian officers had been purged and there was therefore a great need for officers. Within a few months of Hitler's invasion of Russia, Stalin opened wide the ranks of the Officers' Corps to Jews who distinguished themselves as leaders on the battlefield. By 1943 forty-nine Jewish Generals were listed in command of Red Army forces, several of them decorated with the highest orders for Bravery. The Chief of the Soviet Air Force was the Jewish General, Shmushkevich. For the purposes of propaganda abroad the heroic exploits of Jewish officers and men were reported in full detail. Within months of the outbreak of war, the Jewish Anti-Fascist Committee produced a report on 'Jewish Heroes of the Soviet Union' for distribution abroad. The report described how Jews had distinguished themselves in all branches of the armed services. Of the 1,500 'Heroes of the Soviet Union', and the 500,000 recipients of orders and medals for bravery over 10,000 were Jews. This meant that they held 'fourth place among the Heroes of the Red Army'. The Russians, Ukrainians and White Russians held first, second and third places; the Georgians and the Cossacks, always so renowned for their valour, all rated lower than the Jewish fighters.

The same communiqué also stated that Lieut-General Jacob Kreiser (or to give him his full Jewish name Lieut-General Yankel Osher Kreiser), who distinguished himself in the defence of Moscow, was given the Order of Suvorov, the highest military distinction in the Red Army. It added that this great hero was also a member 'of the Jewish Anti-Fascist Committee in the USSR'.[8]

There could be no doubt of the heart-warming effect of these reports on the Jewish reader in America, Great Britain, or indeed, in any other part of the free world. Yet these details were withheld from the Soviet Press. The Russian men and women engaged in the war effort were not told of the patriotism and heroism with which the Jewish soldier also fought against the common enemy. Instead virulent anti-Jewish Nazi propaganda found its way into the ranks and not infrequently affected the relationship between Russians and Jews in uniform. Jews in the Red Army often found themselves blamed for the war. This, of course, was not done openly. Nevertheless, it created an atmosphere of hostility towards the Jew. Polish Jews, who by force of circumstance found themselves fighting in the ranks of the Russian forces, have left records of cases showing that both officers and men in the Red Army often had anti-Semitic tendencies and were prone to humiliate the Jews fighting by their side.[9]

Stalin's anti-Semitic policies in time of war were reflected in an even more damning manner by the attitude and treatment of Jewish partisans who came to join Russian units. A whole literature has grown up about the heroic exploits of the Russian partisan units, and their contribution to the victory over the Germans. Fighting from their hideouts in the vast forests of Western Russia and Eastern Poland and the swamps of Polesia, the partisans played an important part in the war effort by their ceaseless harassing of the enemy forces. Their numbers increased as the war dragged on. Well organized and in almost constant contact with the Red Army which supplied them with weapons, they formed a kind of vanguard of the regular forces. The Russian partisans were under the control of a leading member of Stalin's Military Council. For some time Khruschev was at the head of the partisan units in the forests and managed to visit them occasionally.

Their task behind the German lines was to disrupt communications, blow up bridges and railway lines and cut telephone wires. Often they could also intercept enemy messages. Their role was particularly prominent after the Stalingrad victory. Retreating enemy forces were already partly disrupted and the partisans added greatly to their troubles by harassing them day and night in the dense forests and on the swampy and marshy roads of Polesia.

Jewish partisan units in Poland came into existence quite early in the war. Long before the revolt in the Warsaw Ghetto in the spring of 1943, small groups managed to escape into the forests around Warsaw and Lublin, and in numerous other places all over Poland. As their numbers grew they established contact with Polish partisans and co-operated with them in acts of sabotage against the Germans. Relations were not always friendly. Polish units consisted of peasants who in most cases either possessed arms of their own, which they had managed to hide earlier, or were supplied by the central Polish Underground organization. Explosive materials were always supplied by the High Command of the Polish Underground authorities. But Jewish groups consisted mostly of unarmed town-dwellers. They had no weapons dating from before the war. They had either to buy them from the Polish units or from local peasants at high prices which few could afford. Quite often the peasants, having taken the money, would inform the Germans of the whereabouts of the Jewish units which were then quickly wiped out. Cases like this were reported to have taken place in the large forests stretching from Zamosc, near Lublin, to the villages and townships near Krasnik, Zaklikov, Bychawa, Wilkolaz, Sobieszczany and Belzyce, where small groups of Jews sought refuge in the dense woods, once the property of Count Zamoyski. Some were denounced before they even managed to form themselves into units. Others were hunted down later. All this was the result of the bitter hostility of some peasants. There were even cases which occurred around Kielce in which Polish partisan units of the extreme nationalistic groups themselves attacked and wiped out Jewish units hiding in the forests.

Yet, because of the regular and frequent appeals by the central authorities of the Polish Underground to Polish partisans to accept Jews and help them whenever possible, such occurrences were rare. On the whole the relationship between Jewish and Polish partisans can be described as a friendly one.

But in White Russia, the Ukraine and Volynia the situation was different. As far as can be established, in the absence of any clear instructions from above, the attitudes of the Russian partisan units towards the Jewish units varied considerably, depending largely on the personal views of the local commander of the Russian group. Some were friendly and helpful. But the majority, especially in the early stages, were hostile. It was never easy for Jews to be accepted into the Russian units. There were cases of Jews who had managed to escape into the forests and then been forced by anti-Semitic commanders of the Russian partisans to abandon their hideouts and return to the ghettoes to certain death. Even when Jews were accepted, an anti-Semitic commander could create such a hostile atmosphere for the Jewish members that they feared to go into combat with their non-Jewish fellow partisans.[10]

As foreign correspondent in Warsaw in the years immediately after the war I had many opportunities to meet and interview quite a number of Jewish partisans. They were coming out of Russia together with other Polish Jews, who were being repatriated in their thousands as a result of an official agreement between Moscow and Warsaw. It appeared that as the war continued the number of Jewish partisans increased. At one time they were believed to have numbered between 10,000 and 12,000. Among those I met were survivors who had been fighting, some of them for as long as two years, behind the German lines in Volynia,

Polesia and the dense woods in those areas. To illustrate the high proportion of Jews in the partisan units in those regions, some of them told me of a tragic encounter with the Germans in the Bialowieza Wilderness in the Spring of 1943. The Wilderness, covering an area of some 300 square miles of pine and other trees, was famous for the hunting parties organized there since Tsarist days. The dense forest offered a most suitable hiding-place for Jews escaping from Bialystok, Suwalk, Bielsk, Zambrov and from other ghettoes in the area. Early one morning they were surrounded by German forces near Hajnowka, in the heart of the Wilderness. During a battle lasting for some hours all the partisans except two were killed. One of the two—a Polish Jew—I later met in Warsaw. He maintained that of 69 men in that group, 14 were Russian, 6 Ukrainians, 9 Poles, 5 Lithuanians, 3 Latvians and 2 Czechs. The remaining 30 were all Polish Jews which testifies to the large numbers of Jews who took part in the fighting against the Germans in the forests. According to him, this was one of the most mixed partisan units in the area, and was known as the 'International Commando'.

Only in the French Underground Movement were similar cases reported from certain regions. In the Lyon-Grenoble region, for instance, of 75 members of the Maquis shot by the Germans in one massacre, 15 were Frenchmen, 8 Poles, 8 Spaniards, 2 Germans, 2 Armenians, 2 Hungarians, 1 Swiss and 5 whose nationality could not be established. But 32 of them were Jews.[11]

Quite a number of the partisans I met fought alongside the Russians without disclosing their Jewish identity, because of the anti-Semitic atmosphere that prevailed. Even when accepted into Russian units, the Jews, as in the case of the Polish units, had to provide their own weapons. Another difficulty facing Jewish partisans was that in some cases they escaped into the forest with their wives and children. The families had to be protected and fed, and food was difficult to obtain. Only on rare occasions would local peasants agree to sell bread and potatoes to Jews in hiding. 'We felt,' said one of the Jewish partisans who was the head of a group in the Baranowicze Forest, 'that an appeal on the part of the Soviet authorities to help us could have been of great benefit and saved many lives.'

A member of a Jewish partisan unit organized from a group of refugees who escaped from the Slonim Ghetto claimed without boasting that in certain cases Jewish partisans fought much harder and with a greater determination than others. 'We fought for ourselves but even more so to protect our families who accompanied us into the forest.' But he maintained that even in cases where Jewish partisans displayed much valour in the fight against the enemy they were seldom rewarded. 'The Jews might have been the heroes but the heroic acts were ascribed to Russians. About us there was silence.'

There were, of course, exceptions. Several Jewish partisans managed to save their children through the help of Russian units. Towards the end of the war better relations developed. Some Russian commanders collected small groups of Jewish children hiding with their parents in the woods and managed to transport them to Moscow, and thus save their lives. In several cases the parents actually later managed to trace their children and bring them out of Russia into Poland.

Each of the partisans I interviewed had a harrowing tale to relate. Some of them had spent years in the forests living like hunted animals, hungry, cold and in constant peril. Hard as was their experience I rarely heard them complain of the conditions in which they had lived and fought. What, however, made them feel bitter and disappointed was the fact that they had been shown so little friendship and humanity by the Russian partisans and the peasantry. Only about one-third of the many thousands of Jewish partisans who fought with the Russians escaped.

5

STALIN: 1945-1953

The years between the end of the war and the death of Stalin marked a new period in the history of the Jews in the Soviet Union. Anti-Jewish measures, hitherto concealed, now crystallized into open anti-Semitism. Russia was settling down to a process of reconstruction, as Stalin began a nation-wide effort to heal the wounds of war, to rebuild what the enemy had destroyed. But the wounds suffered by Soviet Jewry, like their contributions on the battlefield, were overlooked, often deliberately so. Soviet Jews returning from the remoter parts of Russia found their homes in the Ukraine and White Russia occupied by their former neighbours, who refused to leave. Over a million Russian Jews had been exterminated by the Nazis. But those coming back from the Far East, where they had sought refuge during the war, found themselves facing fresh difficulties which prevented their return to normal life. They were neither permitted to reconstruct their cultural institutions, nor to resettle in the collective farms and villages in the Crimea which they had built with so much toil and devotion before the war. Yiddish newspapers, theatres, and publishing houses once suppressed were not allowed to reappear. The ravages caused by the war in the Jewish cultural sphere were not to be repaired. In fact, Jews found that more and more measures designed to prevent them from sharing with others in the fruits of victory were being introduced.

When so many Jews had died in Russia's defence, those who tried to pick up the threads after the war could only be horrified by the intensified hostility shown towards them. Many reasons have been suggested for this. When visiting Russia during Khrushchev's premiership, I tried to sound local Jewish opinion on this issue with particular reference to the Stalinist era. I was given many conflicting answers. A Jewish scholar in Moscow believed that Stalin's anti-Jewish sentiments were the remnants of ideas inculcated by the Church when he was training for the priesthood. The Russian Church, he declared, was the most anti-Semitic 'pillar of Tsardom'. Another version was that the anti-Jewish policies were part and parcel of Stalin's general distrust of the minorities, a distrust which continued to influence him long after the end of the war. Reference was often made to his having deported a number of minorities to Siberia during the war. Now that the war was over his distrust focused on the Jewish minority mainly because of their international connections, a disqualifying feature in the cold war atmosphere.

In a discussion with a highly placed Jewish member of the Soviet régime Stalin's anti-Jewish campaign during the last years of his life was attributed to 'a growing deterioration of his mental faculties.' When I pointed out that there was no sign of any mental derangement in Stalin's dealings with other issues the blame for all that happened was squarely put on Beria.[1] A number of non-Jewish Russians with whom it was possible to bring up the issue seemed to follow the same line, and I soon realized how official propaganda in Russia influences even some of the more penetrating and inquiring minds. Besides, submission through the infectious effects of official propaganda has become to most Russians a safe means of hiding their own inner thoughts and perplexities.

Maxim Litvinov's *Notes for a Journal* throws some light on Stalin's personal anti-Semitism. The book consists of notes (some of questionable authenticity) made between 1926 and 1939. The passages relevant here come from the section 1926-28. The following passage is dated May-June 1926 :

I met Schechtmann [the Rabbi of the largest synagogue in Moscow] who complained about the Godless and said they had ransacked two places of worship in Moscow. The Rabbi of Kiev has also been arrested on charges of currency speculation. What nonsense !
I promised to help, although I know how difficult it is. Koba [Stalin] doesn't like me to interfere in questions con-

cerning the Jewish religion. Last time, indeed, he rebuked me severely and threatened to bring the matter to the attention of the Central Control Commission . . .

Litvinov later describes how, at Schechtmann's insistence, he spoke to Stalin :

. . . I gave in and decided to ring up Koba. He was furious and said, 'I don't think we are shooting enough of that Zionist rabble. We must draw up a decree for the banishing to Siberia of all Zionists as class enemies.' Koba also said that he had ordered Artuzov to prepare a full list of all Jews in the USSR who were paying shekel [i.e. contributing to Zionist funds] and that all these persons would be immediately sent to Siberia or given 'minus six'. I tried to explain to him that such measures would bring all the American Jews up in arms against the USSR. He replied that these Jews would always be against us because we were communists and atheists. He added, 'We shall explain that these sons of bitches were banished because they were fiddling foreign currency. There is no need to state that we are applying repressive measures because they are Zionists...'

Litvinov goes on to make his own comments on Stalin's anti-Semitism. Clearly Stalin disliked Jews, he says, but 'in my opinion he understands the absurdity of anti-Jewish measures'. Then he goes on to relate how Lazar Kaganovich recounted that Stalin 'had explained . . . the difficulty of making a Jew, even a Jewish workman, into a true Communist and atheist because the Jews, he said, were typical petty bourgeois with the instinct of ownership developed over the centuries.' Litvinov makes a slight attempt to explain the origin of Stalin's anti-Semitism : 'Of course, Koba's anti-Semitism is the sequel to the support given by the majority of Jews in our party to Trotsky and the opposition. But I have in fact noted that Koba felt some inherent hostility towards us.' He then refers to Grigory Zinoviev's story that Stalin's anti-Semitism stemmed from competition in his childhood between his father and a rival shoemaker in the same town who was Jewish. '. . . Of course this explanation is an over-simplification, but it contains a grain of truth . . .'[2]

Stalin's daughter, Svetlana Alliluyeva, in her *Letters to a Friend*[3] reveals how she personally came up against her father's dislike of Jews. He angrily opposed her first love affair with a Jewish intellectual, and later her first marriage to Grigory Morozov, a Jew. She wrote that he never liked Jews, though at that time he did not express his hatred for them as openly as he did after the war.

When Stalin had first begun to close down Jewish cultural institutions the justification often given for these unconstitutional measures was that Russia was building a new society. The old forms of existence and the traditional Jewish way of life were considered obstacles which had to be removed. No such excuse could be made after the end of the Second World War. By that time the entire edifice of Jewish life in Russia was already in ruins. Yet the drive and campaign against the Jewish minority persisted and grew. Every day some new charges against the Jews, designed to humiliate and degrade them in the eyes of the general public, would appear in the Press. One day they would be accused of being 'ruthless wanderers', another, 'cosmopolitans' —people who had no attachment to their native land. Often these accusations were directed against whole groups of Jews. Writers, poets and members of the Jewish intelligentsia generally, were frequently referred to in the Soviet Press as 'passportless intellectuals'. A new lexicon was created by Kremlin propagandists to cover up the anti-Jewish campaign with a veneer of false accusation. This must have left an ugly stain on the beauty of the Russian language. A more sinister implication of the campaign was that it singled out the Jew and stigmatized him as a stranger, an alien—a mark of dishonour which even fifty years after the Revolution he still has to bear.

Immediately after the Revolution, starvation in the cities, and the campaign to transform the Jewish middle classes into workers and farmers had made thousands of Jews settle in the Crimea. By 1927 there were tens of thousands of Jewish farmers in Central Crimea. In one settlement alone, the village of Friedorf, over half a million acres were farmed by Jews. Plans had been worked out for the establishment of more Jewish collective and co-operative farms to accommodate a quarter of a million people. Some of the Jewish agricultural settlements in the Crimea were among the most advanced in the country, and Russian farmers were often taken for excursions to visit the Jewish farms and learn their advanced methods.

Among the refugees who had fled to the remoter parts of the USSR and who returned to their former homes after the war, were many thousands of Russian Jews who had worked on such farms. But when they tried to return to their villages they were stopped. When Solomon Mikhoels, the well-known actor who was Director of the Yiddish State Theatre from 1923-48 and chairman of the Jewish anti-Fascist Committee, tried to intervene with Stalin on their behalf, he found the Kremlin ruler in a hostile mood. He maintained that in time of war, the Crimea might serve as a landing place for enemy forces. A couple of years earlier he had deported millions of Crimean Tartars because they had proved to be too friendly towards the Germans—Jews, he declared, could not be trusted to resettle there.

Other anti-Jewish measures followed. The Soviet authorities prevented the publication of a 'Black Book' describing the Nazi atrocities against the Jews in the USSR. They also prevented the issue of a volume recording the heroic exploits of Jews on the battlefields. This second project was sponsored with much vigour and determination by Colonel Itzik Fefer, the Soviet Yiddish poet, who was one of the architects and moving spirits behind the Jewish anti-Fascist Committee. The book was to have appeared under the title 'Jewish Heroes in the Struggle Against Fascism', a subject on which Stalin was determined to maintain silence.

In their devotion and loyalty to the Kremlin, Mikhoels and Fefer somehow failed to grasp that the Jewish Anti-Fascist Committee was nothing more than an instrument of propaganda in the hands of the Soviet leaders. As far as the Kremlin was concerned its main purpose was to obtain material and moral aid for the Red Army. Thus when Mikhoels and Fefer were sent on a trip to London and the United States in 1943 it was more of an exercise in Russian propaganda than an indication of a

D

change in Stalin's treatment of the Jewish minority. They did not go as free agents representing the Jewish community in Russia. Their mission was dictated by the Soviet desire to pacify public opinion abroad and to secure aid for the Red Army from American Jewry. The Committee's propaganda slogan was 'the Red Army is the hope of all mankind'. The appeal was to Jews in America and Great Britain to collect money to buy tanks and aeroplanes, and ship them to the Soviet Union. 'A thousand tanks and five hundred bombers for the Red Army' was the title of Mikhoels' appeal in a leading article in *Einikeit*, the only Yiddish journal still permitted. In response, over $3,000,000 was collected in the United States alone. In London a cheque for £10,000 was presented to Maisky, the USSR Ambassador, from the General Federation of Jewish Labour for the Russian Red Cross. Many other contributions were made by Jews but no details were given as to what the money was spent on.

A skilful propaganda trick on the part of the Kremlin was to permit the Jewish Anti-Fascist Committee to re-establish relations, however temporarily, with the Jewish organizations in the free world. At the third plenum of representatives of the 'Jewish people and of the Jewish Anti-Fascist Committee' held in Moscow on 2 April 1944, over fifty messages of greetings were received from Jewish organizations abroad and all warmly applauded. Among those who sent greetings were the Agudas Israel, the orthodox Jewish movement, the World Jewish Congress and the National Jewish Council in Palestine whose message was signed by Ben Zvi, the future President of Israel. Soon, however, the Soviet authorities began to frown on such contacts. Thus an introduction written by Albert Einstein for the proposed 'Black Book' was rejected in Moscow because of its 'Zionist overtones'.

However circumscribed by official manipulation the Jewish Anti-Fascist Committee was gaining authority in the eyes of the Jews themselves. Demobilized Jewish soldiers, although bemedalled and proud, were faced with many problems. Some were searching for their families, others for a new home in which to settle. Their expectations of sharing in the victory of their country were high. But things were in a state of flux and they naturally turned to the only extant Jewish institution for advice and help.

Jewish refugees did the same. In the regions occupied by the Germans, Jewish homes had often been destroyed along with the community. In the smaller townships in the Ukraine and White Russia conditions were such that it was impossible to get help from the local authorities, a good many of whom had been anti-Semitic. In their predicament thousands of Jews thus turned to the Jewish Anti-Fascist Committee in the hope of finding assistance and advice. Quite often they were in need of actual protection. Untiring in their efforts the leaders of the Committee, especially Mikhoels and Fefer, found themselves the recipients of thousands of appeals from Jews all over Russia. They had to intervene on behalf of those who needed rehousing. Jews in Vilna appealed for their help in getting the authorities in Moscow to permit the opening of a Jewish school. From Minsk the Jewish community appealed to them on behalf of the Yiddish theatre which the local authorities refused permission to reopen. Within a very short space of time the Committee became, in fact, whether willingly or not, the central body for Jewish affairs.

But disillusionment soon followed. The more pressing Mikhoels and Fefer became in their appeals and interventions, the less popular they became with the Kremlin. Stalin and his assistants were already busy working out new anti-Jewish measures designed to reduce the status of the Jewish minority still further. While the Committee was still functioning, albeit in a restricted form, Solomon Mikhoels was suddenly struck down. On 13 January 1948 he was killed in Minsk in mysterious circumstances in a car accident. Ostensibly Mikhoels went to Minsk on an official mission. He was sent to distribute Stalin Prizes to the students in the White Russian Academy of Arts. Although his body was brought back to Moscow and he was given a State funeral as one of Russia's greatest actors, many of his friends were convinced that he had in fact been murdered by the MVD.

One of the features of Soviet policy immediately after the war which had led the Jewish minority to hope for better times to come, was the support given by the Soviet representatives at the

United Nations to the creation of an independent Israel. This was a highly emotional issue. The existence of the Jewish Anti-Fascist Committee together with the prospect of an independent Israel had created the impression that the Jews were about to be compensated for their sufferings. Itzik Fefer even suggested a Conference of World Jewry to discuss among other issues the 'problem of Palestine'. But the Israeli Embassy had hardly been established in Moscow when the Kremlin issued a clarification of its policy on the Jewish problem, which warned against expecting much support for independent Israel. Both the re-statement of policy and the warning came in the form of a special article in *Pravda* by Ilya Ehrenburg.[4] As on several other occasions, the Kremlin chose a Jew to outline its policy and express its views.

There have been several attempts by Jewish historians to interpret the article as having been the outcome of a personal clash between Golda Meir, the newly appointed Israeli Ambassador and Ilya Ehrenburg. According to foreign observers, including Western correspondents, the incident occurred at a reception given by the American Ambassador in Moscow, when Golda Meir was supposed to have been rudely insulted by Ehrenburg because she addressed him in English rather than Russian. As is known, Mrs Meir is a Russian-born Jewess. On being introduced to Ehrenburg by the American Ambassador, Walter Bedell Smith, Mrs Meir asked him whether he spoke English. To this he replied, 'I do not speak English, and I have no regard for a Russian-born Jew who *does* speak English'.[5]

In the light of further events it appears that the article was not the outcome of a mere incident at a diplomatic reception. It was an officially-inspired document, a declaration of policy on the Jewish problem in Russia. The Kremlin's choice of Ehrenburg as the author and mouthpiece was significant.

Although the pressures on the Jewish minority had grown continuously ever since the end of the war, Stalin had been careful not to make any official pronouncements on the Jewish issue. His attitude towards the Jewish minority had manifested itself in actions only—in his categoric refusal to permit the reconstruction of Jewish cultural institutions. This was in line with previous practice. For years the Soviet Government had carefully avoided making an open statement on the Jewish question. Nor would it bind itself by any declaration on a specific aspect of the Jewish problem, whether it was religious, educational or cultural. Thus seen in historical perspective Ehrenburg's article was an extremely important document on Russia's attitude to the Jewish problem and contained the basic outline of the measures to come.

It contained three main points. In the first place, it emphasized yet again that the Jews had no right to call themselves a nation. The roots of this idea lay in Marxist theories about the Jews. As we have seen Lenin and Stalin had faithfully followed the same line. A people 'cannot be said to constitute a single nation,' Stalin had written in *Marxism and the National Question*, 'if they are economically disunited, inhabit different territories, speak different languages, and so forth'.[6] He went on to argue that the only basis for a national cohesion between the Jews in Georgia, Daghestan, Russia and America was their common religion. This was written in 1913. But by 1948 the Jews had regained their ancient territory. Could they then claim to be a nation again? This called for a re-definition. *Pravda* was categorical. Even with Israel in existence, Ehrenburg wrote, the Jews were still not a nation. Israel was really like any other country. It was not even truly independent. For its destiny was being shaped by the encroachment of 'Anglo-American capital' and its ruling classes consisted of people 'apt to betray national interest for the sake of the dollar'.

While primarily designed to re-affirm the party doctrine that the Jews, despite Israel's existence, were still not to be considered a nation, the article was political dynamite for another reason. In unmistakable terms it warned Soviet Jewry that the USSR's vote for the establishment of Israel heralded no change in the Jews' own position as Soviet citizens, and their duties towards the State.

Jewish working people [Ehrenburg wrote] like all other working people are strongly attached to the soil on which they are born and on which they grew up . . . Soviet Jews are citizens of a socialist society. They are united with the whole of the Soviet people by a comradeship of arms. They are bound to every inch of Soviet soil . . . and this must look to the Soviet Union which alone leads mankind on the road towards a better future.

Clearly the article was intended to demonstrate to the Jews the dangers of what the Soviets felt was their dual allegiance. The Kremlin leaders were shocked by the warmth with which Moscow Jews had received the Israeli envoy a few days earlier. What were Russian Jews up to when they came in their thousands to welcome Mrs Meir to the Moscow synagogue on a Sabbath morning? What were they thinking of when they brought their wives and children in the afternoon to see and admire the Israeli flag which hung over the Metropol Hotel where the Ambassador and her staff had taken up temporary residence? Did recognition of Israel and the Ambassador's arrival really revive a latent love for Zion among Russian Jews, a fresh attachment to Hebrew both long denounced and forbidden? How incorrigible can Jews really be! Ehrenburg's article cautioned against the resuscitation of either of these passions as manifestations of bourgeois nationalism. Russian Jews must not be misled into expecting any leniency on the part of the authorities entrusted with the task of watching over the loyalty of the Soviet citizen.

Finally, having disillusioned them on the subject of Israel, he threw out yet another grim warning. In ominous conformity with the Party line he denied that there might be any real links between the Jew in Moscow and the Jew in London, Chicago or Tunis. He declared that there was no such thing as allegiance to a 'mystic' Jewish nation. The Jew who lived in Chicago, spoke American and thought in American had really very little in common with the Jew who lived in Tunisia, spoke the local language and thought in Tunisian. Often the only thing that bound them together was the experience of Anti-Semitism. As regards the Russian Jew he was even further removed from other Jews by the fact that a mere admission of any links with Jews abroad, whether in Israel or America, meant a lack of loyalty to the Soviet Union.

Nothing could have been stated more clearly to warn Russian Jews of the official position of their Government and of the consequences for them if they dared to ignore it. It was the voice of the Kremlin speaking through Ehrenburg.

At first people were inclined to underestimate the article's importance. They knew of Ehrenburg's relations with the Kremlin. He had been the most popular author in Russia during the war. They knew that Stalin admired his writing. On one occasion at least he had telephoned Ehrenburg personally to express appreciation of one of his books. Even so some found it hard to accept that what Ehrenburg had written was the latest blueprint of Soviet policy on the Jewish issue, and that he had been chosen as the mouthpiece through which it was announced in the official newspaper of the Communist Party.

But none could fail to see the direction of events by the end of the year. In November 1948, the Jewish Anti-Fascist Committee was dissolved and its newspaper *Einikeit* closed down. The probable murder of Mikhoels by the MVD rendered the Russian Jewish community fatherless. The dissolution of the Committee and the closure of the only Yiddish newspaper deprived them of their only means of expression. Silence fell upon Russian Jewry.

The really crushing blow was delivered in the same year. The MVD arrested all the leading Jewish personalities—writers, poets, artists, musicians and officials in the Government and the Party throughout the country. The entire élite was eliminated, leaving the Jewish minority leaderless and helpless. Within a few days 431 Jewish intellectuals were arrested and put in chains—217 writers and poets, 108 actors, 87 artists and 19 musicians.[7] The majority perished in concentration camps. Only a few returned alive. Among the victims were twenty-four of the most prominent Soviet writers and poets, some of them members of the Communist Party. After several years in concentration camps, they were tried in secret and, according to details established since, were executed on 12 August 1952. The reputation of some of them has since been restored, and their widows have been granted a State pension after an official apology. Only one, Lena Shtern, one of the most prominent scientists in the USSR who was tried together with the twenty-four writers, escaped the firing squad. Set free after Stalin's death and given a pension, she has maintained absolute silence about her experiences in gaol.[8] Details of that tragic event are said to be in the archives of the KGB in Moscow. Attempts made by foreign inquirers, including the present author, to obtain access to the official records have all proved of no avail.

The most well-known victims of the execution were Colonel Itzik Fefer, Leib Kvitko, Perets Markish and David Bergelson. The last two have won world-wide acclaim for their contribution to Yiddish literature. Leib Kvitko is well known today as an author of children's stories and rhymes, his books running into many millions of copies in Russian and many other languages. The first to spread Communism among Jews in the post-revolutionary era, these writers were the cream of secular Yiddish culture. Colonel Itzik Fefer was among the most devoted followers of Stalin. In one of his poems he described him as being 'deeper than water and his height exceeds the mountains'. Love for Russia and loyalty to the Communist Party breathe from every line he wrote and from much of what he said when he visited London during the Second World War. Fefer was the only one of the twenty-four who broke down and 'confessed' during the trial. He was so weakened by interrogations and prison life that he had no strength left to resist. All others denied the accusations brought against them that they were, or had never ceased to be, 'Nationalist Bourgeois Zionists'. This charge was linked up by the MVD with another, even more heinous in Stalin's legal code—the accusation that they were 'agents of American Imperialism' and enemies of the USSR.

The widow of a Jewish writer, Moshe Broderson, wrote a series of articles on the trial of the twenty-four writers.[9] Broderson was a Soviet-Jewish writer of Polish origin, not one of the twenty-four. He was arrested in 1950, released in 1956 and allowed to return to Poland where he died. His widow disclosed that the secret trial lasted from 11-18 July 1952. All the accused appeared in court with clear signs of torture on them. They all denied the charges except one whose name she refused to disclose for the sake of his relatives in Russia. On 12 August twenty-three of them were shot. The twenty-fourth, Benjamin Suskint, an artist, went mad and later died in a mental asylum. Their graves remain unknown. She accused the Soviet Union of Writers, and particularly Konstantin Simonov, then the chairman, of having co-operated with the MVD. Her husband, she wrote, had seen among the papers of his indictment a notice signed by Simonov in which he agreed to Broderson's arrest.

Accusations of the type made against the twenty-four writers were no novelty in Russia in those days, nor are they today. They were levelled against Jews and also against some of the leading intellectuals of other national minorities. Ukrainian and White Russian writers and poets in particular were often accused of propagating nationalist ideas and made to suffer.[10] But in the case of Jewish intellectuals liquidated during that fatal period the Police no doubt acted on instructions from a higher authority. The charges were graver. Colonel Itzik Fefer and his associates were accused of plotting 'a rebellion and the dismemberment of the Soviet State'. When this detail first leaked out from the proceedings of the secret trial, no one could grasp its meaning. It was not until after the 20th Party Congress of February 1956 that the explanation emerged. It was disclosed by Khrushchev that they had been accused of scheming to create 'a Jewish National Bourgeois Zionist republic in the Crimea'. The Russian word actually used during the trial was *Buntovshchiki*—'plotters' against the existence and unity of the Soviet Union.

Although the Jewish writers have been rehabilitated, the charges against them have never been withdrawn. A few of them have had their work published or re-published posthumously. Yet the stigma attached to their names has not been removed and continues to hang over the heads of their families. An additional hardship inflicted upon them—as one realizes on visiting the USSR—is the refusal on the part of the authorities to disclose not only the full details of the trial and execution but also the name of the place where the writers were buried. It is known, for instance, that the relatives of Leib Kvitko and of Itzik Fefer made several applications to the authorities for permission to erect gravestones. A number of artists and sculptors who had been lifelong friends of some of the victims also offered to erect monuments to their memory if their burial place could be discovered.

Of the Jewish intellectuals who escaped the purge, Ilya Ehrenburg was among the most notable. Why was he exempted? Faced with this question after he wrote *The Thaw*, Ehrenburg said that he 'just drew a lucky number'. But this simple answer was unacceptable to many. Only some time later did it become known that on one occasion at least he was publicly accused of co-operating with the authorities when so many of his colleagues were eliminated. The accusation was made at a reception for Soviet writers given by Khrushchev shortly before he was deposed, by Galina Sieriebriakova, the author of a biography of Marx, and the ex-wife of Grigory Sokol'nikov, a former Russian Ambassador in London. She was a Polish-born Jewess who had suffered twenty years' exile, mostly in jail in Siberia. When she saw Ehrenburg at the reception she burst out with such vehemence that she had to be led from the room. 'How did you manage', she shouted, 'to live like a gentleman [*barin*] when so many of us suffered in prisons and camps?'[11]

The fact that Ehrenburg alone had been spared when all the other members of the Jewish Anti-Fascist Committee, except Lazar Kaganovich, were liquidated, gave rise to many rumours. The director of the Yiddish Theatre in Moscow, who was one of the 400 Jewish Intellectuals jailed after 1948, and who subsequently committed suicide, was rumoured to have charged him with dishonourable contacts with the authorities. Ehrenburg's strict silence concerning the fate of the Jewish writers, his refusal to admit that he ever knew some of them, only added to the suspicion that he was not telling the truth.[12] Recalling the trial and execution in 1952 of the twenty-four Jewish intellectuals, and commenting on the strange fact that Ehrenburg was not brought in to confront the victims, one Jewish author accused him of having been the 'finger man in the case'.[13]

Whatever the truth there has so far been no clear evidence

to substantiate these rumours, least of all the accusation that he
played any direct part in sending the Jewish writers to their fate.
Not until the archives of the KGB become accessible to the
student of the Stalinist era, if ever, will the truth be known.

But quite apart from his rumoured activities, there is no doubt
that he exposed the policy of assimilation, which according to
his *Pravda* article had solved the Jewish problem. Ehrenburg
himself was an assimilated Jew. Having spent part of his life
abroad he was anxious to make his presence felt in Moscow,
and rapidly became a highly controversial figure. He had already
lost all traces of Jewishness. He had abandoned the Jewish religion and had no feeling for Jewish history or culture. He knew
no Yiddish; Russian was his mother tongue. What is more he
maintained that Russian Jews no longer had any need for Jewish
schools or cultural institutions. Needless to say, to most Jews in
the Soviet Union he was an extremely unpopular figure. Even
his former colleagues in the Jewish Anti-Fascist Committee read
his article with disgust. Itzik Fefer actually published an essay
opposing Ehrenburg's arguments, especially his denigration of
Israel.[14]

As the ideal assimilated Russian Jew, Ehrenburg was invalu-
able to Stalin and later to his successors. He ranked first among
Soviet propagandists, at home and abroad. During the war his
articles as war correspondent of the Red Army daily kindled
more hatred of Hitler and the Germans than any other writings.
His articles won him great popularity with the troops and were
the envy of other war correspondents. He displayed the same
zeal in advocating assimilation as the solution to the Jewish problem in the USSR. For him there could be no compromise. The
idea of reconstructing Jewish cultural institutions after the war
was an illusion, he argued, from which Russian Jewry had to
free itself.

For many years Ehrenburg acted as an Ambassador-at-large,
travelling around in the West where he had maintained contacts
in intellectual quarters. He was a member of the Soviet-inspired
Peace Council. In addition to his function as a propagandist, his
presence at international conferences and elsewhere was skilfully

exploited by Soviet official spokesmen to prove there was no discrimination against Jews in the Soviet Union.

In one of the few frank conversations I was able to hold with Russians on the subject of the writers' purge, a Russian intellectual, non-Jewish, expressed himself in essence as follows. 'Not all the waters of the Volga will ever wash clean the stain on the honour of Russia and on the conscience of many of our people which Stalin left by the slaughter of the Jewish intellectuals and those of the other national minorities in our country. The best and the noblest were slain. What is perhaps worse is that we must still keep silent. No one is able to raise his voice in open protest.' But the remorse that Russians feel on this issue is not, I found, as widespread as on the matter of the 'Doctors' Plot'. Dark as were the events in Russian Jewish history towards the end of Stalin's rule, the 'Doctors' Plot' is considered to be the blackest and most shameful. On 13 January 1953, the official Soviet News Agency, Tass, announced that the MVD had arrested the night before a group of physicians who had plotted to kill Soviet leaders. In fact, the report stated, a number of prominent officials in the Government and administration had already been the victims of these 'inhuman plotters and doctor killers'.

Six Jews, all with an established reputation in the Russian capital, were prominent on the list of the physicians who, it said, had 'all been arrested and imprisoned'. They were Professors M. F. Vovsi, V. V. Kogan, M. B. Kogan, A. H. Greenstein, I. S. Ettinger and Dr A. A. Feldman. The Russian newspapers added that in arresting the physicians, the authorities had acted on the basis of information supplied by a woman doctor named Lydia Timashuk. Dr Timashuk was stated to have 'learned of the physicians' secret plans' while working with them in Moscow hospitals. As a true patriot, the papers stated, she immediately informed the authorities.

Nikita Khrushchev has since disclosed that Dr Timashuk was an agent of the MVD, but Soviet newspapers described her as a devoted patriot. *Pravda* presented her to the public as an example 'worthy of emulation as well as a symbol of Soviet patriotism'. A week afterwards Dr Timashuk was awarded the Order of

Lenin on the decision of the Supreme Soviet of the USSR. This remarkable honour, the Russian Press wrote, was bestowed upon her for the help she had rendered to the Soviet Government in the 'unmasking of the murderous doctors'.

In order to give the whole affair a sinister Jewish character the 'plotters' were alleged to have acted on behalf of Jewish organizations abroad. They schemed the wrecking of the defences of Russia, and this, it was emphasized, at a time when the threat of war, regarded by Stalin as an inevitability, was hanging over the Communist camp. They had already, it was alleged, caused the untimely death of two outstanding Soviet personalities, A. A. Zhdanov, a prominent member of the Party Central Committee, and A. S. Shcherbakov, a colonel in a key position in the Red Army. This accomplished, they were plotting to cause even more harm, acting on the express instructions of 'the Jewish and American as well as British Imperialist Forces'. *Pravda* actually published 'the revelations' that :

> The doctors . . . admitted that they were connected with the International Jewish bourgeoisie nationalist organization Joint [the Joint Distribution Committee] established by American intelligence . . . to conduct extensive espionage, terrorist and other subversive work in many lands, including the Soviet Union and with a world Zionist conspiracy.[15]

There have been various versions in the Russian Press and abroad as to the exact number of doctors arrested and charged with participation in the plot. A first official report gave their number as eleven. A later version mentioned the figure of thirteen, and was followed by a final announcement that fifteen doctors were involved. After Stalin's death, when the doctors were cleared and released, Russian sources said that twelve had been rehabilitated, although at the time of the arrest the names of only nine had been disclosed. As Russian authorities have so far refused to release the full details of the 'Doctors' Plot' it is still impossible to establish the exact figure.[16] But this very diversity in the numbers given by the Soviet authorities has now come to be seen as part of Stalin's general anti-Jewish plans. He deliberately ordered their number to be kept secret and some of their names not to be disclosed in order to make it appear as a predominantly Jewish plot. True, there was also a number of Russians and Ukrainians among the physicians. Yet their names were not disclosed during the allegations but only after the event. In the case of the Jewish doctors their names were all given in the official reports.

The widespread arrests and purges, as well as the liquidation of Jewish writers, were all manifestations of a hardening hostility towards the Jewish minority. But the 'Doctors' Plot', organized by the MVD only about two months before Stalin's death, has now come to be regarded as the most sinister in the whole chain of anti-Jewish measures. It was also unprecedented in Communist history.

As is customary in the Soviet Union, the public is made to react to any important event, either at home or abroad. Mass demonstrations are organized, and letters sent to the Press, expressing the appropriate reaction. Yet while Communists in Great Britain and France, including Jewish Communists, rushed to condemn the 'doctor killers', the 'spontaneous' expressions of indignation in Russia itself were not as widespread as expected. To the credit of the Russian people only three prominent personalities joined in the campaign of denunciations. One of them was Mikhail Suslov. He was the first of the Kremlin leaders to condemn the doctors as the 'most despicable creatures and deserving of the utmost punishment'. Another was Frol Kozlov, and a third Mark Mitin, one of the last Jewish members of the Central Committee. Of the three only Suslov, who is well-known for his anti-Jewish leanings is still in a prominent position in the Kremlin. Under Khrushchev he was often chosen to be the official spokesman on Jewish affairs, and he invariably voiced the opinion that Russian Jews have already accepted assimilation as a realistic solution to the Jewish issue.[17]

When I asked several people in Moscow what the Jews in Russia felt at the time of the 'Doctors' Plot', they replied that they were gripped by a paralysing fear thinking that the end had come. One member of the Jewish community said that when

the news of the arrests of the Jewish doctors came over the radio
'we felt as if Hitler's armies were once again at the gates of the
city' and there was weeping as on the day of *Yom Kippur* (the
Day of Atonement). Although the plans were kept secret, some
information about a new 'danger to the Jews' seeped through
the Kremlin walls. I met several Jews in Moscow who told me
that they actually had begun packing 'small parcels' a few days
before in anticipation 'of the MVD's knock at the door'. Reports
based on evidence collected in diplomatic circles in Moscow in
the more enlightened atmosphere following Khrushchev's speech
at the 20th Party Congress maintained that during the Stalinist
era the MVD had received orders to prepare camps for 600,000
Jews in Siberia.[18]

The 'Doctors' Plot' was fabricated in order to give Stalin the
desired pretext for mass deportation of the Jews—a final solution
to the Jewish problem. In the view of several Russian Jews,
Stalin was already then under the influence of strong drugs and
suffering from a brain disease which they maintained was the
cause of his death a few weeks later. It is said that Stalin cancelled orders suddenly without giving any reason, and then reiter-
ated them. Clearly he was no longer in full control of his faculties.
Religious Jews in Moscow told me that it was 'a miracle' that
they were saved and that Stalin changed his mind at the very
last moment. But Khrushchev has given a version nearer the
truth. During an official visit to Warsaw in 1956 Khrushchev
claimed that it was he personally who prevented the deportation
of the Jews from Moscow at the time of the 'Doctors' Plot'. In
conversation with members of the Polish Communist Party
Khrushchev said that it was due to his insistence and that of
several others within the Politburo that this measure against the
Jews was cancelled.

Khrushchev did not disclose who were the others who also
intervened. According to a version still circulating among foreign
observers who were in Moscow before Stalin's death, it was Lazar
Kaganovich who also intervened at the time.[19] As one of Stalin's
closest associates and linked with him also by family ties, Kaganovich always carried a good deal of influence in the Kremlin.

When Stalin outlined his plan against the Jews, Kaganovich was reported to have taken out his Party card and thrown it on the table in front of Stalin with the words : 'If you deport the Jews you must also send me to a concentration camp.'

In the fifty years of Jewish life under Communism, the 'Doctors' Plot' was the most malevolent anti-Semitic act on record. But the accusation that Jews could be plotting the death of Communist leaders was not entirely new. A year earlier, in November 1952, Rudolf Slansky, the Jewish General Secretary of the Czechoslovak Communist Party, together with twelve others, ten of them Jews, were hanged in the Pankrac prison in Prague. They had been charged with having 'arranged with a Freemason Physician to shorten the life of President Gottwald'. Slansky 'admitted' that he had been guilty of such a plan. The trial was instigated on directives from the Kremlin. All the evidence was presented in such a way as to emphasize that the accused were Jewish before they were Czechoslovakian. They were charged as 'spies, traitors and embezzlers', 'Jews and Zionist agents'. In addition to the charge of conspiring to poison the President, they were accused of having 'illegal contacts' with the American Jewish Joint Distribution Committee and with international Zionism.[20]

The 'Doctors' Plot' had in fact an historical precedent. Four hundred years earlier, in 1550, Ivan the Terrible, the Russian ruler Stalin most admired, expelled a group of Jewish merchants from Poland charging them with having spread 'poisonous medicine' in order to endanger the lives of the Tsar's subjects. When King Sigismunt August of Poland protested, on the grounds that the expulsion was 'a violation of the Trade Treaty between our two countries' the Tsar replied that 'it is not convenient to permit Jews to come here because they import poisonous medicines'. His prejudice may have been based on wild stories heard from his grandfather, the Russian Grand Duke Ivan III. In common with other princes in those days, Ivan III had in his Court a learned Jew from Venice, a doctor by the name of Master Leon. He was supposed to look after the health of the Duke and of his family. In 1490 the Duke's son fell dangerously ill. Master Leon tried to cure the patient by means of hot cupping-glasses, called *banki.* He assured the Duke that his son would recover, and in an unguarded moment added that 'otherwise you may put me to death'. On 15 March 1490 the patient died. When the forty days of mourning prescribed by ancient custom in Russia were over the Grand Duke ordered the execution of the Jewish physician for his failure to effect a cure. Master Leon was beheaded publicly in one of the squares in Moscow.

Although at the time of writing, some fifteen years have passed since the liquidation of the Jewish writers and the 'Doctors' Plot' neither of these two events has been fully investigated. Only a few of the people responsible have been brought to account in Russia for these crimes. There certainly is no information whether those concerned with the arrest of the writers and with their torture in prison and execution, have been punished. Khrushchev has since disclosed that 'oppressive measures' were used against the doctors to extract confessions.

In his famous speech to the 20th Congress on the 24 and 25 February 1956,[21] Khrushchev said that Stalin had personally issued advice on the conduct of the interrogation and the manner in which the doctors should be treated to extract admission of the alleged crimes. He called the investigating judge and told him of the methods to be used. 'Beat, beat and, once again, beat'. Shortly after the doctors' arrest, Khrushchev said, the members of the Politburo received protocols containing 'the doctors' confessions of guilt'. Stalin even blamed the members of the Politburo for not being more vigilant: 'You are blind like young kittens; what will happen without me? The country will perish because you do not know how to recognize enemies.' Khrushchev also revealed that Stalin called in Semyon Ignatiev, the Soviet Minister of State Security and told him: 'If you do not obtain confessions from the Doctors we will shorten you by a head.'

On their release the physicians were allowed to resume their practices. Some of them took up their former positions as consultants to the Kremlin. But Professor Vovsi, who before the arrest was President of the Academy of Medicine was not reappointed to his post. The victims in the plot received an official apology but were warned not to discuss the affair with anyone.

Dr Timashuk, the police agent employed to make a false accusation against the doctors, was not punished. She was merely deprived of the Order of Lenin which had been awarded to her for the part she played as a police informer.

The planning, arrest and interrogation of the doctors—all were tortured and made to confess—must have involved the participation of a large number of the personnel in the State Security machinery. But as far as can be established only a few have been brought to account. Of the top officials, only the Deputy Minister of State Security, Mikhail Riumin, was discharged from the Central Committee and arrested shortly after the doctors' release. A year later, in July 1954, he was charged with having been the chief perpetrator of the plot, found guilty, sentenced to death and executed. A few minor officials were reported to have been moved to other posts. But no one else was tried. Ignatiev, who next to Stalin was the man who set the whole machinery of the MVD in motion, was allowed to go free, his reputation unblemished. As a result of a Government reshuffle and a merger of the MGB (Ministry of State Security) with the MVD (Ministry of Internal Affairs), following Stalin's death, Ignatiev lost his former position, but he remained a member of the Party's Central Committee. In fact, he remained a close associate of Khrushchev in the Party Secretariat. In response to several protests against him by a number of other members in the Central Committee (including it was rumoured, Lazar Kaganovich), and an attack in *Pravda* in which he was accused of 'political blindness' Ignatiev resigned. A couple of months later he re-emerged and was appointed as First Party Secretary to the Bashkir Autonomous Republic. The fact that he played an important official role, and was directly responsible for the 'Doctors' Plot' affair, has not blocked his way to a political career.

In their strict silence on the circumstances of the 'Doctors' Plot' the Soviet authorities have been much more circumspect than was, for instance, the Czechoslovak Government on the Slansky trial. After Stalin's death and Khrushchev's accession to power, the Czechoslovak authorities re-opened the Slansky affair. This became more evident following the improvement of relations between the Soviet Union and Yugoslavia after Khrushchev's official visit to Belgrade in 1955, and the re-establishment of friendly relations with Marshal Tito. 'Working surreptitiously and treacherously' for the establishment of Titoism in Czechoslovakia was another of the main charges which had been made against Slansky in the frame-up trial. With the revision of the trial, Slansky and the other defendants were rehabilitated. The Supreme Court of the Czechoslovak Republic established that the tribunal which had tried and condemned Slansky and his associates 'violated the Law', and further that the defendants' confessions and self-incriminations were 'mere phrases without concrete instances or sufficient evidence'.

No such revision has taken place in the Soviet Union. The details leading up to and surrounding the 'Doctors' Plot', as those of the arrest and execution of the Jewish writers a few months earlier, are still kept strictly secret. No investigation has ever been undertaken to establish how it was possible that so many crimes could have been committed by a single generation of a nation so humane as the Russian people. As regards the re-emergence of anti-Semitism as an official policy, not even the mere mention of the fact is permitted. In the absence of a comprehensive sociological analysis of the circumstances which prevailed in Russia at that time, and extreme official secrecy, there have been numerous speculative attempts to explain the 'Doctors' Plot'. Among Russian Jews the prevailing version is still, as it was immediately after Stalin's death, that all was 'due to Stalin's illness' from which he was alleged to have suffered towards the end of his days. They called it 'a cancerous growth'. Even if true this can hardly be accepted as the only explanation. Trained diplomatic observers stationed in Moscow at the time of the 'Doctors' Plot' agree that it was a complete fabrication worked out in grim detail and designed to deliver a final blow to the entire Jewish community in Russia. It was not a war against an undesirable or unacceptable group as was the case with the old Bolsheviks whom Stalin liquidated. The 'Doctors' Plot' was a well-prepared plan for the total deportation of Soviet Jewry from the centres of Soviet life to remote Siberia. There have been, of course, deportations of whole national minorities (see pp. 188-9). But these were carried out in the heat of war. They were punitive measures enforced on the Germans and several other ethnic groups who either had co-operated with the Germans, or Stalin feared they might do so. In the case of the Jewish minority, no such justification existed. Without exception Russian Jews remained loyal to the Soviet régime. Had the 'Doctors' Plot' been carried to its logical conclusion it would have meant the elimination of all the Jewish elements in Russian cultural and administrative spheres— even the total disappearance of the Jewish community.

6

THE BEGINNINGS OF DE-STALINIZATION

The brief interlude between Stalin's death and Khrushchev's accession to power was not marked by any spectacular events in the history of the Jewish community in Russia. Georgii Malenkov, who had been Stalin's private secretary, became his successor as Premier in 1953.[1] The Russian people all shared the emotional excitement of Stalin's death; the experience of the 'Doctors' Plot' a few weeks before had left the Jewish minority in a dazed state. A hostile anti-Jewish atmosphere still prevailed all over the country. Malenkov was already Premier but Jews were still afraid. Even after the doctors had been released from gaol—and this was one of the liberalizing steps to Malenkov's credit—there still lingered a belief among Russians that they had been responsible for the death of some Russian leaders. Harrison Salisbury, the American writer, who visited Moscow in April 1953, came across the belief that Jewish physicians were not innocent. 'Everyone in those days', he was told, 'could tell you of a drugstore which they knew had been padlocked because the authorities discovered the Jewish pharmacist secretly mixing poisons in the medicines.' And 'Everyone had a father or a brother or a cousin who had died because a Jewish doctor deliberately bungled an operation or gave a wrong diagnosis.' The taxi-driver with whom he was riding on the day when it had been announced in the papers that the 'Doctors' Plot' had been a fraud, summed up the prevailing attitude by saying 'those *svolochi* [rascals]. They got away this time. But their day will come. We will get those yids!' To Salisbury this was a clear indication of the 'terrible, terrible need of Russia for a scapegoat, for someone or some people on whom to pile the blame and the guilt for the horrors of the Stalin epoch.' And he concludes that this must be what gave anti-Semitism popular appeal and made it attractive to the Government.[2]

However, in the period immediately following Stalin's death, the Soviet Government introduced a number of liberalizing measures which gave the Jews new hope. Malenkov was known for his anti-Semitic feelings before he came to power. The Russian Jewish community had not forgotten that it was after Malenkov's succession in 1948 to Zhdanov's seat on the Secretariat of the Communist Party, that there was a marked intensification of the anti-Jewish campaign in *Pravda* as well as in other Russian newspapers. It was then that attacks on Jews as 'passportless wanderers', 'people without a home and roots', became more frequent. Mikhail Soloviev, the author, relates how once when attending a meeting of Soviet industrial leaders as a reporter for *Izvestia*, he heard Malenkov angrily shout at the Jewish director in charge of nail production on which he had failed to reach the fixed target: 'if these nails were for Stalin's coffin, you'd have them soon enough'.[3]

So it was with relief that the Jews greeted the liberal gestures made by the Government. The most important of these were an amnesty and the release of the imprisoned doctors. The amnesty was proclaimed in a special decree and caused an immediate surge of optimism at home and abroad. The Soviet Government admitted for the first time that under Stalin the prisons and concentration camps had been filled with millions of Russian citizens, including women and even children. For years past all charges made abroad about the existence of concentration camps in Russia had been invariably denied. Such charges, it was maintained, were 'malicious slanders against the freedom-loving Soviet State'. But according to figures collected on the basis of reports emanating from non-Russian sources, including some of the most reputable international organizations, over 21,000,000 Soviet citizens had been deported and had died in Russian concentration camps between 1917 and 1947. During the most severe and brutal Stalin purges of 1937 and 1938 over 1,500,000 had been murdered by the NKVD. These included some 300,000 members of the Communist Party.[4]

The amnesty was only partially effective, but even so it meant the release of millions. Only convicts sentenced to less than five years, and mothers, children and pregnant women, were given complete freedom. Their number was not known, but was believed to be some hundreds of thousands. Prisoners sentenced to more than five years had their sentences halved; the sentences of murderers and counter-revolutionaries were unchanged. So hundreds of thousands still remained in the prisons and concentration camps.

Among the prisoners who benefited from the amnesty in March 1953 were thousands of Jews. In Moscow alone between 70,000 and 80,000 Jews were reported to have been freed. In Leningrad their number was believed to be between 50,000 and 60,000 and in Kiev between 30,000 and 40,000. But tens of thousands were still kept in gaols and concentration camps, charged with counter-revolutionary activities. These included several thousand Zionists who had been imprisoned after 1948 when Israel came to be regarded as an imperialist outpost in the Middle East.

A fortnight after the amnesty, on 4 April, the Soviet Government under Malenkov's Premiership, announced that the doctors charged in the 'Doctors' Plot' had all been released and that the whole affair was nothing but a criminal concoction, the invention of the MVD. On their release the doctors were rehabilitated and some were given back their original posts. Two of them had died under torture, beaten to death by the police.[5]

Another encouraging measure was the re-establishment of diplomatic relations with Israel. Relations between Russia and Israel had become more and more strained in the last phase of Stalin's rule. On 9 February 1953 some unknown person planted a bomb in the Soviet Embassy in Tel Aviv in protest against his anti-Jewish measures. Three days later Stalin broke off all diplomatic contact with the Jewish State. Malenkov had been in power only a couple of months when in July 1953 the Soviet mission returned to Tel Aviv with the status of the Russian envoy raised to Ambassadorial rank. Israel's legation in Moscow also became an Embassy. As a further token of re-established relations Malenkov allowed about a hundred elderly Russian Jews to leave the USSR to be re-united with their relatives in Israel.

These two moves, especially the prompt release of the Jewish doctors, were greeted by Russian Jews as a welcome signal of a change in policy. Having suffered severely under Stalin they considered the release of prominent members of the Jewish medical profession as an initial stage towards a restitution of Jewish rights. They anticipated a reconstruction of the Jewish cultural institutions—schools, theatres, newspapers and facilities for Yiddish literary expression—which had all been liquidated under Stalin. Above all they expected to be given the opportunity of enjoying the same rights as the other minorities in the USSR, and to return to their old status.

Optimism spread abroad. Jewish organizations, especially in the United States, made several attempts to intervene with Malenkov on behalf of Soviet Jewry. Jewish cultural institutions in the Soviet Union were in ruins. Appeals were addressed to Malenkov in the form of memoranda requesting that they be rebuilt. Appeals were also made for the release of those Jewish intellectuals, including thousands of Zionists, who still remained in concentration camps. But Malenkov went no further. All such Jewish appeals were ignored.

Early in 1955 Malenkov was replaced as Premier by Marshal Bulganin. But the man with real power in the Kremlin was Nikita Khrushchev, the Party Secretary. The Jewish minority was still in a state of bewilderment and anxiety. After a quarter of a century of Stalin's rule its status as a national minority had been greatly lowered. In the Russian diplomatic service, the Party hierarchy, the higher positions in the Red Army, Navy and Air-Force there was no longer a place for a citizen with the word *Yevrey* (Jew) stamped on his personal document.

Khrushchev was no Marxist theoretician. It is doubtful whether he ever made any careful study of Marx's essay on Judaism, or indeed of any other of his major works. But he had been for years a close associate of Stalin. He was for many years Moscow's Viceroy in the Ukraine where there was a large Jewish population. As a pillar of the Communist régime he was fully informed of Communist policy towards the Jewish minority. To follow this policy now that he was in power, and continue the process of assimilation, all he had to do was to preserve the state of affairs he inherited. That was exactly what Khrushchev did. He did nothing to alleviate his predecessor's repressive measures; in fact he added a few of his own to hasten still further the process of Jewish assimilation.

Khrushchev had many contacts with Jews, some of them dating back to his early youth. As a turner's mate in Mariupol, a small port in the Ukraine with a large Jewish population, Khrushchev, as he often liked to recall, lodged in the home of a Jewish family by the name of Yenkelevich. As a boarder in a Jewish religious home he was often invited to light the fire in the house of his landlord on a winter Sabbath morning, when the Jews were not allowed to perform this kind of function. The story, which Khrushchev himself helped to spread, was also known of the part he had played in fending off an attack on the Jewish community in the same town. The year was 1913, the year of the Beilis ritual murder trial in Kiev (See pp. 35-6). The event created a pogrom atmosphere in Russia, and the Black Hundred, the most rabid anti-Semitic group in Tsarist Russia, organized an attack on the Jews of Mariupol. Khrushchev was on the Jewish side and was injured in the fight. His Jewish landlady attended to his wounds, and Khrushchev remained a lifelong friend of the family.

With Lazar Kaganovich he cherished close relations for many decades. Kaganovich helped Khrushchev in his political career. At one time when Khrushchev, as Stalin's nominee in the Ukraine, failed to carry out his instructions, Kaganovich actually saved him from falling a victim to the purges. There were many other Jewish Communists with whom Khrushchev maintained friendly relations; his own son was married to a Jewish girl, the daughter of a Kiev doctor, a fact which he often brought up to try to prove that he was not an anti-Semite. Nevertheless, I found in Moscow that opinion about him on this issue was very divided. Some Jews were prepared to defend him against charges of anti-Semitism. At the same time I came across others

who accused him of being 'an inveterate Jew-hater'. They recalled that towards the end of the Second World War a number
of anti-Jewish riots had occurred in Kiev and in several surrounding localities. Khrushchev was then in charge of the
Ukraine. But he did nothing to stop them. The riots broke out
when Jewish families, who had escaped from the Germans in
1941, were beginning to return and to claim back their former
homes. They found them taken over by Ukrainians.

According to one version the riots first broke out when a
Jewish Red Army officer, decorated with war medals, returned
from the front to claim his former home which was inhabited
by a Ukrainian family. The Ukrainians refused to leave and a
fight ensued. Attacked by a large crowd the Jewish officer fired
a few shots in self-defence killing one of his assailants, who happened to be a member of the Communist Party. News of the
event quickly spread through the city and many Jews were
attacked and beaten up, some seriously. The Jewish officer, his
wife and two children were killed. Polish Jews returning home
from exile in the Soviet Union and passing through Kiev at that
time, related that they were not permitted to leave the trains
because of the 'anti-Jewish riots' in the city. It was known that
Khrushchev was in the town at the time, for he attended the
State funeral he had ordered for the Party member shot by the
Jewish officer. The situation in Kiev and in the Ukraine generally became more serious from day to day as the number of
anti-Jewish attacks multiplied. The Kremlin was forced to send a
special delegation to the region to put an end to the disturbances.

Another account quoted as evidence of Khrushchev's anti-
Semitic feelings refers to the period when he was head of the
Ukrainian and White Russian partisan units active behind the
German lines in Volynia and other parts of Western Russia.
Among the partisans were numerous Jews who had managed to
escape from the ghettoes into the forests and swampy marshes.
When the Germans had been driven out and the Russian troops
re-entered the area, a committee consisting of partisans and repre-
sentatives of the local population organized a mass demonstration
to welcome the Red Army. The meeting was held at Sarny, a

town in Volynia, and was addressed by Khrushchev. He thanked
all the partisans for their 'heroic efforts' and paid tribute to the
members of 'many nationalities' who participated in the fight
against the Germans. He then went on to name the various
nationalities, the 'Ukrainians, White Russians, Poles, Czech-Slo-
vaks and Slovaks' but made no mention of the Jews. To the
small group of Jewish Partisans who had fought in the forests
against the Germans and who were present this 'was a bitter
shock and a humiliating demonstration of Khrushchev's anti-
Semitism'. The more so as the mass meeting was held in Sarny
not far from the mass graves holding the bodies of 16,000 Jews
killed by the Germans.[6]

There were other incidents, more recent and of a different
nature, which contributed to the impression among Jews that
Khrushchev, despite his denials, harboured strong anti-Semitic
prejudices. In 1956 he and Marshal Bulganin, then Premier,
visited London. As First Secretary of the Russian Communist
Party this was Khrushchev's first official contact with the British
Government. He was given a warm welcome, as his 'co-existence'
theory found many admirers in the free world. Among those who
sought to meet him were the President and members of the Jewish Board of Deputies in Great Britain who were anxious to intervene on behalf of Soviet Jewry. But he refused to see them. He
adopted the same attitude towards American Jews when he
visited President Eisenhower in 1959. Twenty-one major Jewish
organizations of the United States made a consolidated effort to
meet the Soviet leader. Not even the personal intervention of the
President could influence Khrushchev to meet the representatives.

A more serious event, which illustrates Khrushchev's anti-
Jewish feelings was his attack on Yevgeny Yevtushenko, the young
Russian poet, over his poem on Babi Yar'. The poem was inspired by a visit the poet paid to Babi Yar', the ravine near Kiev
where the Germans killed between 33,000 and 100,000 Jews (the
figure first given at the Nuremberg trials) in mass executions described as the largest in history. Moved by sympathy for the
victims, Yevtushenko condemned anti-Semitism and protested at
the fact that there was no monument to commemorate the Babi

Yar' victims. Some years after the Revolution another young Russian poet, Vladimir Mayakovsky, had also written a poem denouncing anti-Semitism in Russia. It was called 'Zhyd' (The Jew). Stirred by sympathy for the Jews who had suffered during the civil war and after, Mayakovsky had angrily denounced all 'hooligans and pogrom-makers'. His poem had been warmly welcomed as a contribution to the Party's battle against racial prejudices. But from official sources Yevtushenko received only criticism for his poem. The criticism caused much surprise in liberal intellectual circles in Russia and disappointment among Russian Jews. The feeling became even stronger when it was known that Khrushchev had been among the denigrators of Yevtushenko's poetical talents, mainly on account of his Babi Yar' poem. Khrushchev's criticism was taken not merely as another demonstration of his unfriendliness towards the young poet, but as an indication of the official line on the Jewish problem generally. It was recalled in Jewish circles that the details of German atrocities at Babi Yar' had been supplied to the Nuremberg trial by the Russian Commission (of which Khrushchev was Chairman) investigating German crimes in the Ukraine. Khrushchev was therefore fully informed of all the circumstances of the event. Why then should he now criticize the poet for complaining that nearly three decades later there was still no monument to the Jewish victims of the massacre, and that hostility towards the survivors persisted? Was not this, Jews argued, convincing evidence of Khrushchev's personal antagonism and its effect on his official attitude?

One of the most historic events of Khrushchev's rule was his denunciation of Stalin's policies, made at the 20th Party Congress in 1956. If for no other reason he has certainly secured himself a unique place in Soviet history by his courage in exposing to the Russians and to the world outside the true nature of Stalinism. Should ever a better sense of comradeship prevail in the Kremlin, Khrushchev, for this act alone, deserves a monument in the Red Square.

Still, there were elements in the speech which reflected the traditional attitude to anti-Semitism. Khrushchev's denunciation

of Stalin indicated a new enlightenment in general, but the refusal
to admit to anti-Semitism, even to past anti-Semitism, persisted.
Although Khrushchev exposed so many of the crimes Stalin had
committed against Russians and against the minorities, he avoided
making any reference to those committed specifically against the
Jews.

The 20th Party Congress opened on 14 February 1956. When
in his famous speech denouncing Stalin of 24 and 25 February
Khrushchev referred to the Kirov murder of 1934 and the 'Leningrad Case,' as we have already seen, he also gave the first official
details of the 'Doctors' Plot' as the most scandalous final episode
in Stalin's ruthless career. But he did not go so far as to concede
that it was a specifically anti-Jewish plot, referring to it simply
as the 'affair of the doctor-plotters'. He mentioned that Dr Timashuk, the woman specialist who acted as a police agent in denouncing the doctors, might have been acting on instructions.
He referred to Beria, the former head of the MVD as playing
a 'very base role' in organizing the 'various dirty and shameful
cases', and ended by saying that the party must 'restore completely the Leninist principles of Soviet Socialist democracy'.[7]
But he did not make any specific reference to the anti-Semitism
which had motivated the Slansky trial and the 'Doctors' Plot',
and which had characterized the whole of the Stalinist era.

Yet to do him justice, Khrushchev was not alone. His silence
was in line with established official policy. The same pattern
was manifest in Malenkov's refusal even to acknowledge the
appeals made after Stalin's death for the re-establishment of
Jewish cultural institutions in the USSR. In taking stock of half
a century of Jewish history in Russia it is necessary to find the
reason for this conspiracy of silence.

The reason is two-fold. The solution of the minorities problem
is supposedly one of the triumphs of the October Revolution. To
concede that the solution in respect to one national minority
is unsatisfactory might encourage the grievances of others. More
important, it would be an admission that the basic principles
of the Revolution have been dishonoured. The charge of anti-
Semitism not only recalls the most shameful features of Tsarist

rule; it is inevitably associated with Nazi persecution. No one could acknowledge such a charge while the memory of Auschwitz is still alive.

The other reason is more telling. Why were Malenkov and Khrushchev so careful in dealing with this issue? Were they afraid that any further investigation might reveal their own involvement in these affairs and in the whole policy of Soviet Russian anti-Semitism?

The overall impression they created was that it was all due to Stalin, working in association with Beria. From Malenkov's and Khrushchev's declarations and actions, the Russian people were led to believe that Stalinism was the source of all their troubles. Stalinism, as some angry and disillusioned Communists abroad later concluded, was the mongrel-offspring of Marxist-Leninism. But was Stalin alone? Were there not others who co-operated in perverting Marxist-Leninism?

When he addressed the 18th Party Congress in 1939, Stalin had already accomplished his ruthless purges. Yet he assured the Party then that he had a team of men who would work with him for the solution of all problems and the realization of Soviet aims. He spoke of the 'many young men' who had become members of the Central Committee and who would go forward devotedly with him towards the goal of Socialism. The old Bolshevik leaders had been purged. Stalin was surrounded by such men as Malenkov, Beria, Bulganin, Khrushchev and most of the present rulers in the Kremlin, above all by Brezhnev and Kosygin. There were many others; they had all served him faithfully, helping in his rise to power and in the crimes he committed against the Russian people, against the minorities, against the Jews. For more than twenty years Malenkov stood by the side of his master until he himself came to be regarded as Stalin's heir. He was a member of Stalin's personal secretariat from 1934 to 1939—the period of the liquidation of Jewish cultural institutions, and of the most brutal of Stalin's purges. During the Second World War from 1941-45 Malenkov was a member of the Council of State Defence consisting of a small group of Stalin's most intimate collaborators.

After the war Malenkov not only retained his position and power in the Politburo but was made a member of the Presidium with more influence and responsibility in the direction of Soviet policy at home and abroad. In January 1952 he was awarded the Order of Lenin for his 'outstanding services to the Communist Party and the Soviet People'. In a joint tribute paid to him on the occasion the Central Committee called him 'a loyal disciple of Lenin' and a trusted 'colleague of Comrade Stalin'. As a further sign of Malenkov's high position in the Party and State he was chosen to deliver the major address at the 19th Party Congress held in October 1952, the last which Stalin attended. Malenkov was already then actually wearing the *rubashka* or shirt—the high-buttoned Russian jacket Stalin used to wear. At that Congress Malenkov gave a remarkable performance displaying that he was in full command, not only of facts and figures, but also of the direction of Soviet policy. He spoke for five hours on home and foreign policy. It was on this occasion that he openly attacked Israel as 'a puppet of American imperialism'. This was the first time that a Soviet leader had made this accusation against the Jewish State, but it has been repeated by Soviet propagandists ever since.

In his position as Stalin's successor—he was sometimes referred to as the 'Crown Prince' and heir to the 'iron throne' in the Kremlin—Malenkov not only had full knowledge of Stalin's discriminatory measures against the Jews but must himself have contributed to them.

If in a different capacity, Nikita Khrushchev also played his part. He was First Secretary of the Party Committee of Moscow, and Second Secretary of the Moscow region from 1935-8, the period of the most severe and brutal purges. In the Second World War he was also a member of the Military Council with special responsibilities for the partisan units and the conduct of political propaganda among them. As we have seen earlier the Russian partisan units cherished no special sympathy for the Jews. After the War from 1947 onwards, Khrushchev was First Secretary of the Central Committee of the Ukrainian Party, and later also became Chairman of the Council of Ministers. He virtually held the office of a viceroy. It was during those years that many of the anti-Jewish measures, including the arrest of whole groups of Jewish writers in Kiev, took place. In the light of the above it is easy to see the reason why, when these two leaders re-opened the wounds of Stalin's crimes after his death, they refused to allow the opening of any debate.

Although Khrushchev had been so careful to avoid any direct reference to the treatment of the Jews under Stalin, nevertheless his speech at the 20th Party Congress played an important part in the process of uncovering what had really happened to the Jewish intellectuals arrested in 1948. It was only after he had revealed the true nature of Stalin's authority that more of the truth about the purge of the intellectuals emerged. For the three years since Stalin's death, silence had been enforced on official spokesmen everywhere, and the families of the victims had been terrorized into keeping the secret.

All efforts to obtain news about the fate of the Jewish writers from the Soviet Embassies in London and other capitals had met with the reply that such rumours were 'the usual anti-Soviet slanders'. Letters addressed by Jewish journalists to the Soviet Embassy in London following the rumours of the arrests were never even acknowledged. Only on two occasions, both at receptions given by the Soviet Embassy in London, did officials acknowledge that they had received these communications, and then they still denied all knowledge of any arrests of Jewish writers in the USSR.

In America the Committee of Jewish Writers Artists and Scientists, sent its Seceretary Joseph Brainin, and Ben Zion Goldberg, Sholem Aleichem's son-in-law, to seek information from the Russian Ambassador, Panushkin. When told of the concern abroad over the fate of the Jewish writers the Ambassador was greatly offended that anyone could even suggest that in Russia writers could be arrested without cause. He categorically denied any knowledge of the arrests. Having failed with Panushkin, the same representatives approached the Soviet Foreign Minister, Mr Gromyko, who came to New York for a special session of the United Nations. He, too, denied any knowledge of the arrests.

But the rumours persisted. Soviet officials continued either to ignore them or, in an attempt to dispel them, went so far as to claim that they had seen some of the Jewish writers in Moscow. In July 1955 at a Press Conference in Geneva, Leonid Ilichev, Press Chief of the Ministry for Foreign Affairs and a member of the Secretariat of the Central Committee, stated that he had met the poet, Perets Markish, 'in the street only recently'. Ilya Ehrenburg, when approached by foreign journalists abroad, either denied knowing Itzik Fefer and the others, or asserted that nothing had happened to them. In the autumn of 1955 Molotov received a delegation of the Jewish Labour Committee of the United States and suggested that they visit the Soviet Union, thus implying that nothing untoward had happened. Shortly afterwards an official delegation of the Soviet Union of Writers visited the United States. It was led by Boris Polevoy, the Union's Chairman. Asked what had happened to the Jewish writers, Polevoy declared that the rumours were 'just anti-Soviet propaganda'. As regards Leib Kvitko, Polevoy said that he had seen him shortly before he left Russia, because they lived in the same apartment house.

During those years of silence, quite a number of people in Moscow, it became clear, had known of the writers' fate. Communists who had been associated with Fefer when he was secretary of the Jewish Anti-Fascist Committee during the war, had been imprisoned with him and since released. Through them it was reported that Fefer had been heard reciting his poem 'I am a Jew'. One rumour went round that he died with the words 'I am a Jew' on his lips.

Perets Markish, another Soviet Russian poet to share the same fate, is reported to have refused to be blindfolded before execution, saying that he wanted 'to meet death face to face'. David Bergelson, already a broken man, is stated to have called out 'Comrades it was all a terrible mistake'. It is of course impossible to establish what truth there is in these stories about the behaviour and mental state of the Jewish writers.

The truth about them, or at least part of the truth, was first revealed in the Yiddish daily in Warsaw, the *Folks-sztyme* (The

E

Voice of the People). The *Folks-sztyme* was the official organ of the Jewish section of the Polish Communist Party. A few weeks after the 20th Party Congress, and encouraged by its revelations, it published an article entitled 'Our Sorrow and our Consolation'. The article appeared on 4 April 1956, and contained details which in essence confirmed the rumours. It had an immediate effect. Until then it had only been the capitalist Jewish newspapers in the West which had dealt with the issue. Now there was confirmation from a Communist paper. The *Folks-sztyme* was edited by Hersh Smolar, a Communist of unquestionable loyalty to the Party. The rumours could no longer be ignored. Jewish Communists in the West who previously had refused to believe them, and on many occasions had denounced them as slanders against the Soviet Union, had to concede the truth. Many of them resigned from the Party.

The resignations, which were accompanied by open protests in the West, caused consternation in Moscow. Puzzled as to how the news could have reached the Yiddish daily in Warsaw the Kremlin ordered an immediate investigation. It soon transpired that it had been received through the same channels by which Khrushchev's secret speech at the 20th Party Congress had reached the West. Polish diplomats were blamed for the whole affair. Unable to persuade the *Folks-sztyme* to publish a retraction, the Kremlin decided on direct action. Leonid Ilichev attacked the *Folks-sztyme* in a statement to the *National Guardian* in America. He charged the *Folks-sztyme* with 'slanderous anti-Soviet propaganda', and accused the editors of mixing 'truth with rumour', suggesting that they had been the victims of false information, and that by publishing it had harmed the Party and the Soviet Union.

But the Jewish Communists in Warsaw remained firm. They had in their hands authentic accounts of the liquidation of the Jewish writers in Russia. For apart from diplomatic sources, they had also accounts given to them by Polish citizens who had returned from the Soviet Union, where they had been imprisoned together with the Jewish writers. Some of them had served long sentences in Russian concentration camps. At the insistence of

Polish Communist leaders, the editor of the *Folks-sztyme* sent a letter to Ilichev containing the actual details, and expressing regret. At the same time he requested that Ilichev should withdraw his unjustified attack on the newspaper. For six weeks the *Folks-sztyme* and the leaders of the Polish Communist Party waited patiently for a reply. But Ilichev remained silent. A polite reminder sent to the Kremlin through a member of the Polish Embassy in Moscow failed to produce a response, and so on 3 November 1956, the Yiddish daily published an 'Open Letter to Comrade Leonid Ilichev'.

The letter was an admission on the part of Jewish Communists of their disillusionment. After challenging Ilichev to retract his condemnation of the *Folks-sztyme*, the Open Letter pointed out that the original article had been written and edited by Communists of long standing. 'We fought for many years in defence of the Soviet Union. We are accustomed to insults . . . But those came from our enemies. How disappointing it is when such treatment is meted out by friends!'

The substance of the letter was the accusation that Ilichev's attitude was a continuation of Stalinist anti-Semitism:

> . . . don't you feel, Comrade Ilichev, that the deplorable contents of your views have in themselves elements of that terrible period of the Stalin cult, when anyone who protested against injustice and the violation of Leninist policy in respect of the minorities, was immediately condemned and denounced? Can you really answer the tragic question which we discussed in our article by merely declaring that it was 'anti-Soviet slander'? Whom will such a declaration really convince? No one!

To back up this charge the letter referred again to the sufferings of the Jewish minority under Stalin, and challenged Ilichev to deny the truth of the revelations the paper had already made.

> Can you disprove the fact that in the period after the 17th Party Congress—the majority of whose delegates have since disappeared without trace—and especially in the years 1937 and 1938, all Jewish schools have been closed down by

administrative decisions? Can you disprove that in those years leading Jewish personalities, and even others not in the forefront of the movement, but who have served the October Revolution with body and soul, have all been liquidated? . . . Is it not true that in the years 1948 and 1949 there took place in Russia the wholesale destruction, without exception, of all Jewish social and cultural institutions, including the Jewish anti-Fascist Committee which played an important role in the Second World War, the Jewish publishing house . . . the newspaper *Einikeit*, and the Jewish State Theatre in Moscow? All these institutions were liquidated because they were Jewish institutions.

While conceding that Jews were not the only minority to have suffered under Stalin, the letter emphasized that 'the greatest Jewish writers and leaders in the sphere of Jewish culture were arrested and murdered, that Jewish cultural and social life in the Soviet Union was liquidated.' The letter went on :

Do you know, Comrade Ilichev, that your interview in which you condemned the article in the *Folks-sztyme* as slander and anti-Soviet material, has caused damage to the Soviet Union? To present the real friends of the Soviet Union as slanderers in fact hinders the process of making good the injustices of the past . . . Your interview, Comrade Ilichev, is a clear demonstration not of new developments but of a return to the old !

The letter ended with a re-affirmation of the paper's determination to expose the truth, so that 'the Jews in the Soviet Union shall be given as before, the natural rights to develop their social and cultural life in accordance with Leninist principles.'

The analysis of the Jewish position in Russia which the letter presents is as valid today as it was when it was written. The whole affair became known as the 'Ilichev Episode'. Ilichev himself ignored the letter. He was reported to have described the protest as 'a voice from the Warsaw ghetto'. The Soviet Government too, although they were known to have been informed of its contents, remained silent.

KHRUSHCHEV AND ANTI-SEMITISM— BIRO-BIDJAN

The first major statement Khrushchev made on the Jewish issue in Russia came some five months after the famous 20th Party Congress and his denunciation of Stalin. Khrushchev was then already fully established in power as the First Secretary of the Communist Party. In this position he was both the originator and the chief supervisor of the new post-Stalinist policies both at home and abroad. In August 1956 he received a delegation of the Progressive Labour Party of Canada to whom he gave an interview on the Jewish issue defining Party and Government policy. The Canadian delegation was one of the first sent by pro-Soviet groups abroad to learn from the Kremlin of the new policies which were to have been mapped out for guidance in the post-Stalin era. It had among its members a Jewish Communist, J. B. Salzberg, a leading figure in the Provincial Parliament, who came specially to study the position of Soviet Jewry. It was in concession to his explicit request that Khrushchev agreed to deal with the Jewish issue and to have it 'threshed out in an amicable manner'.

Altogether the Canadians spent some fourteen hours in discussions with Khrushchev on various issues. During the discussions Khrushchev was accompanied by Suslov, Pervukin and Ponomariov, all prominent members of the Central Committee. The meeting devoted to the Jewish question took place in Khrushchev's own office in the Kremlin and lasted for some two hours. Khrushchev himself spoke for most of the time. He appeared to have been well informed in advance of the feeling of uneasiness which prevailed among the members of the Canadian delegation in regard to the Jewish question in Russia. He was particularly aware of Salzberg's own special interest in the subject and showed that he was eager to give a full explanation.

Khrushchev opened the meeting (as the delegation later reported) with a denial of all 'allegations and accusations abroad that there is anti-Semitism in Russia'. He maintained that such allegations against him personally were 'false'. To prove them false Khrushchev pointed to Lazar Kaganovich who then occupied a high position in the Soviet Government, and added, 'my own daughter-in-law is Jewish and I have a grandson who is half-Jewish'. He then went on to deny 'the existence of any Jewish problem for the Jewish question in Russia has already been solved'. 'The majority of Jews', Khrushchev claimed, 'has already been assimilated and integrated into the general stream of Russian life. That is all to the good. For integration is a historical process while separation is reactionary'.

When it was put to him that, as part of the new liberalization policy, Jewish schools like those which had existed under Lenin might be re-established, Khrushchev gave a categorical reply: 'I cannot agree with the thought of creating schools for Jewish children alone.' He then went on to point to the benefit Jewish children would derive from attending Russian schools. He mentioned Lvov where Ukrainian parents preferred to send their children to Russian schools rather than to the existing Ukrainian ones. In the same city, the capital of Western Ukraine, he maintained as well that 'Russian theatres compete most successfully with the local Ukrainian theatres'.

Obviously somewhat anxious about the chilly impression he had created on the delegation by his categorical refusal to reopen Jewish schools, Khrushchev embarked on a discourse on the 'good and bad characteristics' of various nationalities. 'Every people', he said, 'has positive and negative qualities'. As regards the 'negative qualities of the Jews', he recalled that after the First World War when Rumania had seized a part of Russian territory, the Jews had opted for Rumanian rather than for Russian citizenship. When after the Second World War the Red Army liberated the same areas, they found the streets of Chernovits full of refuse. The Jews, however, refused to take part in the cleaning up of the city, arguing that this kind of manual labour was usually done by the non-Jewish section of the population. As a further illustration of Jewish 'negative' qualities, Khrushchev pointed out that 'whenever a Jew settles in a place he immediately builds a synagogue'.

Writing later about his interview in *Morgen Freiheit*, Salzberg remarked that Khrushchev made these charges not in anger but by way of explanation and comment. Yet the Canadian delegation, and especially Salzberg himself, came away from the meeting with the firm conviction that Khrushchev was 'no friend' of the Jewish people. What finally convinced Salzberg—a loyal friend of the Soviet Union—of Khrushchev's hostile feeling was the reply he gave concerning the pre-war farming Jewish colonies in the Crimea (see p. 93). Salzberg had clearly heard complaints about Stalin's refusal to permit the return of Jewish settlers to their homes in the Crimea. When he mentioned the subject to Khrushchev he received the blunt reply that the new Soviet leader was 'in full agreement' with Stalin. Khrushchev was against the resettlement of Jewish farmers because, like Stalin, he feared 'that in case of another war the Crimea might become a landing-place and the enemies' bridgehead against the Soviet Union'. Khrushchev added that Solomon Lozovsky, an old Jewish Bolshevik and former chairman of the 'Red Trade Union International', was 'an innocent victim because he was drawn into the Crimean Affair'. Lozovsky had died with the Jewish writers executed on 12 August 1952. Toward the end of the discussion Khrushchev advised Salzberg 'in a comradely manner not to be influenced by the bourgeois and the Zionists.' But Salzberg later wrote the following comments:

I am greatly perturbed by Khrushchev's views because they express old prejudices towards the Jews as a people. They are in sharp opposition to the Marxist way of thinking and to a certain extent resemble Stalin's attitude towards the smaller nationalities at the time of the Second World War when whole communities suffered for the sins of a few individuals. Khrushchev himself exposed these facts at the 20th Party Congress. In my opinion Khrushchev's words are of the order of Great Russian chauvinism, which Lenin fought against all his life. I think also that Khrushchev's approach to the Jewish nationality is an unforgivable violation of Socialist Democracy because it does not lead to voluntary integration, which is an historic process, but to forced assimilation.

Salzberg was particularly hurt by Khrushchev's remarks about Jewish resettlement in the Crimea.

If Khrushchev's lack of faith in the loyalty of the Soviet Jews is to be considered as a general rule then this would mean a terrible accusation, not only against Soviet Jewry but against Stalinist crimes and against the deformation of the nationalities issue generally, and the Jewish problem in particular. It is high time that we should begin to speak openly and enter into public polemics with the Soviet leaders concerning this very aggravated problem. After Khrushchev's declarations to our delegation there can no longer be any doubt that this is an aggravated issue.[1]

Khrushchev's interview with the Canadian delegation on the Jewish issue was one of a series. Earlier in the same year, in May 1956, he had received a delegation of French Socialists with whom he had discussed the position of the minorities, including the Jews in Russia. To the French delegation, as to the Canadian, he denied any existence of anti-Semitism in the Soviet Government or Communist Party. Again he pointed to Lazar Kaganovich, 'the Jew in the Soviet Government'. But when confronted with the question of why there were so few Jews in the administration, when in former years there had been so many, Khrushchev gave the following explanation:

At the outset of the Revolution [he said] we had many Jews in the leadership of the Party and State. They were more educated, maybe more revolutionary, than the average Russian. In due course we have created new cadres and should the Jews want to occupy the foremost positions in our republics now it would naturally be taken amiss by the indigenous inhabitants. The latter would not accept these pretensions at all well, especially since they do not consider themselves less intelligent or less capable than the Jews.

Elaborating a little further on the same theme, he added,

> . . . when a Jew in the Ukraine is appointed to an important post, and he surrounds himself with Jewish collaborators it is understandable that this should create jealousy and hostility towards Jews.[2]

The implication was clear. Khrushchev differentiated between the Jew and the indigenous population as if the Jew were an alien.

Contrary to his expectations, the interview with the Canadian delegation failed to pacify Jewish opinion. Shortly after the interview twenty-six leading American progressive Jews, including the editor of *Morgen Freiheit*, the Pro-Communist Yiddish daily in New York, addressed a memorandum to Premier Bulganin and to Marshal Voroshilov, the President of the USSR, appealing for a change in Russia's policy towards the Jewish minority. Claiming to have been lifelong friends of the Soviet Union, and speaking in the name of an important section of the five million Jews in the USA the signatories to the memorandum expressed their deep anxiety over the treatment of Jewish culture and cultural institutions in the Soviet Union. They were greatly perturbed, they wrote, by the fact that Jewish cultural institutions destroyed under Stalin had not been re-established. They also expressed anxiety over a statement made by Yekaterina Furtseva, the Minister for Education. In an interview with a representative of the *National Guardian* she was reported to have stated that the number of Jews in the Soviet Government had to be reduced because there had been too many.[3] 'Does this mean', the memorandum asked, 'that there are going to be quotas based on race and nationality?'

In 1957 Khrushchev gave another interview dealing with the Jewish issue to a visiting group of American professional men. When they asked if Jews could open theatres and publish newspapers anywhere in the Soviet Union, Khrushchev replied:

This is a very old question. There used to be many Yiddish theatres in many cities—Moscow, Odessa, Kiev, Lvov. You have seen in your travels the culture and customs of many different republics: Georgia, Kazakhstan and Uzbekistan and Tajakistan. But the Jews are dispersed throughout the Soviet Union. We wanted to unite them and established Birobidjan for this purpose. All that is left now in Birobidjan are signs in Yiddish at the railroad stations but there are no Jews there. There are many Jews in the government and even in the Central Committee of the Party. They are assimilated into the Russian language and culture.

Khrushchev then went on to discuss the matter of Jewish schools:

If we had seven-year schools for Jews in the Jewish language where could the graduates go? We would have to establish ten-year schools, special universities for them. Other republics have their own territory and their own language and we encourage this, but the Jews are dispersed and engulfed in the culture where they live. They enjoy all the benefits of the Republics where they live and complete equality in economic and political respects. What other freedoms can there be? They can live and work freely and there can be no greater freedom. Our position is that it all depends upon the will of the Jews. If they want to create a state within our borders like Birobidjan, nobody is against this and it exists to this day, but the initiative must come from the Jews there. They could have their own language, school and traditions. The state language would be Jewish and they would have the benefits of anything they wanted. But to set up separate schools all over Russia would be too expensive.[4]

The Biro-Bidjan issue was brought up again by Khrushchev in a subsequent interview he gave to a French journalist, M Groussard, in the spring of 1958. Serge Groussard, the editor of *Le Figaro*, was on a fact-finding mission to Moscow. His visit coincided with a crop of rumours which were circulating in Russia as well as abroad, to the effect that the Soviet Government was preparing a new drive to settle Jews in Biro-Bidjan, the so-called autonomous Jewish region. At that time Lieut-General Kreiser was Commander-in-Chief of the Russian garrison in the Far East. The appointment of a Jewish Commander to the area was interpreted as a political move designed to persuade Russian Jews to settle in Biro-Bidjan in larger numbers. The French editor therefore brought up the subject with Khrushchev during the course of the interview. Khrushchev gave the following reply :

> The Soviet Union was the first in the world to decide to help the Jews not only as individuals but also as a people. We have chosen for this the territory of Biro-Bidjan, a region sparsely populated in Siberia, north of Manchuria. We have put at the disposal of the Jews a large territory and granted it a special status. It was a remarkable gift. The land of Biro-Bidjan is the most fertile there is. The climate is meridional—Southern—and the cultivation of the soil a pleasure. There is water and sun. There are immense forests, rich lands, minerals in abundance, and rivers swarming with fish. And what happens? At first the Jews went to Biro-Bidjan in large numbers. They were enthusiastic and exultant. From all corners of the Soviet Union, and I could say from all countries of Europe which they could leave to escape persecution, Jews rushed to Biro-Bidjan. And then? And then very few remained. Lately the arrivals and departures continue. But one must recognize the fact that the departures have grown larger and larger and now exceed the arrivals. How many Jews remain in that beautiful region? That I could not tell exactly in the absence of documentation. But there must remain a large enough number still. Why, in 1955 I passed through Biro-Bidjan myself, and contrary to your informants I saw many inscriptions in Yiddish on the station, and in the streets near the station. I must, however, admit that if we were to strike a balance, we would have to state that the Jewish colonization in Biro-Bidjan was a failure. Colonists arrived there full of fervour, aflame with enthusiasm and then one by one they left.

Groussard asked Khrushchev why he was 'so pessimistic' and how it was possible to explain this failure of Jewish colonization in Biro-Bidjan? Khrushchev put 'this disagreeable phenomenon' down to 'historical reasons'.

> The Jews [he said] have always preferred artisans' trades; they are tailors, they work with glass or precious stones, they are tradesmen, druggists and carpenters. But if you take, for instance, construction and metallurgy where people work as a team you would not find a single Jew to my knowledge. They do not like collective work, or group discipline. They have always preferred to be dispersed. They are individualists[5].

During the decade he was in power, Khrushchev made several other statements about Jews and the Jewish issue generally. Some of them were serious, others jocular. Those quoted here were the most important for they reveal the essence of Soviet thought on the Jewish issue, and the basis of Kremlin policy. In fact they still retain their importance today. For they are not merely the views of one ruler in power. They are an expression of the fundamental approach to the Jewish minority which has all along informed official policy.

To put Khrushchev's comments on the question of Biro-Bidjan into perspective, it is necessary to trace briefly the history of the whole project. The idea of providing a separate area for Jewish colonization was first mooted by Soviet leaders in 1928. It arose out of the necessity of finding employment for the millions of Jewish small businessmen and artisans who had been forced out of their occupations by the Revolution. The new system which abolished private trading and placed nearly everything under the control of the State called for a complete transformation of the Jews' mode of existence in Russia. One way to make this possible was to settle large numbers of them on the land. Agriculture was to become a constructive occupation which would turn the Jewish bourgeoisie into a productive element of the new Soviet society.

This approach recalled the earlier attempts of the Tsars to deal with the Jewish issue. Tsarist rulers had also considered that the practical method of changing the Jews' way of life was to settle them on the land. According to the views expressed by Tsar Nicholas I such a 'corrective method' would lead ultimately to a complete change in the Jewish personality, and his fusion with the rest of the population. To him and to his followers this was the correct method of solving the Jewish problem. So, early in the nineteenth century a scheme was initiated which provided for the settlement of Jews on the land. A few areas in the Pale of Settlement were opened to Jewish farming. Pieces of land taken away from 'disloyal subjects'—a frequent occurrence in those days—were allocated to Jews. The first to benefit from this scheme were Jewish soldiers who had completed twenty-five years of military service in the Tsar's army.

At first the Soviet authorities, working in close co-operation with the Jewish Communists in the *Yevsektsiya*, directed the declassed Jewish element to farming areas in the Kherson, Driepropetrovsk and Kiev regions, where some thousands of Jews had settled in Tsarist days. As the number of Jewish would-be farmers grew they were also given land in the Crimea, where within a short time they became the most efficient and progressive farmers in Russia. The number of Jewish collective farms and State farms increased rapidly. But when as a result of the revival of anti-Jewish sentiments the Russian peasants began protesting to the Government that 'the best land was being allocated to Jews', the Kremlin decided on the novel idea of settling Jews in Biro-Bidjan.

As large as Belgium and Holland put together—over 22,000 square miles—Biro-Bidjan takes its name from its two rivers, the Bira and Bidjan, tributaries of the Amur River, which forms the boundary with Manchuria. It is 5,000 miles from Moscow, nearer to Peking and Tientsin. The land is rich in natural resources but has an unpropitious climate. It has vast forests and, like all Siberia, is rich in deposits of coal, iron ore, marble, diamonds and even gold. It forms part of the Khabarovsk territory, and is served by the Trans-Siberian railway.

When it was first opened to Jewish colonization in 1928 the territory had a total population of just over 30,000—Russians, Ukrainians, White Russians, Koreans, Chinese and even groups of nomads like the Nanai and Evenki. There were less than three people per square mile. Although difficult the climate was described by the first Jews to settle there as healthy, and the soil as very fertile.

Jewish settlement in Biro-Bidjan went through three distinct phases. The first was from 1928-34, the second from 1934-37, and the third from 1946-48. During the first phase only a trickle of Jewish settlers arrived. After two years the number of Jewish immigrants was 2,700, as opposed to 3,200 Koreans. The Koreans had four national village councils, the Jews only three.[6] The Government furnished aid in the form of building materials, and also helped with farming machinery and housing. But conditions were severe, and many of the settlers left, unable to acclimatize. Among the first settlers were numbers of Jews who had been disfranchised by the Communist régime on account of their 'unproductive' occupations. Former Tsarist policemen, small shopkeepers, middle-men, money-lenders, religious teachers and rabbis, were among those declared unproductive and deprived of some of their former rights and privileges in the new society. They could, however, enjoy equality if they joined 'the toilers' on the land in Biro-Bidjan. For this reason thousands of Jews in the Ukraine and other parts of Western Russia chose to go, to see what could be made of the new opportunities.

In 1934 the Soviet Government gave a further stimulus to Jewish settlement in Biro-Bidjan. By a special decree signed by Mikhail Kalinin, the President of the Soviet Union, Biro-Bidjan was proclaimed a Jewish Autonomous Region. The Soviet Union has 16 Autonomous Regions within the 15 Union Republics. 9 of these, including Biro-Bidjan are within the territory of the Russian Republic.

The proclamation of a Jewish Autonomous Region promised a splendid 'future for the Jewish people'. Official propagandists described it as 'the new Palestine in the Far East'. The Government was interested in attracting new settlers to the vast empty spaces in the areas bordering on China, due to fear of Chinese infiltration and of possible Japanese aggression. New efforts were made therefore to encourage Jews to settle in Biro-Bidjan. The idea of a new Jewish territory even in such a remote corner of Siberia stimulated new hope among Russian Jewry whose leading members were quick to set a fresh propaganda campaign in motion among Jews, believing that opposition to Communism would soon disappear as a result. The proclamation was interpreted as a manifestation of the Government's good-will towards the Jewish minority—a positive step towards making the Jews equal in status with others.

The arrival of larger numbers of Jewish settlers soon created the demand for Jewish schools and other cultural institutions. Yiddish was the official language used by the administration together with Russian. In December 1936 the decision was taken to hold a special congress on Yiddish language and culture in Biro-Bidjan. The Jewish Scientific Institute in Kiev opened a branch of linguistics there, and in addition to the building and maintenance of Yiddish schools for Jewish children, Moscow gave a grant of 100,000 roubles towards a Yiddish theatre. Half a million roubles was also offered for a house of Yiddish culture.

Jewish writers and poets came in large numbers to admire, describe and laud this new country which was to become 'a rival to Zion'. More than a dozen books were written during this period about Biro-Bidjan and what it offered to the Jew who settled there. Among those who wrote poems in praise of the new country were Itzik Fefer and Shlomo Halkin, and even such non-Communist Jewish writers and poets abroad as Abraham Reisen, Leivik and Leyeles. Books about the 'Jewish pioneers and Robinson Crusoes' of Biro-Bidjan appeared all over Russia and reached the Jewish public abroad. In Poland, where anti-Semitism was on the increase, there was talk of a possible emigration of Jews to the region.

But then the purges started. The Jewish Autonomous Region was immediately affected. Professor Joseph Liberberg, the Jewish chairman of the Executive Committee of the Region, was arrested in August 1936 and disappeared without trace. He was believed to have been executed by the NKVD. Another of the local Jewish leaders, Matvey Khavkin, was also arrested together with hundreds of other Jews, and charged with nationalist bourgeois ideas and Trotskyism. A good many of them disappeared into concentration camps and Siberian labour camps. The Jewish Library, Jewish schools and Jewish newspapers were closed. Immigration was practically brought to a halt as special permission was required from the NKVD. Stalin's anti-Jewish policy took a heavy toll of the small Jewish community in Biro-Bidjan which numbered about 20,000 in 1936.

During the Second World War no new Jewish settlers were allowed in. But when the war had ended a fresh campaign was begun to encourage Jews to go to Biro-Bidjan. A new wave of immigration resulted. Among the newcomers were many of the Jewish farmers who, although they had survived the war had not been permitted by Stalin to return to their villages in the Crimea. Other newcomers were from the Ukraine where anti-Semitism had spread widely after the Germans' departure. Jews who were afraid to remain in the smaller towns and who were unable to obtain new homes in the larger towns also decided to emigrate to the region. Then there were others who felt they could not remain among the mass graves in the Ukraine and White Russia where their relatives had been massacred, and so left for Biro-Bidjan.

Soon, however, this fresh wave of immigration was cut short. The anti-Jewish measures introduced by Stalin in 1948 clamped down on the Jewish Autonomous Region. The newly-opened Jewish schools were closed again, and fresh purges among Jewish leaders, writers, poets and intellectuals began.

Today the total Jewish population of Biro-Bidjan is just over 14,000, 8 per cent of the entire population of the area. The census in 1959 showed that there were 127,000 Russians, 14,000 Ukrainians, some 2,000 White Russians, and various other national groups.

Without Jewish schools and without any other cultural institutions Biro-Bidjan is now Jewish in name only. Officially it is still referred to as the Jewish Autonomous Region. Soviet propagandists continue to point to Biro-Bidjan as a territory in which the Jews enjoy equal rights and opportunities. As in other parts of Siberia Jewish skill and training has made a definite contribution to progress and modernization. Biro-Bidjan has one of the largest clothing factories in the region, and its products circulate all over the area. Furniture from its factories, organized and run by Jewish labour, can be seen in nearly every home in Khabarovsk, Komsomolsk and other cities along the Amur River. The Soviet authorities have shown their appreciation of the contribution Jews have made towards the industrialization of the whole area by appointing a number of them to managerial positions in the region's factories and collective farms. The central railway station still bears its name 'Biro-Bidjan' in Yiddish letters. Many streets in the capital still have Yiddish names. There is a Yiddish newspaper published three times a week with a circulation said to be between 1,000 and 1,500; once a week there is a broadcast in Yiddish. The Sholem Aleichem Library is reputed to have about 20,000 volumes translated into Yiddish but only a few hundred original Yiddish works—the works of Marx, Lenin and Engels—are on the shelves. All the others are hidden in the cellar. In his recent book, *Between Hammer and Sickle*,[7] Ben Ami describes how when he offered to leave several books, written in Yiddish, such as *The Diary of Anne Frank* and an album of the Dead Sea Scrolls by Professor Yigdal Yadin, a Jewish librarian at first refused to accept them. She obviously thought them to be dangerous literature. In Russia even today 'the storing of literature calculated to produce national or religious hostility or discord' is punishable by up to two years' imprisonment. The librarian must have been aware of this and feared to accept Jewish books even as a gift from an Israeli visitor. Only after he had assured her that a film about Anne Frank was being shown in Moscow and that the Dead Sea Scrolls had been studied by Soviet scholars did she agree to accept the gift.

Among the many reasons which contributed to the failure of Biro-Bidjan as a Jewish colonization project was that the Soviet Government would not shake off its habit of taking away with one hand what it gave with the other. But the Kremlin never admits failure. And so the Jewish Autonomous Region survives in name. Soviet propaganda can still point to Biro-Bidjan as an example, however misleading, of Jewish equality. Khrushchev's admission that the Biro-Bidjan project was a failure ran true to form, for he blamed the Jews. Their individualism, he maintained, made them prefer dispersal to living together in one area.

An official Soviet publication which tries to answer the question of why there are so few Jews in Biro-Bidjan maintains that one of the main reasons is due to the fact that by the end of the thirties, especially in the war years, there was no longer any need to leave their homes in Vinnitsa, Kiev or Sverdlovsk to find work elsewhere. The Jews were thus not compelled to emigrate to Biro-Bidjan.[8] The idea that it is still a Jewish territory is also maintained in other Soviet publications. An article published in *Sovietish Heimland*, the Yiddish monthly in Moscow of which Aaron Vergelis (himself a native of Biro-Bidjan) is the editor, still proclaims that Biro-Bidjan is a 'land of milk and honey'.[9]

But from the Jewish point of view, the reason why Biro-Bidjan is a failure is not that there are so few Jews in the territory. Other nationalities who inhabit their own Autonomous Regions within the Russian Republic are sometimes in a minority there. What makes those regions specifically national is the culture which flourishes within them. In Biro-Bidjan cultural facilities are denied to the Jews. They are not permitted to establish the schools, teacher training colleges, libraries, publishing houses, clubs and newspapers which other national minorities enjoy in their respective Autonomous Regions.

8

THE JEWS UNDER KHRUSHCHEV AND HIS SUCCESSORS

Set in its proper perspective Khrushchev's policy towards the Jewish minority appears to follow Stalin's rather than Lenin's principles. At the same time, he himself contributed a good deal towards a deterioration of the Jews' position, hastening the process of Jewish assimilation by various measures of his own design. He brought greater pressure to bear on Judaism and on its followers in the Soviet Union. He intensified the campaign against Zionism, and increased hostility towards Israel.

For a brief period immediately after Stalin's death, an atmosphere of greater tolerance had prevailed. This was the period when Malenkov introduced his various liberal measures—notably the amnesty and the release of the doctors. At the same time, thousands of priests and religious leaders of many denominations, who had been arrested by Stalin, were also released and allowed to return to their posts. Here and there a few churches which had been closed for years were re-opened. The period became known as the 'thaw'; but it was relatively short, and the drive against religion was soon renewed with vigour.

During Khrushchev's rule the number of synagogues in Russia was reduced from 500 to 97.[1] The rapid decline was officially justified by the fall in the number of religious Jews due to the war havoc and the death of the older generation. Greatly reduced in numbers as the remaining worshippers were, they were stated to be no longer in a position to maintain the buildings in the required state of repair. 'Town planning' was often given as another reason for the mass closure of Jewish houses of prayer. Owing to war damage many Russian cities had to be rebuilt and replanned. This involved the demolition of whole quarters. But in some cases where synagogues were closed as a result, this was seen as a deliberate move to weaken still further the Jewish religion and to destroy the feelings of communal identity which persisted among the Jewish population in many towns. Very often the closing of a synagogue was accompanied by other repressive measures. Thus the baking of *matzos*—the unleavened bread used by Jews at Easter—was greatly restricted under Khrushchev, in several cities being forbidden altogether, although it had never been interfered with under Stalin. Restrictions were also imposed on the Jewish custom of burying their dead in separate Jewish cemeteries. This again was an interference in traditional Jewish rites which not even Stalin had ventured.

It would, however, be incorrect to suggest that the campaign against religion which intensified in the latter part of Khrushchev's rule was directed against Judaism alone. Other minority denominations, and even the Orthodox Church, experienced similar treatment if in a less crude and humiliating fashion. Figures collected by the leaders of the Orthodox Church in Russia who claimed to have still between 40,000,000 and 50,000,000 practising followers show that the number of churches was greatly reduced during the years Khrushchev was in power. At the time of Stalin's death, it was estimated that under the authority of the Patriarchate there were 25,000 churches and 3,500 chapels in the Soviet Union. By 1959 20-22,000 were still open. But at the beginning of 1962, the official figure given was only 11,500. This was due to measures taken by the authorities during the period 1959-61 to close down as many churches as possible. 'Thus less than three years after the beginning of the persecution nearly 10,000 churches had been closed to worship.' The same source maintains that 'in the first months of 1964 a further 2,000 churches were shut'.[2]

Catholics, Baptists, Lutherans, and most of the long-established religious denominations were likewise subjected to repressive measures. Propaganda against religion was carried on in the form of special publications—books, pamphlets and periodicals—of a militantly atheistic nature. In addition numerous anti-religious films were shown all over the country, anti-religious programmes relayed on radio and television, and museums and special 'houses of atheism' established in the larger towns and cities, all designed to discourage religious practices and to combat the belief in God. One of the anti-religious measures taken during this period was the republication of Emilien Yaroslavsky's *The Bible for Believers and Unbelievers*.[3] It was Yaroslavsky who had founded the League of Militant Atheists shortly after the October Revolution. He was in the vanguard of the fight against religion for many years and editor-in-chief of numerous Soviet atheist periodicals. His treatment of religion was often crude and frivolous, and the re-issue of his books in 1959 was an ominous indication of Kremlin policy towards the faithful.

As a multi-national State the Soviet Union is also a country of many religions. At least forty have been accounted for. Strange though it may sound, there are in Russia today more religious sects of various kinds than in the United States.[4] Some are traditionally Russian, like the Old Believers, the *Khlysty* or Men of God, the *Subbotniki or* Sabbatarians, and the *Dukhovrynye liudi* or Spiritual Christians. The Old Believers have their own Archbishop in Moscow, elected in 1960, and are the only Church to own a printing press of their own in the USSR today. They are split into two main bodies the *Bezpopovtsy*, or priestless, who as their name suggests have no priesthood, and the *Popovtsy*, literally 'Presbyterians', who are fragmented into several sects. The Men of God live around Tambov and in Kazakhstan, and are split into two different communities, 'the Old Israel', and 'the New Israel'. The first abstains from drink, the second practises flagellation, and both shun *Kolkhoz* (collective) farming. The *Subbotniki*, or Sabbatarians, are also characterized by Jewish traits, and are divided into two bodies : the *Bezshapochniki* pray with their heads uncovered, the *Shapochniki* with their heads covered. Amongst the sects attached to the Spiritual Christians are the *Dukhobors*, a group similar to the Quakers. Oppressed in Tsarist days, several thousands of them emigrated to Canada, but some 4,000 are still living in Georgia. They, too, oppose collectivization.

Other sects, such as the Pentecostals, the Mennonites, and those attached to the Baptist and Evangelical Christian groups are Western in origin. The majority of their adherents inhabit the areas of European Russia around Smolensk, Tula Saratov and Kazan', though there are smaller groups in the Far East. The Tremblers, who are an off-shoot of the Pentecostals, are found in Siberia, where secret cells of Jehovah's Witnesses have also recently been uncovered.

Finally there are numerous schismatic sects which have sprung up since the Revolution. Far from arresting the growth of sects the post-revolutionary period seems to have created an atmosphere favourable to the birth of new schismatic groups. About a dozen emerged immediately after the Revolution. Others arose later partly as a result of religious persecution and the upheavals of the civil war; the Second World War produced more. According to one report at least twelve new religious sects had been formed by 1957 in the Ukraine alone.[5] The membership of such sects varies from a few hundred to tens of thousands. Some are recognized by the Soviet authorities, others not. Most of them have accepted their position in the Communist State, but quite a few refuse to co-operate. Thus the *Krasnodrakonovtsy*, or Sects of the Red Dragon, identify the Soviet Government with the dragon of the Apocalypse and exhort members to resist the socialization of life. Of this group the *Cherdashniki* have the express aim of replacing the Soviet régime by the 'Laws and Institutions of the Gospel', and the *Chernokhristovtsy*, or followers of the 'Black Christ', who are active in the Ukraine refuse to touch Soviet papers or money with their hands. Another post-revolutionary sect, the True Orthodox Christians, who sprang from the True Orthodox Church, a right-wing schism of Orthodox Christians, hold strong monarchist views. Most of their members live in the Tambov region and hold prayer meetings in the open air, in woods and near wells.[6]

Confronted by such diversity, Khrushchev began with an intensification of the anti-religious campaign. But while he mobilized new men for the army of militant atheists he urged restraint in respect of the great religions. He also advised against attacking the leading personalities in the churches.

Only in the case of the Jewish religion was nothing barred. Khrushchev instituted a campaign against Judaism which gave the ordinary Russian a wholly distorted picture of Jewry. Forced to remain silent, the Jews could voice no protest against Khrushchev's accelerated attacks. The young were no longer really interested in religion, and the older generation lived still in fear, burdened with the memory of Stalinist terror. While advocating restraint towards others, Khrushchev sometimes went out of his way to demonstrate his hostility towards Jewish religious leaders. He gave vent to this hostility early in his political career. In the summer of 1956 a group of American rabbis led by Rabbi David Hollander, Honorary President of the Rabbinical Council of America, visited the Soviet Union to study the Jewish position. A request for an interview with Khrushchev was refused. When an opportunity arose for the American rabbis to meet Khrushchev at the Fourth of July Party given by Charles E. Bohlen, the American Ambassador in Moscow, Khrushchev deliberately turned his back on them.

A notable characteristic of the campaign against Judaism was the publication of a whole series of books, pamphlets and articles denouncing Judaism as a crude, primitive, reactionary and even sinister faith. The Old Testament—the basis of the Jewish religion—was denounced as a book full of strange cults and barbarous customs, such as circumcision. The Jewish God was made out to be 'a revengeful deity' who inflicted all manner of punishments—hail, fire, plagues and floods—on his chosen people. And it was on their God's commands, the Russian reader was told, that the Jews of former ages 'mercilessly destroyed their neighbours'. Officially this new drive against the Jewish religion was justified by the argument that it was merely part of the Government's fight against religion.

Among the publications attacking Judaism which made their appearance in Russia during the Khrushchev decade one of the most damaging was a volume entitled *Judaism Unembellished*.[7] Its author was Professor M. K. Kitchko of Kiev University. It contained the most crude accusations against Judaism, some of them reminiscent of the 'Secret Protocols of the Elders of Zion' forgery of Tsarist days. It depicted Judaism not merely as a religion fostering greed over money, a hypocritical and barbaric faith, but also as an ally of Zionism, of Israel, and of the capitalist world, and as such an enemy of the Soviet Union. Published in 1963 under the auspices of the Ukrainian Academy of Sciences, the book contained a set of drawings resembling in detail those used in the anti-Jewish Nazi publications before and during the Second World War. Even Jewish Communists abroad were shocked and protested to Moscow. So numerous and persistent were the protests voiced in France and the United States that the ideological department of the Party ordered the withdrawal of the book from all bookshops in the USSR. Khrushchev himself maintained absolute silence on the affair. But his son-in-law, Alexei Adzhubei, who was at that time editor of *Izvestia* admitted that the publication of this volume was a mistake.

Another publication attacking the Jewish religion was a volume entitled *The Reactionary Essence of Judaism*, by M. U. Shakhnovich, published by the Soviet Academy of Sciences in Moscow. Officially it was described as a guide to the ideals and practices of the Jewish faith, but condemnation was expressed in the very title of the book. A third publication of the same character was a book entitled *Criticism of the Judaic Religion* by Moshe Solomonovich Bielenky. Sponsored by the Soviet Academy of Sciences it was crowded with crude interpretations of the principles of the Judaic faith, and the practices of orthodox Jews. All three volumes appeared between 1960 and 1963 when Khrushchev was in power. A characteristic habit of Kremlin Propagandists is that they frequently use Jews to further their anti-Jewish campaigns. Bielenky is a Russian-Jewish writer who has been in the service of the Party propaganda machine for some years. He has written a second book, also sponsored by the Soviet Academy of Sciences and published in Moscow in 1963, entitled *What is the Talmud?* This also presents the Talmud and Judaism generally as a collection of 'reactionary ideas and anti-social principles'. The Talmud is accused of propagating 'the exploitation of men by men', and of teaching 'contempt for the worker and the manual labourer'. The rabbis, the author explained, have always regarded the workers as 'inferior beings'.

As if this were not enough, the Soviet authorities published a translation of Holbach's *Gallery of Saints*. Paul Holbach's book against religion with its particular bias against Judaism was first published in Paris by the French Encyclopaedists in 1770. It was an attack against the Church containing many passages of an anti-Semitic nature. He accused Moses of having taught the Israelites 'to cherish a venomous hatred for other peoples' and to be 'cruel, bloodthirsty and avaricious'. The Children of Israel, Holbach wrote, 'were treacherous, rebellious, fanatical and untruthful'; 'their religion taught them that they were ordained by heaven to plunder to steal and to murder'. The re-publication in Moscow in 1962 of a Russian translation recalled how frequently these accusations had been repeated in Tsarist literature 150 years earlier, and could only be interpreted as another manifestation of official hostility towards Judaism and the Jew.

Articles denouncing the Jewish religion and its practices accompanied the publication of these volumes. They appeared at intervals in the Soviet Press in the areas most densely inhabited by Jews, such as the Ukraine, White Russia, and Moldavia. There were hundreds of articles of this nature. In all of them the Jewish religion was presented as being anti-social in essence, and its followers as fanatical parasites ill fitted to be members of Soviet society. Judaism was described as a reactionary force, hindering the advance of science and enlightenment; religious Jews were labelled as the enemies of progress and the servants of imperialism. The synagogues where the remaining religious Jews congregated were described as 'dens of secret machinations, where half-tipsy bearded Jews gathered to enjoy the fruits of their deals in foreign currency'. It was in the synagogues, so it was alleged, that 'illegal sales of *matzos* and deals in graves on the Jewish cemeteries were being transacted'. In short the synagogues were made out to be the meeting-places of the dangerous anti-social elements in the community. To close them was therefore for the benefit of progressive Russian society.

The campaign against Judaism went hand-in-hand with propaganda against Israel. This, too, became more pronounced under Khrushchev. Diplomatic relations between Israel and the Soviet Union had been broken off by Stalin shortly before his death, but re-established almost immediately by Malenkov. Nonetheless the attitude towards Israel remained hostile. Khrushchev did nothing to improve the position. At the time of Suez the strongest and most threatening protest addressed by the Soviet Government to the powers engaged in the war was that sent to Israel. Communism has always been the enemy of Zionism. But under Khrushchev official policy towards Israel was made to fit more closely with Communist doctrine than ever before. A notable event in the anti-Israel campaign was the publication in Moscow of a volume entitled *The State of Israel—Its Position and Policies*. Like the attacks on Judaism, this was written by two Jewish authors and gave rise to numerous articles denouncing Israel as 'the tool of imperialism'. Recalling Lenin's early hostility towards Zionism the authors presented Israel as a country 'guided by interests alien to the Jewish workers'. 'Israel', they wrote, 'was not being led along the road of national independence but was tied to the chariot of the doomed world of the imperialists'. In the Russian Press the Israeli diplomats residing in the Soviet Union were often accused of organizing 'subversive anti-Soviet propaganda, or distributing nationalist Zionist literature harmful to the Soviet Union'.[8] They were supposed to 'exploit' the synagogues for the purpose of distributing this kind of harmful Zionist literature.

All Israel's attempts to re-establish friendly relations with the Soviet Union were invariably repulsed by Khrushchev. An offer made by Ben Gurion when he was Prime Minister to go anywhere in order to meet the Soviet leader was rejected in an offhand manner. Suggestions of an exchange of Israeli-Soviet ministerial visits were greeted in the same way.

Though Russian Jews were still partially in the grip of terror from Stalin's days, and harassed by new measures brought into operation by Khrushchev, there was a clear upsurge of pro-Israel feeling amongst them. Not only the older generation but the young too became more interested in the future of the Jewish State.

These sentiments were strengthened by thousands of Russian Zionists who were returning from concentration camps after Stalin's death, and by the visible existence and prosperity of the Jewish State. 'No matter what happens there is an ocean of love in our hearts for Zion'. This is how an elderly Jew who was released after nine years in a concentration camp in 1956, described to me the sentiments he, and many like him, felt for Israel. He maintained that there were at least 30,000 Zionists imprisoned in Russia when he was in gaol. But not even the hardships and torture of the concentration camps could erase their love for Zion.

Among the Jews released from concentration camps was Joseph Barzilai, a co-founder of the Communist Party in pre-war Israel, who went to the Soviet Union before the Second World War. He had been sentenced to twenty years in a concentration camp but was released after Stalin's death. In his memoirs he recalled that he saw many who perished in the Nurilsk concentration camp but who remained faithful to Zionism until their last hour.[9] One young Russian Jew, called Eli Zelibansky, sang the *Hatikvah*, the Jewish National Anthem, on the way to his execution in the same camp. Before he was taken out of his cell to be shot he asked an inmate to tattoo the Star of David on his forehead. The existence of Israel only stimulated still further the pro-Zion feelings which the Soviet authorities were anxious to dispel.

After some half a dozen years in power Khrushchev became aware that his two-pronged assault on Soviet Jewry—the dual attack against Judaism and Israel—had failed to break completely their resistance to his policy of assimilation. New measures were called for. His realization of failure coincided with a poor harvest in Russia. There was need to find a scapegoat and, following the well-tried practice of Tsarist days, the choice fell on the Jews. Stalin had done the same in the late twenties when economic failures and shortages became most acute. And so with the 'blame the Jew' tradition in mind a country-wide drive was instituted all over Russia against 'speculators and illegal traders in State property'. The majority of the offenders were found to be Jews.

A wave of police arrests began, followed by 'economic trials' and death sentences. The death sentence for economic offences was a measure introduced under Khrushchev's administration. Like other measures of an anti-Jewish nature it is still in force today. Under the Soviet régime economic offences have always been treated as serious crimes. Theft of personal property was made punishable by imprisonment for anything between three months and five years. Pilfering of State property was considered a much more severe crime. By a decree published in 1932 State property was declared to be 'sacred and inviolable'. Theft of State property was made punishable by 'deprivation of liberty for not less than ten years and the confiscation of the offender's property'. Only under 'certain aggravating circumstances' was such a crime punishable by death. But in 1947 the Soviet Union abolished capital punishment altogether. The penalty for theft of State property was changed to imprisonment for a term of from seven to ten years in a correctional labour camp. Punishment could be with or without confiscation of property. Only in the case of theft of collective farm produce or co-operative property was the term of imprisonment longer. But not even if the act of stealing was carried out by 'an organized gang' and on 'a large scale' was the maximum penalty fixed by the Soviet Criminal Court greater than twenty-five years imprisonment. The only persons still liable to death in Russia were 'spies, traitors and diversionists'.

In May 1961, on Khrushchev's bidding, the death penalty for economic offences was reintroduced. The Presidium of the USSR Supreme Soviet adopted a decree reintroducing the death penalty for the misappropriation of State property and for illicit trading. At the same time the application of the decree was greatly extended. It was made to include a greater variety of offences from trading in pilfered or other State property to dealings in foreign currency. Indeed any illegal dealings became an 'economic offence' and could incur the maximum penalty.

In Soviet Russia all consumer goods are State-produced and therefore State property. Distribution and sales are carried out through State employees. The opportunities for misappropriation and corruption are enormous. Temptation increases in proportion to shortage and encourages the vast black market which spreads over the whole of the Soviet Union. Since the days of the New Economic Policy in the early years after the Revolution, 'fiddling' has been a widespread feature of Soviet economic life. To obtain goods wanted, even parts needed to complete a Government order, it was often necessary for managers and directors of State factories to resort to 'fiddling'. They had to employ special men capable of discovering and securing the necessary articles in the quickest possible way, a piece of machinery or a quantity of raw materials. Such people were, and they still are, equipped with what is called a special pull to 'fix anything'.

The possession of this much-needed quality, to be able to 'fix and arrange' things and deal with the many difficulties encountered in daily life gave birth to a new idiom which Russians use very frequently. *'Blat vyshe Sovnarkoma'*, *'Blat* is higher than a Soviet Commisar'. It means that anyone who can practise *Blat*, which is a kind of graft, is blessed with powers exceeding those of authority. Millions all over Russia have found themselves in the position where only by the use of *Blat* have they been able to overcome shortages and carry on with their task.[10] By Khrushchev's new law a whole series of offences previously punishable by imprisonment were placed in the same category as treason, entitling the courts to inflict the death penalty. It soon emerged from some of the trial proceedings reported in the Russian Press that in some cases it was left to the discretion of the KGB to decide which of the offences came under the new law. The illegal possession of a few foreign coins or paper money, the unauthorized manufacture of goods or the possession of them could invoke the death penalty. So could the misappropriation of State property. As a result the Russian courts sentenced to death 163 offenders, 88 of them, or some 60 per cent, were Jews. All these sentences were passed between July 1961 and August 1963. Altogether eighty-one trials of persons for economic offences took place in Moscow, Vilna, Lvov, Kishinev, Chernovtsy and in forty-three other cities. Hundreds of offenders were alleged to have been involved. In cases in which the KGB played a dominant part details were often withheld. Sometimes the names of the alleged offenders were mentioned twice, which accounts for the fact that the exact number cannot be established. Only the KGB knows the true figures. But from all accounts based on reports of the trials published in the Soviet Press the majority of the alleged offenders were Jews.

Whether the economic trials actually helped Khrushchev in his effort to divert public attention from the prevailing economic difficulties only he himself knows. Judging by events which took place about twelve months after the main wave of arrests and trials had stopped, they clearly failed to produce the expected results. For in the Summer of 1964 a poor harvest and resultant shortages were the main reasons for Khrushchev's own downfall. In a country such as Russia bad harvests are serious events of a special political significance. Ironically the succession of crop failures for which Khrushchev made the Jews a scapegoat, contributed to his own disappearance from the Kremlin.

The economic trials constituted a singular feature of the Khrushchev decade. They did considerable harm to the image of the Jew in the eyes of the Russian people and stimulated a revival of anti-Semitic sentiments. Throughout the years of Communist rule the Russians have developed a sixth sense through which they can discern whether the Government is pro- or anti-Jewish. They can do so without waiting for official announcements or declarations. In Stalin's days the campaign against 'cosmopolitans' and 'passportless citizens' was a clear indication to the Russian people of official hostility towards the Jewish minority. If anyone was slow to realize who was meant by such descriptions the Russian Press took good care to inform the reader that they applied to Jews. Whenever the person criticized —a writer or an artist—happened to be a Jew who had adopted a Russian pseudonym the Press invariably also printed his or her original Jewish name. A similar practice was adopted during the economic trials. To make absolutely certain that the reader was left in no doubt of the Jewish origin of an alleged offender, the Russian Press would print the patronymic—Abramovich or Israelevich for instance—after the name. As all such offences were considered highly unpatriotic, the Jews were subjected to particular opprobrium and attack. Nothing brings greater disgrace in Russia than lack of patriotism; so the reputation of the Jews suffered greatly. Instead of eradicating racial antagonism the economic trials merely emphasized and solidified them. It cannot have been coincidence that many of those accused adhered to the Judaic faith and engaged in religious practices, or maintained contact with Israel and Jews abroad. There were several cases where attention was focused on such individuals.

At the beginning of 1962 eight persons were tried in Vilna on currency offence charges. Their names, as given in *Sovietskaya Litva*,[11] were Fedor Kaminer, Mikhail Rabinovich, Aaron and Basia Rezhnitsky, M. Melamed, R. Vidri, M. Kaminer and Z. Zismanovich. It was emphasized by the Prosecution that Basia Rezhnitsky had brothers in Israel and the United States. Four of the accused, including Aaron and Basia Rezhnitsky, were sentenced to death, the latter being the first woman to be sentenced to death under Khrushchev's rule. (Her sentence was changed to life-imprisonment as a result of many protests abroad, including Lord Russell's letter to Khrushchev discussed below, but her subsequent fate is unknown.) The case was widely reported in the Russian Press including *Pravda* and *Izvestia*. According to these newspapers some of the deals in foreign currency were carried on in the local synagogue, and the rabbi too played an illicit role in the transactions.[12] He was accused of having acted as the 'arbitrator' between the 'gang' of currency dealers when they fell out with each other over profits. Thus the rabbi, the synagogue and all elements of religious life were presented as playing a part in criminal offences of an unpatriotic nature.

The anti-Jewish charges in the Vilna case were insidious and subtle; they were much more overt in a trial in Lvov, in March 1962, when out of five Jews tried two were sentenced to death. The Lvov case was typical of the way in which the economic trials were exploited for the anti-Jewish campaign. It was reported in an article entitled 'Prayer and Speculation', which appeared in *Lvovskaya Pravda*.[13]

The article starts by describing how 'a well-dressed middle-aged man alighted at the Lvov railway station and made his way to the Lvov synagogue. He stood there for a few minutes assuming a detached appearance and seeing that nobody paid any attention to him entered the building.' Inside, the article said, there were only a few elderly Jews 'mumbling their prayers'. The visitor, Benjamin Gulko, who was described as 'an inveterate currency speculator'[14] soon found the person he was looking for and a 'haggling over the price of golden Tsarist five rouble pieces began'. The other man, the article stated, was Kontorovich, described as a warden of the synagogue and the local *shokhet*, the ritual slaughterer of animals to provide kosher meat for the religious Jewish community. Kontorovich was also said to be a member of the *Dvatsatka*, the minimum quorum of twenty Jews which by Soviet Law was necessary for the establishment and supervision of a synagogue or religious assembly.

After thus introducing the two principal figures in the trial, the paper stated that Gulko had declared in his testimony that 'crooks and speculators of all types gather in the synagogue where they strike up acquaintances and conclude all sorts of transactions.' The synagogue had been turned into a black market where, with the blessings of Kontorovich and other pillars of religion, criminal transactions were conducted 'without ceremony'.

While some of the religious Jews were presented as a clique of speculators and currency dealers, others attending the synagogue were accused of exploiting the place of worship for illegal dealings in spirits and wine. They were charged with owning a 'bootlegging plant' and doing a brisk trade selling 'holy wine to Believers'. Others were deriving a profit from the sale of reserved seats to parishioners. Income was also derived from the sale of prayer books and religious calendars 'at inflated prices'.

Having depicted the synagogue as the centre of illegal deals in foreign currency and gold coins, and other criminal offences, the article made the further accusation that 'members of the Israeli Embassy in Moscow come as a rule to the synagogue on their visits to Lvov. They come not to pray to the Almighty. They come to distribute to Believers prayer books, calendars, and propaganda pamphlets on the "Israeli paradise" which are printed in the State of Israel'. In the Vilna trial the fact that some of the accused maintained contact with Israel and Jews abroad had been brought into the case to stiffen the charges. Similarly in the case at Lvov the existence of the Israeli Embassy in Moscow was cited as additional grounds for closing the synagogue, which was subsequently done.

The Press campaign which accompanied the trials had a number of standard features characteristic of the Khrushchev period. Jewish gatherings of a religious nature, whether in synagogues or elsewhere, were invariably depicted as occasions for illicit and nefarious dealings. It was implied that the leaders of the Jewish community, sometimes including the rabbi himself, were exploiting their positions for criminal purposes. The Rabbi of Vilna was said to have acted as arbitrator between gangs of offenders. One rabbi who was alleged to have traded 'in gold and foreign currencies' in Piatigorsk was sentenced to death in 1963.[15] His sentence was later reported to have been commuted to fifteen years imprisonment.[16] The synagogue had thus reputedly become a mere meeting-place for Jews to establish undesirable contacts and carry out criminal activities. The participants in such gatherings were a bunch of crooks, the enemies of society, and moreover the synagogues had become centres for anti-Russian propaganda furthered by Israeli diplomats.

The titles alone of some of the articles which appeared at this time demonstrate the anti-Semitism which was whipped up by the economic trials. Thus, 'Slaves of Gold' (*Pravda Ukrainy*, 1 August 1962), 'Worms in the Gold' (*Radianska Ukraina*, 13 June 1962), 'Dirty Gold' (*Literaturna Ukrainia*, 15 June 1962), 'Gold Fever' (*Pravda Ukrainy*, 9 October 1962), 'The Golden Key' (*Trud*, 12 September 1962), 'The Golden Husband' (*Sovietskaya Moldavia*, 18 July 1962), 'The End of a Joint-Stock Corporation' (*Tashkentskaya Pravda*, 25 July 1962), and 'The Millionaire from Arbat' (*Trud*, 25 January 1963). The emphasis in articles such as these was on the anti-social nature of the offenders' alleged behaviour. Jews were depicted as a people standing apart from Soviet life, interested only in personal gain, and without any respect for State laws or State property.

F

In 'Slaves of Gold', the Kiev daily newspaper described a group of seven Jews, six men and one woman, who, 'thirsty for gain and profit', were alleged to have been collecting for years gold ingots, gold articles, gold coins, and American and Canadian dollars. The chief defendant, named M. Poisner, was pictured as a person 'dried out by avarice', dirty, a despicable old man who 'denied an overcoat to his son' but collected gold in vast quantities which he kept in jars and boxes, buried deep in the earth. Poisner and another Jew named Sh. B. Kuris were sentenced to death, the remaining five to terms of imprisonment ranging from seven to fifteen years.

Literaturna Ukrainia in the article 'Dirty Gold' described a group of Jews as 'greedy and voracious vultures' who dealt in gold, dollars and pounds sterling. They were all tried by the military court in Odessa. Two of them, Benjamin Gulko and Foka Fuks, whose wives were also among those accused, were sentenced to be shot. They had revealed themselves, the report said, to be 'servants of dirty gold so distant from our Soviet reality and from the character of our life, that it is impossible even to see them as Soviet people'.

The article entitled 'Gold Fever' in the same series dealt with a group of fifteen Jews who were depicted as arch-worshippers of gold, swindlers and speculators, 'beasts who got what they deserved'. Six of them, including an eighty-one year old Jew named Bornstein, were sentenced to death and shot. The writer pointed out that 'Gold blinded, closed them off from the entire world'. He chided them for their ingratitude to the State which had given them free education and good professions which they had misused for their own evil gains.

These are just examples of the massive anti-Jewish campaign. It was started in an attempt to find a scapegoat for the failure of government policy but as it gained impetus it was used to justify the severity of the sentences. The Press usually reported that the sentences had 'received the unanimous approval of all persons present in the courtroom'. Thus singled out, how could the Jew defend himself from the anti-Semitism which swept the country?

Foreign visitors to the Soviet Union during this period found the Jewish community in an anxious and perplexed mood. Quite a number feared that a revival of Stalinism was at hand. This feeling was particularly strong among religious Jews. But the economic trials also caused great disappointment and shock abroad. It was this feeling of revulsion that prompted Bertrand Russell, Professor Martin Buber and François Mauriac to send a joint appeal to Khrushchev which was released to the Press in April 1962. After assuring the Soviet Premier that their appeal was motivated by 'principles of humanity' and their opposition to the death sentence generally, they declared that they were 'very concerned' that for the past nine months there had been a number of sentences in Russia passed by Soviet tribunals for economic and similar offences. 'We believe', the appeal continued, 'that such social and judicial practice does not benefit a great progressive and cultural nation'. They called upon the Government of the Soviet Union to abolish this method of dealing with economic offences. 'We anxiously call upon you to prevent the carrying out of the death sentences that have been imposed by the courts'. The document also contained a strong reminder to the Kremlin that the present policy might contribute towards a reawakening of anti-Jewish feeling in Russia. The Russian authorities were further assured that in sending the appeal they were also motivated by concern 'for the good name of the Soviet Union'.[17] In the months following Lord Russell wrote several more letters to the Soviet Premier both on the issue of 'economic offences' and on the wider question of anti-Semitism in Russia. On 21 February 1963 he received a lengthy but evasive reply to a note he had written on 2 February. The letter, signed by Khrushchev himself, denied the existence of anti-Semitism in Russia and justified the drastic measures taken by the Soviet authorities in dealing with 'people who appropriate values belonging to the society, who live idly at the expense of other people's labour'. 'Such people' he declared, 'are prosecuted by law based on the morality of labour'. He denied that the decisions of the courts were directed against 'people of a definite nationality' pointing out that among the offenders were also Russians,

Georgians, Ukrainians, White Russians, and people of other ethnic groups. And he finally sought refuge by pointing to the Soviet Constitution which 'proclaims equality regardless of nationality and race. Advocacy of racial or national discrimination is punishable by law.'

Khrushchev's main emphasis was on the difference between the capitalist and Communist approach to the question of labour and property. Unlike the capitalist system, he wrote, 'our State and our society by means of law, protect honest working people against the parasite and sponger who violate the morality of our Socialist society.' For this reason 'It is known that bourgeois propaganda resorts to slander and falsification in order to denigrate our socialist system and our morality.' He appeared to be particularly hurt at the suggestion in the appeal that the trials were a manifestation of anti-Jewish policy. 'There is not, and never has been, an anti-Semitic policy in the USSR',[18] he declared, clearly disregarding a quarter of a century of Stalin's anti-Jewish measures. Only a few years earlier, in 1956, while discussing the Jewish issue with a delegation of the French Socialist Party, he had admitted the existence of anti-Semitism among the people in Russia as 'a remnant of a reactionary past.' (see p. 230, note 2.)

Nonetheless the appeal of the intellectuals was not in vain. One immediate effect was a reduction in the number of trials and a relaxation of anti-Jewish propaganda in the Soviet Press. The very fact that Khrushchev replied to the appeal was significant, for it demonstrated the Kremlin's sensitivity to criticism abroad. The exchange of documents between Lord Russell and the Soviet leader was not published in the Russian Press. But those members of the public who normally listen to foreign broadcasts soon learned of their contents. They could not fail to draw the conclusion that anti-Semitism was no longer as commendable as the economic trials and the accompanying Press campaign had led them to believe.

Perhaps most important of all was the effect the appeal produced on Khrushchev himself. He did not change his policy but he became more aware of the preoccupation of liberal opinion abroad with the position of the Jewish minority in Russia. Had he remained in power for several years longer, it is very likely that Kremlin policy would have been affected.

As it was, the appeal came too late. The anti-Jewish attitude which Khrushchev had inherited from his predecessor had hardened and become a firm element of Soviet policy.

One reason why anti-Semitism has become so entrenched is that Khrushchev's successors—no less than Khrushchev himself—are followers of Stalin. Both Alexei Kosygin and Leonid Brezhnev held high positions under Stalin.

A member of the Politburo for many years, Alexei Kosygin was appointed Vice Premier and later Premier of the RSFSR (Russian Federative Socialist Republic). This must have given him an insight into the way in which Stalin established himself as the sole ruler, and have also enabled him to play a role in the framing of policies. From 1935-38, Kosygin was Mayor of his native Leningrad and Chairman of the Executive Committee of the Leningrad Soviet. Stalin must have been satisfied with him for he was soon promoted to higher office. After a brief spell in several important branches of the State administration—he was Minister of Finance for a time —he was made a Vice-Chairman of the Council of Ministers of the USSR. Throughout this period he retained his importance in the Politburo.

Highly favoured by Stalin his skills and experience in the art of government were also appreciated when Khrushchev came to power. In 1960, some time after Marshal Bulganin had left the Premiership, and when several other former Bolsheviks had been ousted from the Party, Kosygin was appointed to an even higher policy-making position—First Deputy-Chairman of the Council of Ministers of the USSR.

During the period when Kosygin held these high positions, before becoming Premier, the status of the Jewish minority in Russia worsened. He was Chairman of the Council of Ministers of the RSFSR from 1946-53. The RSFSR occupies 6,500,000 square miles, three-quarters of the total area of the USSR, has a population of 129,000,000, and the largest Jewish population of all the Republics. As its head, Kosygin was in charge of policy towards the Jews. The arrest of so many Jewish intellectuals, writers and poets in Moscow must have been made with his authority to a certain extent. As for the 'Doctors' Plot' however much it was the criminal concoction of the MVD, it could not have taken place without Kosygin's knowledge, if not his actual participation.

Leonid Brezhnev, Kosygin's contemporary in the Kremlin, is also no stranger on the Soviet political scene. His career too dates from Stalin's rule. An active member of the Communist Party from his early youth, Brezhnev held many responsible positions in the administration before the war. From 1941-45 he was first deputy, then head of the political department of the Fourth Ukrainian Front and was later made Major-General for his services. He became a member of the Central Committee early in his career. In 1950 Stalin appointed him head of the central body of the Communist Party of Moldavia. While in Kishinev, the capital, Brezhnev was responsible for anti-Jewish measures there, in particular the arrests of Jewish writers and intellectuals. Faithful to Stalin he also won favour with Khrushchev. At the 22nd Party Congress Brezhnev was elected to the Presidium of the Central Committee on Khrushchev's recommendation.

It was no accident that when two years later on 14 October 1964, Khrushchev was forced to give up power on the pretext of 'age and ill-health' his office, with his powers divided in two, was assigned to Kosygin and Brezhnev. Like Malenkov and Khrushchev before them they were the pillars of the Stalinist régime. They helped him to shape his policies, and then to execute them. These four were the men Stalin most favoured. With all anti-Stalinists and true Leninists exterminated, only those who helped directly in that process have been left to introduce de-Stalinization. Is it possible to expect former Stalinists to throw themselves wholeheartedly into the process of de-Stalinization? Although the open terror of Stalinist days has ceased, the Russian people—the millions who suffered and hoped for freedom—received only a fake freedom. What they have been granted is a deceptive imitation of what the civilized world understands as real freedom. Suppression is still the rule of the day. Criticism and protest are regarded as crimes. The few courageous writers and poets who have dared to express their views have been made to pay with prison sentences. And where the Russian people suffer and must keep silent, the silence of the Jewish minority, humiliated for decades, is more complete and more crushing.

9

NATIONAL MINORITIES IN THE USSR—I

Contemporary students of Russian history investigating the position of Jews in the Soviet Union often show a tendency to treat the Jewish issue in isolation, not as part of a general policy. They approach the subject from too narrow a viewpoint. Although sometimes this is because of inadequate methods of investigation, it also reflects the Jewish historians' traditional approach to the history of the Jewish minority in Russia, which concentrated on Jewish suffering and persecution. Among the leading Jewish historians writing in this tradition is Professor Simon Dubnov.[1]

To a certain extent this emphasis is due to the absence of any really reliable data about the labyrinthine problem of national minorities. Constant changes in official policy towards the Jewish minority make information more scarce and less reliable. The treatment of the Jewish issue in even the most authoritative Soviet publications had always depended on the prevailing official attitude towards the Jews. In 1932, when Stalin was only just beginning to demolish the Jewish cultural structure, the large *Great Soviet Encyclopaedia* allocated 150 columns to the entry on 'Jews', *(Yevrei)*; two decades later this had been reduced to four.

Successive Russian governments have placed all kinds of difficuties in the way of research into the Jewish problem. But they have not succeeded in making a study of the Jewish problem entirely out of the question. One of the most fruitful approaches is to compare the situation of the Jews with that of other national minorities. Clearly, Soviet policy cannot be accused of discriminating specifically against the Jewish minority, unless a comparison with the experience of other minorities reveals that in fact the Jews have received markedly worse treatment. Historians have tended to overlook what was happening to other national minorities during the same period. Under the Tsars, Ukrainians, White Russians, Poles, Lithuanians and numerous other so-called Western minorities were also subjected to laws restricting their rights and robbing them of their national dignity. Further afield, the Georgians, Tartars, Yakuts, Koreans, Chuvash and many other ethnic groups were treated as second or third-class citizens. If they did not actually suffer the pogroms which were inflicted on the Jews, other minorities did come up against various forms of discrimination.

At the time of the Bolshevik Revolution more than half the population of Russia was made up of national minorities. Of the 160,000,000 inhabiting the Tsar's vast empire only 70,000,000 were Russians, or Great Russians as they are called. But they were the ruling element. The liberation of the oppressed national minorities from political, economic and social discrimination, became one of the redemptive promises of the October Revolution.

The exact number of nationalities under the Tsar's rule has never been fully established. On the official list only about a hundred were accounted for, but this did not include the smaller ethnic groups living in remote Siberia, nor all the nomadic and semi-nomadic tribes in the Far East. Only after the Revolution was a determined attempt made to modernize the way of life of these groups.

Broadly speaking, the non-Russian nationalities in pre-revolutionary Russia were divided into two main groups. The Ukrainians, White Russians, Poles, Lithuanians, Jews and Finns were among those in the Western section who, like the Russians themselves, had a high level of culture and social development. The more primitive groups—the Tartars, Kirghiz, Bulgars, Mordvinians, Kazakhs, Samoyeds, Yakuts, and a whole host of others—lived in the Eastern section. Both groups were deprived of full rights of citizenship which were reserved as the privilege of the Great Russians. Lenin called Tsarist Russia 'a prison of nations', which he promised the Revolution would unlock and deliver to freedom. The solution of the nationalities problem and complete equality of citizenship were the two major pledges of the October Revolution which had a universal appeal. More than any other pledge the hope of winning freedom for the oppressed minorities made ever-growing numbers follow Lenin.

Fifty years later Soviet leaders celebrated the Jubilee of the Revolution. The solution of the nationalities problem figured as a major triumph. The tone was set by the Central Committee of the Russian Communist Party in Moscow on 21 June 1967. In a statement on the 'Fiftieth Anniversary of the Great October Socialist Revolution', the Central Committee declared: 'The Leninist programme for the solution of the national question was implemented and the socialist fraternity of the peoples of our country was established in the course of socialist construction.' It claimed to have solved the question of the national minorities, who 'During the building of Socialism . . . acquired their own statehood, put an end to the economic and cultural backwardness and gradually adopted the highest socialist forms of economy and culture . . . All the peoples of the Soviet Union recognize that the Russian working class and the Russian people as a whole played a huge role in implementing the Leninist national policy'. Inaugurating the official jubilee celebrations, the Central Committee assured the people of the Soviet Union that they were 'consistently working to overcome the survivals of national narrow-mindedness, parochialism, nationalism and chauvinism.' The characteristic features of the peoples of the USSR were 'allegiance to the communist cause, profound internationalism and Soviet patriotism, respect for national dignity, friendship and fraternity.' 'All Soviet peoples', the statement went on to declare, 'have their own culture, that is national in form and socialist in content.' Claiming that after the October Revolution, more than forty nationalities had been helped to evolve a written language of their own, the Central Committee stated, 'Socialism has created conditions for the burgeoning and mutual enrichment of national culture. Preserving and furthering their best national traits and traditions and surmounting obsolescent forms, each national culture fruitfully draws on the cultural achievements of other nations.' The Central Committee went on to claim that 'The Russian language has become a medium of exchange of scientific knowledge and cultural values between nations. The advancement of national cultures and languages gives each nation every possibility to use and absorb the cultural wealth of all Soviet peoples'.[2]

At the point which Jewish history has now reached in Russia, these claims of the Central Committee are of particular significance. At the same time the emphasis on the national minorities issue, and especially the claim that it has been successfully resolved, indicates sensitivity to public opinion at home as well as abroad.

The resolution of the Central Committee was one of a series of official Soviet statements. The same theme dominated the special anniversary publication, *The Soviet Union*,[3] brought out in Moscow as an historical record of the major achievements of the fifty years of Communism. It opened with a dramatic account of the crucial first forty-eight hours of the Bolshevik Revolution and went on to list its major triumphs since. First there was a special article by Anastas Mikoyan claiming that Russia had solved the nationalities problem. Then there was an article by Yekaterina Furtseva, the Minister of Culture of the USSR on Soviet attainments in the spheres of education and culture. She presented these as the acid test of the success of the Bolshevik Revolution. To Furtseva the 'cultural renaissance' in the Soviet Union is best manifested by the fact that there are in Russia today 25,000,000 people employed in educational and academic establishments.

Mikoyan's approach was even more fundamental. His contribution was entitled 'The Soviet Union—a Family of Nations' thus suggesting that one of the most important liberalizing pledges of the Revolution has already been redeemed. That a member of a minority nationality should make this claim is significant. Anastas Mikoyan, a Georgian born in 1895, did much towards the framing of Stalin's Constitution. Thereafter he became First Deputy-Premier under Khrushchev, and Chairman of the Presidium of the Supreme Soviet—the titular Head of State. He resigned in 1965. It was he who had first claimed in the post-Stalin era that the Jewish problem had been solved. In 1959 when he was First Deputy Premier he had seen representatives of the American Jewish Committee while visiting America. In a statement to a Press Conference (15 January 1959) he claimed that all the peoples of Russia enjoyed cultural freedom. However, the Jews, he said, had become so closely merged with the Russian people that they participated in the same culture, many of them considering themselves Russian and preferring the Russian language. He claimed that this development had come about in spite of the provisions made by the régime for the development of their own distinctive culture. Yet the number of books, journals and other publications published in Yiddish is infinitesimal compared with the amount published for other nationalities or minorities in their own languages, nor do theatres, schools, or classes in the Yiddish language exist.[4]

In his contribution to *The Soviet Union's* anniversary publication Mikoyan wrote: 'The victory of the Socialist Revolution in Russia was also the victory of the national liberation revolution of the peoples who had been languishing under Tsarism's dual tyranny of class and national oppression.' He claimed that 'long before the October Revolution, Lenin had worked out a programme for the emancipation of all oppressed peoples living in Russia's multi-national state'. The first point in the historical 'Declaration of the Rights of the Peoples of Russia', issued immediately after the Bolshevik Revolution, laid down 'the Principle of Equality and Sovereignty of the Peoples of Russia.' It further declared that the free development of national minorities was another of its major objectives.

Listing the various measures employed since to transform these principles into reality, Mikoyan claimed 'unprecedented success' for the Soviet Union. Not only had there been notable achievements in the economic field, in industrialization and technological advance, and in the standard of living of the various nationalities, but particularly in the sphere of national culture and education. He was specially proud of what had been done for the national minorities in the North Caucasus, Central Asia and the Far North, where people who had no alphabet in Tsarist Russia had been helped by Soviet rule 'to create and develop their own alphabets, their own national literature and culture.'

Summing up, Mikoyan asserted that the 'Fifty years of Soviet rule has shown just how powerful our multi-national country is. In our Socialist homeland the nations are flourishing as never before. They are drawing closer together, enriching each other's culture, building up friendly ties and a stirring sense of Soviet patriotism.'

Elaborating on the theme, Mikoyan admitted that at the 23rd Party Congress the question of nationalities and the Government's future policy had come up for discussion. This in itself was clearly an admission that the issue still called for consideration. But he assured the reader that the 'Party would continue to attend to the interests and national peculiarities of each of the peoples.' It was in this spirit that, Mikoyan concluded, the people of the Soviet Union 'greet the Fiftieth Anniversary of the Great October Socialist Revolution.'

The theoretical blueprint of the nationalities policy under Communism had been laid down long before the Bolsheviks came to power. It had been defined by Lenin and elaborated by Stalin in the essay written at Lenin's instigation before the First World War (see pp. 54-5). But this article by Mikoyan in the Jubilee publication was the first to make such bold and far-reaching claims for the minorities policy. It was the first time that it had been presented as an accomplished fact when only two years before it had figured on the agenda of party meetings for consideration and adjustment. The need for revision of the Stalinist minority policy and a 'return to Leninism' first voiced at the 20th Party Congress, had become an almost constant item for discussion within the Party, and in the leading historical and philosophical Russian journals, Mikoyan recalled that at the 23rd Party Congress the need for revision had been unanimously agreed on and he claimed that it had since been carried out. How then do the official claims look when held up against reality?

Especially against the reality of Jewish life in the Soviet Union today?

On the fiftieth anniversary of the Bolshevik Revolution the Soviet Union was the home of something like 130 different nationalities and ethnic groups, who varied in numbers and in culture.[5] Despite the tremendous advances in the field of education they also still vary in their level of technical achievement. Collectively their populations total 234,000,000 an increase of about a third since Tsarist days. They form one-seventh of the world's total population, and occupy one-sixth—8,662,400 square miles—of the world's inhabitable land surface.

The people of the Soviet Union speak 120 languages and dialects. Despite fifty years of official atheism they still appear to profess forty different religions and faiths. Numerically the largest are the Russians, otherwise known as the Great Russians, totalling over 100,000,000. Next in size are the Ukrainians with over 40,000,000. The Jews are the eleventh largest group among the nationalities. The majority of them—nearly a million—live in the RSFSR, the largest of the fifteen republics occupying over 6,000,000 square miles, where the vast majority of the Russians and thirty-two other nationalities also live.

Of the groups living in this republic the following were given a script of their own after the Revolution : Abaza, Abkhazian, Adyge, Aleut, Altai, Avar, Balkar, Bashkir, Chechen, Cherkess (Circassian), Chukchi, Dargin, Eskimo, Even, Evenk, Ingush, Itelmic, Izhor, Kabardi, Kalmuk, Karachai, Kara-Kalpak, Ket, Khakass, Khanty, Kirghiz, Koryak, Kumandu, Kumyk, Kurdish, Lak, Lezghin, Mansi, Mordvin, Nanai, Saami, Selkup, Shor, Tabasaran, Tat, Tuva, Udi, Udmurt, and Vepsiek.[6]

Under the Tsars these people used primitive dialects in their tribal communications. None of them had a proper written language. Three-quarters of the entire population of pre-revolutionary Russia were illiterate. The first task the Soviet authorities set themselves in the initial seven-year plan was to introduce general education and an alphabet for those who had no script of their own. Only by providing them with a proper instrument for their education could these peoples be given a chance to benefit from the emancipation the Revolution promised.

In addition to these groups with no written means of communication there were dozens of other national minorities which, although no longer living on a tribal or nomadic level, nevertheless clung to the old forms. To the inaugurators of the new régime their social and economic patterns were so various, and in some cases so primitive, that they were unable to adapt to the new Communist system. This meant a total reshaping of their cultures. To make the new system acceptable and workable, a degree of homogeneity had to be created. This called for a vast programme of education. Theoretically Lenin and his associates had worked out a general outline of the nationalities problem well in advance. But in practice they encountered many difficulties. One of the first steps the Bolsheviks had taken as soon as the Civil War in Russia ended was to list, classify and embark on the education of the more backward groups in the various parts of non-European Russia. Where the Tsars had used repression to assert their authority over these minorities, the Bolsheviks used education to bring them into line with the more civilized groups in the country, and hence to establish their new ideas.

It was soon discovered that over forty ethnic groups from the Adygei in the north-west Caucasus to the Evenki in Central Siberia had no proper alphabet. Leading Russian linguists sent down from Moscow and Leningrad succeeded in the course of a few years in giving the dialects of these people the form of a modern civilized language. In this way they could absorb and convey the meaning of the new terminology, technical as well as ideological, which the Revolution suddenly brought into daily use.

Accounts of these achievements from members of the minorities concerned, were collected and published during the Jubilee year of the Revolution. Interviews appeared in the Press under the title 'What the October Revolution Brought my People'.[7] Here are extracts from three such interviews, all with members of national minorities whose language was only alphabetized after, or shortly before, the Revolution.

Khizir Eredzhibok, an Adygei engineer, recalled the rapid advancement in the life of his tribe since the Revolution. Marked progress, he said, had been made by his people not merely in the industrial sphere, but in the building of a new culture. The Adygei people now live in their Autonomous Region in the RSFSR, with a population of 353,000, less than a third of the total population in an area of 400,000 square miles. They have a national life of their own furthered by their own cultural institutions. Before the Revolution they had no educational system, no health service and no written language. There might be one person in the village who had had some education. 'Today we have many specialists, and yet one person in ten is a student. Many are studying at young workers' schools, dozens are students at technical higher and secondary special schools.'

Under the same heading, 'What the October Revolution Brought my People', A. Pisarev, 'an Honoured Worker in Culture', of the Udmurian Autonomous Soviet Socialist Republic, told of the progress which his people had achieved as a result of the Revolution. The Udmurts, too, had no written alphabet before. In fact Pisarev recalled—to underline the contrast between the past and the present—that at the end of the last century the Tsarist government had falsely accused the Udmurt peasants of 'ritual human sacrifices'. Since the establishment of Soviet power, he said, the Udmurts had produced numbers of gifted people, scientists, doctors and teachers. Illiteracy had been wiped out. Out of every 10,000 people, 1,600 were studying. The Udmurts had 'five institutes, over 20 secondary special educational institutions, and a ramified network of general and vocational schools'. There were '1,100 rural and trade union clubs, and 679 public libraries with a total stock of some 7 million volumes'. After listing the names of numerous Udmurt writers who had won prominence since the October Revolution, Pisarev stated that in the capital, Izhevsk, 'we have the Udmurt Musical Drama Theatre, a Russian Drama Theatre, a puppet theatre, a Republican Philharmonic Society, a circus . . . We live a cultured, creative, prosperous and happy life. It was brought to us on the wings of the new power, whose fiftieth birthday we are going to celebrate later in the year.' The Udmurt ASSR, with a territory of 25,000 square miles, has a population of 1,376,000, of which about half are Udmurts and Ugro-Finnic people of the Russian Orthodox Church.

Similar interviews published under the same heading, were conducted with representatives of minority groups who had managed to attain a level of culture even under Tsarist rule. Thus a member of the Buryat-Mongols listed the 'many blessings' which the Revolution had brought to his people. The Buryats, numbering about a quarter of a million, have their own Autonomous Republic in south-east Siberia. They also live in other regions outside their own autonomous territory. For centuries they were to be found in the transbaikal territories where they professed Lavaism and led a semi-nomadic life. They had no written language until the beginning of the twentieth century. Today, Dugar Naidanov told *Moscow News*, in the Aginski Buryat National Area where some 60,000 Buryat-Mongols live, they have their own elementary and secondary schools, teachers' training colleges, a music school and other cultural institutions. Some 60,000 children, he stated, attend 50 schools in the area; 800 Buryat teachers are employed. Many of the Buryat farmers in the collective villages have been able to send their children to study at Moscow University as well as in Ulan-Ude, formerly Verkneudinsk. There are today many Buryat economists, doctors, teachers and agricultural engineers. 'The people do not only enjoy the benefits of culture,' he concluded, 'they are creating it and helping its progress.'

Written languages were created for these minorities to enable them to participate in the process of transition from Tsarist to Communist society. They had to be provided with a language as the basic channel through which the new ideology could be conveyed and understood. Other minorities, already in possession of a language, were made to accept linguistic changes. This was officially justified as an essential part of the development of the national minorities and as a step towards their integration with the rest of the population, as visualized by Lenin. The Yakuts, the Kirghiz, the Uzbek, and a number of the other Turkic minorities had to give up the ancient Arabic alphabet they had used for centuries and adopt the Latin one instead. At least ten of the national groups changed from Arabic to Latin in the early stages after the Revolution. A decade or so later they faced the further change from the Latin to the Cyrillic—i.e. Russian—alphabet. The change was made in stages so as to avoid excessive opposition, and the accusation that they were being Russified too quickly. In Uzbekistan the Cyrillic alphabet was introduced in May 1940 and a month later into Tadzhikistan; sixteen months later, in September 1941, the Latin alphabet was changed to Cyrillic in the Kirghiz and Kazakhstan Republics.[8]

With the Jewish minority the question of language has always been much more complex than with the other minorities. Jews had a dual linguistic allegiance. Hebrew was the sacred language of biblical days and has remained so. But even in biblical days the Jews in their homeland had frequently changed to other languages, especially to Aramaic. Driven out of Spain into Western Europe, they had developed Yiddish out of German. Yiddish had then come to be considered as a force for the preservation of the Jewish national identity. It was no longer a question of semantics alone. Before the Second World War when more than half the total Jewish population in the world lived in Eastern Europe and spoke Yiddish, it was the language which best expressed the Jewish philosophy of life. It was a vital part of the Jews' *Weltanschauung*. Since then the fate of the Jewish communities in Eastern Europe during the Second World War has invested Yiddish with a special emotional and historical importance.

While retaining its place as a language of prayer, Hebrew in Tsarist Russia was the tongue of the past; Yiddish became the language of the present. After the Revolution Hebrew was restricted to the synagogue. To the Communists the Jewish past was unacceptable, for it was thought necessary to officially separate the people from their bourgeois nationalist traditions.

In the case of the Jewish minority the linguistic reforms were carried a stage further. During the first post-war revolutionary decade Yiddish had to play an assigned role. It was the only effective instrument through which the Party could disseminate and propagate Communism among the Jewish population.

At the same time the Yiddish language was purged of all the Hebrew expressions with which it was richly coloured. The spelling of the Hebrew words which had crept into the Yiddish language by way of prayer and study was deliberately disfigured so as to erase all links with the past. Even Hebrew names like Abraham and those of the other patriarchs had to be re-spelt. Jewish Communists played a prominent part in this campaign.

With the exception of the elimination of Hebrew the Jews were at first granted facilities for the development of cultural institutions on the same lines as the other minorities. In the late twenties and early thirties, to give only a few examples, there were in the USSR nearly 1,000 Jewish schools with Yiddish as a language of instruction. In the Ukraine alone some 90,000 Jewish children attended classes in 765 Yiddish schools. There were also 3 teachers' colleges, 16 Technical and 5 agricultural institutes, 116 libraries, 47 reading clubs, 3 theatres and a children's theatre in Yiddish. In addition, there were Yiddish departments at some Universities and Institutes of Higher Education. The All-Ukrainian Academy of Sciences had an Institute of Jewish Proletarian Culture attached to it, and the White Russian Academy of Sciences had a Jewish sector.[9]

There were a number of courts, civil as well as criminal, where Yiddish was the official language. Official statistics for the whole of the Soviet Union published in the first decade after the Revolution showed that there were no less than 80 Jewish newspapers and periodicals. The State maintained over 40 Yiddish State theatres. There was a Yiddish stage in almost every large city in the USSR. As regards the publication of books, in 1925—to quote the figure for only one year—when Stalin was not yet in full control of the Kremlin, 208 Yiddish books were published in Russia. That was nearly half the total number of volumes in Yiddish published that year in the rest of the world.[10]

Under Stalin, then under Khrushchev, the Russification of all minorities continued. We have already seen how the enforced process of linguistic assimilation was prolonged over several decades to avoid opposition. Nevertheless, the minorities resented it, often strongly. In the official Kremlin version these measures were justified officially, as they are still, by the rapid progress in industrializing and urbanizing the country. Nevertheless, the minorities were not unaware of the other motives which lay behind the official policy. For in spite of Lenin's warning against Russian chauvinism it quickly became apparent under Stalin's rule that the pressures on the minorities towards Russification were growing in intensity. The Russian language which was compulsory in all Soviet schools began to take precedence. It soon became an advantageous vehicle towards a better position in the factory, office and the State machinery generally. Aware of this advantage more and more pupils adopted Russian in place of their native language. Despite all assurances and constitutional guarantees of equality for every language, the younger generation quickly realized that Russian secured for them positions which other languages could never win.

As Stalin's influence grew, the motives behind the assimilation policy became coloured with national prejudice. What Lenin had envisaged as a positive trend leading to co-operation and fellow-feeling between the peoples of the USSR, became under Stalin a pattern of suppression and violence which could only disrupt relations. The ideals of Communism as Lenin tried to activate them required the national minorities to submerge much of their cultural identity in the new way of life. Had he lived longer assimilation might have been achieved without violence. But Stalin used the assimilation policy as a vehicle for his own hostility to the minority groups. With his specifically anti-Semitic prejudice, and the residue of Tsarist anti-Semitism in the country as a whole, this could only mean that the Jews were to suffer even more than the other minorities.

The culmination of Stalin's antagonism as far as many of the minorities were concerned was the mass deportations which took place during the Second World War. The Crimean Tartars, the Karachi, the Kalmuks, the Chechens, the Ingushi, the Balkars, and of course the Germans were all uprooted from their native territories.

This was bad enough. But no other minority suffered the kind of terror to which the Jews were exposed, from the pre-war purges, through the war, to the 1948 liquidation of Jewish intellectuals and the 'Doctors' Plot'.

NATIONAL MINORITIES IN THE USSR—II

After Stalin's death the Communist Party displayed a real inclination to revise official policy towards the national minorities. In
a multi-national, multi-lingual State the issue was vital. The
general relaxation demanded a new approach. The 20th Party
Congress marked a definite break with the past. At that famous
gathering Khrushchev among others brought up the issue for
discussion, prompted largely by the desire to return to what he
called 'Leninist nationality policy'. The 22nd Party Congress
subjected the issue to an even closer review. Stalin was accused
all along of having 'violated' Leninist principles. This demanded
an immediate reversal. In the welcome new atmosphere Khrushchev made it clear that 'A national flavour is quite natural in
literature and art. But all too often', he said, 'we have encountered archaisms in this respect.' In regard to the linguistic problem, Khrushchev declared that 'we impose no restrictions whatsoever on the development of national languages. But their development must not lead to any accentuation of national barriers;
on the contrary it should lead to a coming together of nations'.
He then went on, however, to emphasize the importance of the
Russian language as an agent to assimilation. 'The Russian language', he explained to the Congress delegates, 'has in effect become
the second language of the peoples of the Soviet Union, a medium
of mutual intercourse, an avenue whereby each nation and
nationality achieves access to the cultural accomplishments of all
the peoples of our country and to world culture.' He admitted—
Khrushchev liked to appear as a frank father figure, especially
at this kind of gathering—that there were 'people, of course, who
deplore the gradual effacement of national distinctions.' But he
went on to declare that 'Communists will not conserve and per-

petuate national distinctions. We will support the objective process of the increasingly closer rapprochement of nations and nationalities'.[1]

Laid down thus by the First Secretary of the Russian Communist Party and the head of the Government this line of policy was later incorporated in the fourth chapter of the New Party Programme. The issue was soon being vigorously discussed in the Russian Press.

Ached Agayev, writing in *Izvestia* and in *Literatura i Zhizn*, called for the liquidation of all the literature of the non-Russian nationalities and the introduction of Russian as the only creative language for all.[2] This appeal did not go unchallenged. A. G. Yegorov angrily denounced Agayev's demands.[3] He was supported by another prominent Soviet writer, Vladimir Solouchin, who interpreted Agayev's theories as a dangerous call for a *Gleichschaltung* of languages and cultures.[4] Strong opposition also came from prominent writers among the nationalities. V. Chalmayev, the Kazakh literary critic, called this proposal 'an insult' to the national minorities.[5] Similar opinions were voiced by a group of other writers in various republics. Most notable among them was that by M. S. Dzunusov who denounced Agayev's theories as 'highly chauvinistic and anti-Leninist'. It is true, he wrote, that some chauvinists now mask their views with Communist phraseology. They call it internationalization, fusion, and 'the greatness of the Russian language'. Others urge it on the grounds that all peoples should unite under the flag of proletarian internationalism. Nonetheless, declared Dzunusov, we must oppose it.[6] The discussion on this subject has now almost disappeared from the leading Soviet journals. This is itself an indication that Russification proceeds.

To the minorities in Russia, and in particular to the Jews, the line of policy on the minorities issue laid down at the 22nd Party Congress was another call for speedy Russification. Khrushchev made it perhaps more palatable. He associated this policy with the reforms in industry and Government. Educational and linguistic changes, he explained, were only part of the new measures necessary to hasten the building of Soviet society. It meant the fulfilment of the Communist ideal. But official statistics disclosed in greater detail after the Party Congress, showed the havoc caused in the linguistic and educational domain of national minorities by the Stalinist policy of giving priority to the Russian language. The census of 1959 had revealed that in all fifteen republics more and more children of the various minorities gave preference to the Russian language over their own mother tongue. Fluency in Russian ensured quick advancement to a better career. In the Ukrainian Republic, for instance, despite the strong nationalistic tendencies of the Ukrainian population, a large percentage of Ukrainian children preferred to go to Russian schools rather than to their own. There were at that time 29,361 schools, out of which 4,008 used Russian as the language of instruction. 16·9 per cent of the population in the Ukrainian Republic was Russian. But over 26 per cent of the children accepted Russian as their first language. An even higher percentage of children opted for Russian in the Republics of Kazakhstan and Kirghizia.[7] In the Uzbek Republic 23·7 per cent of all pupils attended Russian schools while the percentage of Russians in the Republic only came to 11·6 per cent. The situation in Moldavia was even worse from the point of view of the local language. There nearly 30 per cent of the children were receiving instruction in Russian while the total number of Russians in the Republic was just over 10 per cent. Even in the Baltic Republics—Lithuania, Latvia and Estonia—where national sentiments were deep, a high percentage of children also preferred to attend schools where Russian took precedence as the language of instruction over their own native tongue.[8] Small ethnic groups like the Shorians, about 20,000 in number, have almost abandoned their own language in favour of Russian. They live in their own national district, the rich iron-ore Kuzbas region. They first became bi-lingual, made a show of struggling to retain their own language, but finally gave it up altogether. The majority of them now speak Russian only.

The vocabularies and structures of the national languages show the influence of Russian domination. Ukrainian etymologists have concluded that Russian words, especially modern scientific and technological terms, are now included in the Ukrainian vocabulary. 30 per cent of the Yakut vocabulary has also been supplanted by Russian words. According to a recent publication by the Yakut branch of the All Union Academy of Sciences the very syntax of the Yakut language has been affected by the Russian language. Official Soviet opinion describes this result as progress towards internationalization and co-operation between all nationalities. In conformity with this view the publication bore the significant title of *The Progressive Influence of the Great Russian Nation on the Development of the Yakut People.*

Linguistic assimilation among Jews was clearly much more thorough than among other nationalities. Although nearly four-fifths of the entire Jewish minority live in three republics—the Russian, Ukrainian and White Russian—they are still considered as a dispersed nationality. Now there are no longer any schools using the Yiddish language as a medium of instruction anywhere in the Soviet Union there is no way of establishing which language Jewish pupils, or parents for that matter, prefer. But at the 1959 census nearly half a million Russian Jews gave Yiddish as their mother tongue. Only the Polish minority, of which 442,905 out of a total of 1,500,000 gave Polish as their mother tongue in the same census, appears to have submitted to the same extent.

The linguistic changes in the Soviet Union came under close analysis at a conference in October 1963, held at Frunze, the capital of Kirghizia. The conference was a follow-up of the decisions on linguistic reform made at the 22nd Party Congress, and during the subsequent discussions among the members of the General Committee. Among the participants at the conference were leading social scientists and linguistic experts from many parts of the Soviet Union. They had come to consider the nationalities issue in the light of the changes following Stalin's death. Eighty papers were read and six committees appointed to study the problem of the national minorities with particular reference to language and culture. No clear-cut decisions were taken, for the delegates realized that despite the attempts of decades to solve the nationality problem there were still 'many difficulties' to overcome. These were not clearly described. But from subsequent discussions in leading historical and philosophical journals it emerged that the main theme was the revision of Stalinist policies and the demand for 'a return to Leninism'. No full report of the Frunze Conference has ever been published. From fragmentary accounts, however, appearing in the official journals of the Lithuanian, Estonian, and other republics, it was made apparent that one of the dominant themes was the question of language. An appeal was made to Soviet philosophers, sociologists, and lawyers 'to study the intricate problem of fusion of nations and peoples' in the multi-national State.

It transpired that in 1963 only sixty-six languages were recognized and in daily use among the peoples of the Soviet Union. So it seems that more than half of those listed after the October Revolution have officially disappeared, either eliminated altogether or lingering only as a local dialect. Comparisons with earlier figures reveal how rapid the decline in the use of these languages has been. In 1938, for example, some schools in the Uzbek Republic where nationalities were very mixed used fourteen or even more languages of instruction. Before the Second World War schools in Tashkent had provided instruction to pupils in the following languages: Uzbek, Russian, Tadjik, Kazakh, Tartar, Ukrainian, Korean, Armenian, a Jewish dialect called Tat, Uigur, Gypsy dialect, Persian, Khirghiz, Kara-Kalpak, Turkic, Turkmenian, Kipchack, Ossetian, Chechen, Bulgar, and Latvian.

It seems to have been the realization of how far Russification had already engulfed the various national minorities which made the authorities withhold publication of the full conference details. It must have come as a surprise to the delegates themselves, to find so little had been done to restore the balance disrupted by Stalin. Even if only negatively Stalin's successors had followed in the direction which he had taken.

As we have seen discussions on the minorities issue have now almost ceased in the leading Soviet journals. Khrushchev's successors in the Kremlin avoid making any official declaration. But the process of Russification continues. Any protest, whether it comes from national minorities in the Western parts of the USSR, such as the Ukrainians or Latvians, in the Eastern areas from the Yakuts or Georgians, or from members of the Jewish minority, are ruthlessly suppressed and silenced.

As in all other spheres of Soviet administration Brezhnev and Kosygin have proved themselves to be faithful continuators of the policy of Russification and assimilation. Both are former members of the Kremlin élite. They were intimately connected with all important Government decisions in Stalin's days and faithfully assisted in their realization. Stalin spared their lives, because they co-operated in carrying out his plans to liquidate all real and imaginary opponents of his régime.

The process of Russification through the linguistic erosion of national languages is thus part of official Soviet policy affecting all minorities in the USSR. The Jews are in many spheres discriminated against more severely however, and this can be best understood by comparing them with the other minority groups. Of these the Germans offer the most striking comparison. Most of the other nationalities came under Tsarist rule as a result of war and conquest. The Jews and the Germans were newcomers. Persecution drove the Jews out from the West in search of shelter in Poland and Russia. A smaller number fell into the hands of Russian princes as a result of their conquest of the Khazars by the end of the first millenium. The Khazars, or Kizrim as they were called in Jewish history, were an Asiatic people who settled on the Volga and whose rulers introduced Judaism towards the end of the eighth century as the dominant religion in their extensive realm.

German settlers came in by invitation. While making every effort to keep the Jews out and by subjecting those under their jurisdiction to all kinds of restriction, the Tsars were always anxious to bring in foreigners with technical and agricultural skills to teach the Russians and to settle in the vast empty spaces of their empire. Catherine the Great who issued the famous manifesto permitting all foreigners to settle in Russia except the Jews (*Kromie Yevreyev*) granted the Germans special privileges to encourage them to come to Russia. They were given land, were exempted from taxes and military service, and enjoyed other rights which were absolutely denied to the Jews. Even when the Jews were allowed to enter the country they were restricted to living in prescribed areas in Western Russia. The Germans on the other hand had complete freedom of movement. Within a short period of time they managed to settle in several parts of Russia, mostly on the Volga, where they carried on a communal life of their own, preserving their native language and national culture.

Not until the First World War, when Russia and Germany were on different sides of the battlefield, did the German minority experience any difficulty in Russia. In 1914 they were looked on with suspicion, and in 1916 the Tsar signed a decree for their deportation to Siberia. Only a small number were actually deported, and not as many from the Volga region as from Eastern Poland, Volnyia and other areas in the Western parts of the Russian empire. In the *Great Soviet Encyclopaedia* this measure was later denounced as 'barbarous'. A decade or so later during the Second World War, the Soviet authorities resorted to the same method but with greater thoroughness. All the Volga Germans were deported.

Under the Communists the Germans submitted to collectivization, though not without a struggle. Like so many other national minorities they were granted autonomous status and an autonomous territory where they enjoyed complete equality of citizenship. In 1939 Stalin signed a pact with Hitler. Relations became friendly. But their position changed suddenly, after the German army invaded Russia. Two months later, in September 1941, the President of the Presidium of the Supreme Soviet of the USSR, Mikhail Kalinin, signed a decree for the deportation—lock stock and barrel—of all the Volga Germans. They were given two hours to pack, were loaded on to special trucks and sent to start a new life in Siberia. The total number of Germans deported in one move was about three-quarters of a million.

The official reason for their deportation ran as follows:

According to trustworthy information received by the military authorities there are among the German population

living in the Volga area tens of thousands of diversionists
and spies who, on a signal from Germany, are to carry out
sabotage in the area inhabited by the Germans on the
Volga . . .
As none of the Germans living in the Volga area have
reported to the Soviet Authorities the existence of such a
large number of diversionists and spies among the Volga
Germans, it is clear that the German population of the
Volga area conceals enemies of the Soviet people and of
the Soviet authorities . . .
In the case of diversionist acts carried out on a signal from
Germany by German spies and diversionists in their midst
the Soviet Government will be compelled to take punitive
action against the whole of the German population on the
Volga . . .
In order to avoid undesirable actions of that kind and to
prevent bloodshed, the Government has found it necessary
to transfer the whole of the German population living in the
area for resettlement in the arable lands in the Novosibirsk
and Omsk Provinces, the Altai territory, Kazakhstan and
other neighbouring localities allotted.[9]

Subsequent Government orders dispersed the Volga Germans
over fifteen regions west of Saratov and seven regions in the
Stalingrad province.

As minority groups the Germans and the Jews have had one
thing in common. Government policy towards the Jewish as well
as towards the German minority has been dictated by Russia's
attitude towards their people outside Russia. The reversal of
Kremlin policy towards Israel went hand in hand with anti-
Jewish pressures at home. A desire to foster good relations with
the Germans abroad, especially with the German Democratic
Republic, the DDR, dictated an improvement in conditions for
the German minority in the USSR. Within the decade following
Stalin's death, the Germans in Russia managed to regain a status
which in the cultural sphere put them in a far more favourable
position than the Jews. Although not permitted to return and
re-settle on the Volga, they have been given the facilities to carry
on a cultural existence of their own—schools, teachers' colleges,

newspapers, libraries and clubs—which have been denied to the Jewish minority.

Signs of a definite reversal of policy towards the German minority were already visible when the West German Chancellor, Dr Konrad Adenauer, paid an official visit to Moscow in September 1955. Two months later, on 13 December, the Supreme Soviet issued a decree removing many of the restrictions, such as police supervision and registration, enforced on the Germans in the territories to which they had been confined. There followed new concessions to publish and to broadcast. The final step came in August 1964, shortly before Premier Khrushchev was to pay an official visit to Bonn. The Supreme Soviet issued a decree fully rehabilitating the German minority. 'Accusations made against the Germans by Stalin', the decree stated, 'were unfounded. Many Germans made patriotic sacrifices during the war and helped in the building of Communism'.[10]

No detailed information on the many cultural opportunities now enjoyed by the German minority in the USSR is available. But their extent can well be gauged from the fact that at the present time they have 4 newspapers, 5 radio stations broadcasting in German, and 3 television programmes. The foremost German journal in the USSR is a sixteen-page weekly called *Neues Leben* (New Life). Published in Moscow by *Pravda* it has a wide circulation in all areas inhabited by Germans. Two other weeklies in German are the *Rote Fahne* (Red Flag), and the *Wochenschrift* a literary weekly. A third called *Arbeit* (Labour) is published in Barnaul, a principal city of the Altai territory. Two half-hour broadcasts in German are given daily by Moscow Radio. German language programmes are also heard from the radio stations of Alma-Ata, Saran, Omsk, Frunze, and one called Radio Kazakhstan which is devoted mainly to the German language and German music. As with other media, much of the material is political propaganda. A good deal, however, is of literary and cultural value, expressly designed to strengthen the national identity of the Germans. For political reasons these broadcasts often emphasize the link between the Germans in Russia and those outside. In fact, the Germans in Russia are encouraged to identify themselves with their nationals abroad, particularly with those in Communist East Germany. Corresponding links between Jews are frequently denounced as treason. Identification on the part of Soviet Jews with Israel or with Jewry abroad can even be a punishable offence.

Siberia occupies nearly half of the territory of the Soviet Union. In that vast territory, rich in all kinds of mineral resources, the German element, deported thither by force, is beginning to play an increasingly important role. Centres of German culture are springing up in ever increasing numbers in cities and villages in several Siberian Republics. Tomsk, with a growing engineering industry, has a flourishing German cultural centre with its own libraries, schools and clubs. There is another in Kansk and a third in Novokuznetsk. There are German centres in Dzhambul, Kokchetav, Saran, Pavlodar, Ossokarovka, and in the Orenburg and Karaganda areas. A 'German Circle' for students exists in Nebit-Dag, the new oil centre in Turkmenia, and another in Ufa, the capital of Bashkiria. There is a richly equipped German library in Perm, and a 'German Section' of the Soviet Union of Writers in Krasnoyarsk. The network of schools for Germans is growing. Some 50,000 pupils receive regular daily instruction in the German language in schools in Kazakhstan. There are also specially organized German courses for adults.

The wide panorama of German cultural life in the USSR today is best reflected in the German Press. *Neues Leben* reported that in 1966 no less than 574 poems contributed by its readers from all over the Soviet Union were published in its columns. Seven authors received awards.[11] There is an abundant supply of books and textbooks to meet the need of the German minority, and there seems to be a kind of 'Watch Committee' which ensures that supplies are constant. Books are also imported from Eastern Germany—another privilege which no Russian Jew can enjoy. According to the same weekly, books from Eastern Germany involved an annual expenditure of nearly 3,000,000 roubles (over £1,000,000).[12] At least eighty bookshops in the USSR sell German literature. At the beginning of 1967 the journal reported that Soviet German authors were so numerous that the publishing house, Progress, was to bring out seven collected volumes of their work. The Kazakhstan State Publishing Institute was to publish an additional ten books.[13] 'Large editions are being printed and very quickly sold out.' The paper has a regular feature entitled 'Our Bookcase'. To mark the fiftieth anniversary of the October Revolution the biographies of Karl Liebknecht and Clara Zetkin were published in German. Special editions of German classics including Lessing, Schiller and Heine also appeared. Books in German are so popular that the Druzhba bookshop in Alma-Ata was reported to be selling at least 400 roubles worth of German books on delivery day. 'Those who came the following day found that all had been sold out.'

In the field of German education a great effort is being made to train teachers. About 500 German teachers qualify each year but still fail to meet the constant demand for instructors in German. As far as possible it is met by students of the German faculty of the Pedagogical Academy at Omsk and from German teachers' training courses established in Karaganda, Orenburg, Slavgorod, Saran and Issyk-Kul.

In an attempt to reflect the full gamut of German life in Russia today, *Neues Leben* recently introduced a new feature in its columns entitled 'Witnesses of Glory'. Its purpose is to record the military contribution made by the German minority towards the building of Communist Russia. Deportation meant, of course, that the Germans made little contribution during the Second World War. The feature, therefore, recalled earlier events. It published a few records recalling the names of Germans who had fought against the remnants of the Tsarist forces in the civil war immediately after the Revolution. One reader brought to the notice of the German public the names of several of his old comrades who, he wrote, had defended the homeland and been decorated for their part in the fight against the Fascists. Another recorded the part some Russian-Germans had played in the Spanish Civil War. All this was designed as one of the correspondents suggested, to ensure that 'our dear comrades shall not take the last seat at the festive table at the time of the 50th Anniversary'.

For the Jewish minority there was no need to go so far back

in history. The Jews' activity in the Red Army during the Second World War is best demonstrated by the fact that they held fourth place as recipients of decorations for bravery on the battlefield (see p. 88). Official Soviet figures given during the war listed the names of forty-nine Jewish generals serving with the Red Army, one of whom, General Shmushkevich, was Chief of the Soviet Air Force.

The last Jew to hold a high position in the armed services was Lieut-General Yankel Osher Kreiser. He holds the title of Hero of the Soviet Union and several of the highest orders in the Soviet Army, including the Order of Kutuzov and the Order of Suvorov. He distinguished himself in the defence of Moscow and was placed second on the list of Red Army generals praised by Stalin in his Order of the Day broadcast on 8 September 1943. Lieut-General Kreiser was Commander of the Red Army units in the Far East after the war, but retired in the early 1960s. As far as can be ascertained, Jews no longer hold any of the higher posts in the Red Army, Navy or Air Force. In view of the policy of keeping all but a very few Jews out of the higher military academies and cadet training schools, this is not surprising.

Another revealing comparison presents itself on the question of how dispersion has affected the Jews and the Germans. Second in size to the Jewish, the German minority numbers 1,619,000 and lives in four republics spread across Central Asia and Northern Siberia. Like the Jews, therefore, they are appropriately considered a dispersed minority. Yet, even so, the Germans are in a very different position from the Jews. The situation in the Tselinny territory in the so-called Virgin Lands demonstrates this. The Virgin Lands stretch over an immense expanse from the Volga to the Russian Far East across the South Urals to North Kazakhstan. The Tselinny territory, or Tselinny-Krai in Russian, has an area of some 10,000,000 acres. Germans and Jews are among the many nationalities working in the area. In Tselinograd (formerly Akmolinsk) which is now an industrial city and the principal centre of the territory, they form part of a mixed population. Here, as in the surrounding areas, Jews and Germans are both making their contribution to the territories' development and industrialization. The Germans in Tselinograd have a newspaper called *Freundschaft* and enjoy a communal life of their own. The city has four institutes of higher education one of which teaches the German language. Evening classes in German are held in other educational centres in the city.

Jews are no strangers to Siberia. Deported in batches with others in Tsarist days for political and revolutionary activities, quite a number remained.[14] During the Second World War, thousands of Jews from the Ukraine and other parts of Western Russia invaded by the Germans found refuge there. The number of Jews in Siberia in 1946 is estimated to have been between 250,000 and 300,000. The Siberian population has grown from 8,000,000 to 20,000,000 since the October Revolution. Although there are not as many Jews now as there were immediately after the Second World War, Jewish participation in the development of the area is still considerable. A special volume sponsored by *Sovietish Heimland* and published in Yiddish in 1964 drew attention to the role of the Jews in the development of the area.[15] Samuel Gordon, a Soviet Yiddish author, contributed a long essay in which he sang the praises of the Virgin Lands and Soviet achievements there, and described the Jewish participation in the development of the Tselinny territory. The essay speaks of Jews from Moscow, Rostov, Minsk and other Russian cities who responded to Khrushchev's call and went to work on farms and in cities in the Virgin Lands. As managers of collective farms, as directors of co-operatives, and in many other ways they share with the Germans and the other nationalities in the work of reclaiming the vast barren territories for agriculture. But by contrast with the Germans who enjoy cultural facilities and a national life, Gordon reveals the isolation of the Jews. Although there are many thousands of Jews living and working in the same areas as the Germans they have no outlets for a corporate expression of their national, linguistic or cultural distinctiveness. They have retained their names and the author even stresses the point that they show a taste for 'national Jewish cooking', but these are the only features of Jewish life they can still enjoy. They have no schools, libraries or even social clubs of their own, although these are provided for the Germans and the other minorities in the same regions.

I visited Russia in Khrushchev's time and was thus able to try and find out for myself how anti-Semitism affects the Jews in daily life. In Germany or in Poland hostility towards the Jews before the war could easily be expressed by avoiding business relations with them. But under Communism in Soviet Russia this kind of anti-Semitism cannot find expression for the simple reason that all shops and institutions are in the hands of the State. One significant fact is that the Jew often fails to reach the leading position in the factory or other State establishment in which he is employed. He usually gets no further than deputy-chairman. A great part of the information concerning the leading figures in Russian industry, is, of course, still secret. But of eight Jews whose names appear in a recent Soviet publication seven are described as deputy chairmen or deputy ministers of their departments. Only one is chairman.[16]

For the ordinary Russian, the manifestation of his anti-Jewish feelings can only be through propaganda, by direct insult or attack, or by the avoidance of social relationships. I therefore made a point of asking as many Jews as possible in Moscow and in some other cities whether they themselves had experienced any such occurrences. The question I put to them was: 'Have you yourself heard any anti-Jewish remarks in the last twelve months or so?' Out of fourteen Jews in Moscow two replied that they had witnessed anti-Jewish manifestations of this kind. But in Kiev half the Jews I questioned had either witnessed or been themselves the victims of anti-Semitic actions. In one case the Jewish director of a State factory had been called 'dirty Jew' by an angry employee when he had reprimanded him. In the second case an insulting remark against Jews generally had been made by a local post office official to a Jew who was collecting a parcel from a relative abroad.

The frequency and the severity of anti-Jewish outbursts fluctuates. Much depends on the political atmosphere. An article in the Press attacking Judaism or denouncing Israel is bound to increase hostility towards the Jews generally, and I came across quite a number who admitted that they take good care not to appear in public on the day such an article is published. It is not always a question of direct insults, still less attacks. But the fellow next to you in the train will recognize a Jew—and surprisingly Jews in Russia are still recognizable—and may make some nasty remark about Israel or Jews generally. It would be dangerous to react. When a Jewess in Leningrad was insulted on a bus by a fellow passenger, a young man standing by tried to defend her. Though he did not look Jewish, he too was insulted. Elderly Jews, who are more recognizable, avoid using public transport on days when the Press shows hostility towards Israel.

When I enquired whether anyone had heard of a Russian or Ukrainian being taken to court for calling a Jew by the insulting name of *Zhid* I found that no such case had been recorded for the last few years. After the 20th Party Congress of 1956 a worker in a Moscow factory was sentenced to six months loss of freedom for insulting a Jewish fellow worker. But he was neither imprisoned nor deprived of his job. His wages were reduced by 20 per cent for a period of six months. It appeared that the management intervened on his behalf. Significantly it was not the Jew who complained, but a non-Jewish comrade who witnessed the incident. Jews are afraid to complain for fear that it may cause what one of them described as an 'unhealthy anti-Semitic climate', and so make trouble for other Jews.

This fear prevents Jews from protesting against the disabilities from which they suffer. Five decades after the October Revolution they dare not risk voicing their dissatisfaction with their position. One illustration of the prevailing atmosphere was the silence of Jewish writers in two important Russian cities during their meetings with Sholem Aleichem's son-in-law, Ben Zion Goldberg. Accompanied by his wife Miriam, Goldberg went to Russia to take part in the fiftieth anniversary commemoration ceremony of Sholem Aleichem's death in the summer of 1966. Both the Goldbergs are well-known personalities in their own right, quite apart from their family connections with Sholem Aleichem. Goldberg is a distinguished journalist and author, progressive, and a great admirer of the Soviet Union. He was a prominent member of the special committee in America organized during the Second World War to help the USSR. He had visited the Soviet Union several times, and written warmly of Communist achievements. So he felt he had a bond of comradeship with the writers in the Soviet Union.

When he visited Kiev, the Union of Ukrainian Writers, together with the Jewish writers, organized a special reception in the Goldbergs' honour. A large gathering attended. The Goldbergs were warmly welcomed by Smolich, the chairman of the Union. Towards the end of the reception Goldberg expressed a wish for 'a friendly chat' with the Jewish writers. Smolich and the Ukrainians left the gathering and he remained alone with the Jewish writers. But none would enter into conversation with him. No one dared to break the silence.

The same thing happened in Chernovits a few weeks later. A large number of Ukrainian and Jewish writers gave a reception in honour of Goldberg and his wife. As long as the Ukrainians were present at the journalists' reception, there was free interchange between the American visitor and his hosts. But when the Ukrainians had left and Goldberg could talk alone with the Jewish writers in Yiddish as he had requested, 'a doleful silence' prevailed. The Jews were afraid to enter into conversation with a visitor from abroad. 'I could establish no contact with them at all', he said. He and his wife were preparing to leave when the chairman, a Ukrainian, reappeared in the hall and 'the tongues of the Yiddish writers loosened up again. Fear left them'.[17]

After years of Stalinist terror, most Russians, not just members of minority groups, show a certain reserve on meeting foreigners. Contact is difficult to establish. It came as a 'deep shock' Goldberg said, to find that nearly a decade and a half after Stalin's death Jewish writers were still gripped by a fear which paralysed them into silence in the presence of visitors from abroad.

Jews are further hindered from expressing their discontent by the lack of proper channels of communication. Compared with the number of Jewish newspapers—in Russian, Hebrew and Yiddish—in circulation in Tsarist days (see p. 29), the position of the Jewish Press in the USSR today looks very bleak indeed. The only Jewish papers are a Yiddish monthly called *Sovietish Heimland* published in Moscow, and a two-page sheet issued three times a week in Biro-Bidjan, the so-called Jewish Autonomous Region. This means that the Jews are treated on a level with the smallest ethnic groups who until the Revolution, were still leading a nomadic life and had no alphabet to their dialect. Among the other groups with only one newspaper or journal in their native language are the Nenets with a population of 25,000, and the Chuckchi with a population of 12,000. But the Kurds with an Islamic population of some 50,000 in the Caucasus have 3 newspapers. The 100,000 Tuvinians in Central Siberia, also Islamic but of Turkic strain, have 10 newspapers, the Buryat-Mongols in South-East Siberia numbering about a quarter of a million have 6 newspapers, the Kara-Kalpakians in Central Asia numbering 200,000 have 12 newspapers, and all in their native language.

At the 1959 census there were 2,268,000 Jews in the USSR. Of that total 472,000 gave Yiddish as their native tongue. Various experts, including Soviet official spokesmen such as Solomon Rabinovich now estimate the figure at about 3,000,000.[18] In regard to the Press the Yakuts, a Turkic minority of the Russian orthodox faith in North-East Siberia who numbered about a quarter of a million in 1939, appear to be the most privileged of all. Official Soviet sources state that they have 45 newspapers, and 2 periodicals. In Tsarist days the Yakuts had no written language.[19]

From a humane point of view the wall of isolation which Communist rulers have erected around Russian citizens is one of the most depressing features of the system. Contact with foreigners can be maintained only through controlled channels of the Party, in fact through the KGB, and this has had a chilling psychological effect on the Russian and his sense of fellowship. If harsh on the Ukrainian, Georgian and Pole, it is doubly so on a member of such a dispersed nationality as the Jews. Most Jewish families in Russia today have relations abroad but are effectively prevented from keeping in touch. On one occasion when I was visiting the first synagogue in a Russian city I suddenly felt a stranger's hand in my overcoat pocket. He took nothing. But he left a little note with the address of his 'uncle in New York' asking me to let him know that his nephew in Russia was still alive and wanted to hear from him. After a fortnight in the USSR I had quite a collection of these pathetic notes. It appeared that most Jews in State employment have to state whether they have relatives abroad. But it is often dangerous to do so, as it can affect their position, or even their livelihood. This often prompts them to ask their relatives not to write; significantly it is only the old people who dare to maintain regular contact with relatives in America and Israel.

This is another sphere where comparison with Tsarist days is revealing. In the history of Russian Jews there has only been one definite period when contact with their fellow Jews abroad was forbidden as an act of disloyalty. When Napoleon convoked the Great Syndhedrion in 1806 the Tsar's Minister of the Interior instructed the administrators of the western governments to prevent contact between Russian Jews and the Syndhedrion in Paris.[20] Since that occasion Russian Jews have been free to communicate with their relatives abroad—until the present. This policy creates among them a feeling of solitude and deepens their sense of alienation from Jewry in the world outside.

Finally there is the question of emigration, and here the contrast between Tsarist and Soviet Russia is sharpest. Following the wave of pogroms in Tsarist Russia mass emigration of Jews was a daily occurrence. Between 1905 and 1908 over 230,000 Jews left Russia, emigrating mostly to America, with a trickle to England and France. Tens of thousands went to Africa. The latest figures released from Moscow maintain that from 1881 to 1914 some 'two million people emigrated from Russia—one-third of the Jewish population of the country'.[21] Large numbers of them left the country without official documents or permits. They were simply smuggled across the borders of the Tsarist Empire into Austria or Germany.

There are no such opportunities in Russia today. Emigration is barred. The measure applies not only to Jews but to other citizens as well. But as in other spheres the Jews are hardest hit.

They are deprived of the chance of greater freedom which even the Tsars had not denied them.

Is there any social anti-Semitism? The situation varies from city to city. In the Ukraine which has often been called 'the power-house of anti-Semitism' the Jew is by and large not accepted. Occasionally Jewish journalists or writers will be invited to the homes of their non-Jewish colleagues for a festive occasion or family event, and vice-versa. But on the whole Jews keep to themselves. They do not adhere to a special diet, so this creates no problems. Jews and non-Jews will happily meet for a meal. The relationship is regulated by an unwritten law which confines each section to its own ethnic group. In Moscow and Leningrad the rule is not as rigid as, for instance, in Kiev. Nonetheless there, too, the tendency, except among a small group of progressive intellectuals, is to keep apart.

One factor which stimulates good relations is inter-marriage. This is very common nowadays among the Russian intelligentsia in the urban localities. There are no official statistics on mixed marriages. But in Leningrad, for instance, I was told that at least one in every three Jews marries outside the faith. The marriage register in the Sverdlovsk district in Moscow shows that 50 couples were married between 15 July and 31 October 1966. Only 17 were unmixed marriages while 33 were mixed.[22] The older generation maintained that divorce is more frequent between mixed couples than between those of the same faith. The younger generation did not share this opinion. Disagreement on this as on many other topics is common between Jewish parents and their children. Some parents are resentful when their children inter-marry, and may even break with them. It should not go unsaid, however, that some non-Jewish parents adopt corresponding attitudes.

From all the talks I had with Russian Jews there emerged what can be described as a list of grievances constituting the root and essence of Soviet official policy designed to aggravate their position.

The most discriminating of these is that with very few exceptions Russian Jews are no longer permitted to hold high positions in the Russian Communist Party. Ever since Khrushchev's days the Higher Party School of the Central Committee in Moscow is closed to Jews.[23] As we have seen similar restrictions apply to them in the Russian Military and Naval Colleges where very few gain places. They are not tolerated in the more responsible posts in the Army, Navy or Air Force, and are no longer admitted into the Russian Diplomatic Service. Such restrictions put them at a grave disadvantage and reduce them to second-class citizens. They are considered unworthy and not to be trusted and are unreservedly placed under suspicion of disloyalty. I have not met a single Russian Jew who did not feel bitterly humiliated at being discriminated against in this way.

Another grievance listed concerns the restrictions they face when applying for admission to the Universities and institutes of higher education. Even in Stalin's days Jewish youth faced no obstacles in the way of higher education. Today their numbers at the universities are limited, often rigidly so, especially in Moscow and Leningrad where the figure is between 3 and 4 per cent.

There are no Jewish schools of any kind in the whole of the Soviet Union. No facilities exist for the study of Jewish history, Yiddish or Hebrew languages, or indeed any literature which would communicate the Jewish past, ancient or modern, to the younger generation. The situation in this sphere is so aggravated that Jews feel their position is worse than that of those minorities and ethnic groups who, before the Revolution, did not even possess an alphabet of their own. In this way they are being hindered from perpetuating their national existence guaranteed in the Soviet Constitution. They feel that such a policy threatens their very survival as an historic nationality.

In contrast with other national minorities the Jews in the Soviet Union today are not permitted to have their own communal organizations nor any political, cultural or social associations. The Buryat Mongols, living 4,000 miles away from Moscow, for instance, have their own schools, libraries, cultural and social clubs, when all such facilities are denied to the Jews in Moscow or anywhere else in the USSR. The complaint about the lack of any Jewish group life is one of those most frequently voiced by Jews in Russia.

The only form of group life recognized is that of the synagogue. But even here restrictive measures have been working against the existence of the synagogue. At the time of Stalin's death there were still about 500 of them in the USSR. Under Khrushchev their number was reduced to less than 100 and since his departure only 62 are officially recognized.

Soviet Jews are not allowed to maintain any sort of connection —political, cultural, social or religious—with Jewish organizations abroad. At the same time other minorities, and especially religious organizations in Russia such as the Orthodox, Catholic and Protestant Churches are permitted to maintain regular contacts with similar bodies abroad.

The list of grievances also includes that relating to the reunion of families. There are tens of thousands of Jewish families living in Russia who have been separated by the war. They have relations in England, America and many in Israel. While in Russia I met an elderly Jew who had lost three sons, all officers in the Red Army, who fell in the war against Hitler. He had a brother in America and a sister in Israel. For years he was endeavouring to obtain a permit to leave the USSR and join either of his relatives. But no such permission was granted. Thousands of Jews living in Israel appealed to Moscow, via the Soviet Embassy, for permission to be given for their relatives in Russia to join them. Only a very small number succeeded, and the promises by Soviet Leaders to reconsider this policy on humanitarian grounds have brought no results.

On top of all these grievances and complaints are the rigid restrictions placed on Soviet Jews in regard to Zion and Israel. Zionism and the Hebrew language were forbidden soon after the October Revolution. This ban has never been lifted or mitigated in any way. Not even the establishment of the Jewish State of Israel has brought about any change in Russian policy, and since the War of June 1967 and Russia's diplomatic rupture with the Jewish State the position has been greatly aggravated. Along with the re-arming of Egypt and other Arab States goes a severe and virulent anti-Jewish Press campaign of unprecedented crudeness. All the leading Soviet newspapers publish regular attacks on Israel and Zionism which is being presented as an international Jewish organization of a pro-imperialist and anti-Communist nature.

At Moscow's bidding this propaganda has now spilled over from the Soviet Union into the satellite countries where, notably in Eastern Germany and in Poland it is accompanied by large-scale persecution of Jews by the expulsion of Jews from the Party and administration and by forced emigration. The bitter anti-Zionist campaign has revived old animosities and hatred and is undermining the very existence of Jews in the Soviet world. For throughout all this anti-Israel, anti-Zionist propaganda in the Russian and the other Communist States there runs through a dark threat of anti-Semitism reminiscent of Tsarist days. Thus once more the fateful chain linking the Russian and the Jewish people which began centuries ago has come full circle.

At the beginning of this century over 6,000,000 Jews were living in Russian and Russian-occupied lands. That meant that the destiny of nearly half of the total of the Jewish people was controlled by the Tsar and his administration, and subjected to his oppressive discriminative rule suffering from all kinds of Laws and restrictions. Today, fifty years after the Tsars' downfall, there are only about 3,000,000 Jews in the Soviet Union. But with Russia's growing influence in the Middle East and her constant support of the Arabs and their enmity towards Israel she has penetrated right up to the very frontiers of the Jewish State. Her armaments now threaten Israel's very existence. Once again Russia throws what Einstein has called her dark shadow on the lives and destiny of millions of Jews.

POSTSCRIPT: RUSSIA AND ISRAEL

Since the establishment of Israel in 1948, Soviet-Israeli relations have gone through three phases. When an independent Israel was first proposed the Soviet Union adopted a favourable attitude. This was unexpected. Although Tsarist Russia had always been expansionist and Soviet Russia anxious to disseminate Communism, there was at the same time a long tradition of anti-Zionism. From 1947-53, however, the Soviet authorities appeared to favour Israel. But with the Suez crisis, Russia's allegiance with Egypt and antagonism towards Israel became apparent. Finally the June war of 1967 and its aftermath revealed Russia's outright hostility to Israel.

Russia's interest in the Middle East began with the Tsars. Territorial expansion was their main objective. But they backed up their territorial claims by championing the Christian minorities in Moslem countries. The 'Eastern Question', which dominated the nineteenth century arose partly from Russia's territorial aspirations and her incessant conflict with the declining Turkish Empire. The Tsars maintained that it was their duty to guard the religious freedom and human rights of the Orthodox subjects in Turkey. The Crimean and later the Russo-Turkish wars were frequently justified by Russia as a self-imposed duty to defend the interests of the Slav minorities—Bulgaria, Serbia, Herzegovina, and other ethnic groups. 'Pan-Slavism' was the Tsar's political slogan. Turkey became 'the sick man of Europe' and the chief victim of Russian expansionist moves. Russia was constantly seeking an outlet into the Mediterranean and beyond, and became involved in the great rivalry between Christian and Moslem for the control of the Dardanelles which would give her a trade route to the Orient via the Suez Canal. Towards the end of the nineteenth century Russia began to build monasteries and churches in the Holy Land, thus establishing herself as the protector of the Holy Places, a position formerly held by France, the guardian of the Catholics in the Turkish Empire.

Tsarist aggressive plans went a stage further when Russia made a secret treaty with Britain and France during the First World War. The treaty provided for the partition of the Turkish Empire. Russia was to receive some territories adjoining her boundaries and Constantinople, while France and Britain were to have control over Egypt, Syria and Palestine. The plan ultimately led to bitter rivalry between France and Britain over the control of Palestine.

When Great Britain was drawing up the Balfour Declaration during the First World War, to provide for a Jewish National Home in Palestine, she discussed the issue with Sazonov, Nicholas II's Foreign Minister. Sazonov seemed uninterested in Palestine as a territorial issue, but emphasized the Tsar's vital preoccupation with the protection of Russian Orthodox religious institutions. For several decades before, Russia had spent vast sums of money buying up land in Jerusalem to establish Orthodox institutions to provide shelter and homes for Russian pilgrims. In fact Tsarist Russia (followed by Germany) had more influence than any other of the European powers in the religious life of Palestine. She maintained and ran the greatest number of religious institutions, and sent the most pilgrims.

With the downfall of the Tsar, Russia's drive for the partition of the Turkish Empire waned. In fact Lenin, when he became head of the first Bolshevik Government, exposed the secret Tsarist plans for the partition of Turkey and denounced them as an imperialist plot. But Russian interest in the Straits was maintained. Karl Marx once described them as the 'stepping-stones to Russian world domination'.[1]

As for Stalin, he was preoccupied with building Socialism in Russia and did not at first show any special inclination to seek new territories in the Middle East. It was not until the Second World War that Soviet leaders began to realize that the Bolshevik Revolution and Communism offered a new potential for the extension of Russian influence. Towards the end of the war Stalin acquired Polish and German territories, and even made a bid, which proved unsuccessful, to gain territory in Iran. And he kept an eye on the Straits, as appears from Litvinov's role at the Straits Convention held in Montreux in 1936.[2]

Although territorial expansion was not a prime motivator during the first thirty years after the Revolution, the other main influence on Russia's attitude to Israel, anti-Zionism, flourished. Lenin, the early Bolsheviks, and then Stalin were all opponents of Zionism. To Lenin those who upheld the idea of a Jewish nationality, the essence of traditional Zionism, were 'reactionary philistines'. As he saw it, assimilation was the only possible solution to the Jewish question. 'The best Jews, those who are celebrated in world history, and have given the world foremost leaders of democracy and socialism', he stated, 'have never clamoured against assimilation'.[3]

Jewish Communists were of the same opinion. The leaders of the *Yevsektsiyas* were fully aware of the great attachment to Zion of the Jews in Russia. Entrusted with the task of re-educating them and enlisting their co-operation in the building of a Communist State, the *Yevsektsiyas* made every effort to combat and eliminate the Zionist movement and its influence. They branded Zionism as a 'counter-revolutionary and clerical nationalist organization', as an 'instrument in the hands of the Entente imperialism in its war against the proletarian revolution'.[4] Addressing the first All Russian Conference of Jewish Commissariats and Jewish Sections in October 1918, Semen Dimanshtein, the head of the Commissariat for Jewish Affairs, asked 'why remember Zion, the vassal of British imperialism?' when, as he put it, the Jews could build 'a Palestine in Moscow'.[5] The Jewish Communists' anti-Zionism grew increasingly bitter and violent. But as the campaign intensified, their zeal outstripped that of the Soviet leaders themselves. Disappointed, they became even more aggressive. By 1925 their anti-Zionist militancy had reached such a pitch that they even hesitated over the plan to create a Jewish region in Russia for the settlement of the dispossessed Jewish masses whom the Revolution had thrown out of their former occupations.[6]

Despite the intensity of the *Yevsektsiya's* antagonism, Zionism

continued as a movement some years after the Revolution. Outlawed, it was driven underground. In 1923 and 1924 the Soviet
police arrested about 3,000 Zionists in 150 Russian cities. Public
show trials at which Zionists were charged with 'criminal offences'
and sentenced to up to ten years' hard labour in isolation camps
became a frequent phenomenon. But for every public trial there
were many more held in camera, and Russian concentration
camps in Siberia were filled with Jews who remained faithful to
Zion. A large proportion of the victims of these trials and deportations were young Russian Jews, many of the members of the
illegal *Tzeirei Zion* and *Hapoel Hatzair*. In some concentration
camps the Zionists made up more than 10 per cent of the political
prisoners. In 1941 a Jewish writer, a former inmate of a Soviet
concentration camp, related that he had met Zionists there who
had spent between sixteen and seventeen years as prisoners.[7]

So it came as something of a surprise when in 1947 the issue
of an independent Jewish State came before the United Nations
and the representative of the Soviet Union, Andrei Gromyko, gave
Russia's unqualified support to the idea. Mr Gromyko was at that
time a deputy foreign minister. Addressing the United Nations
he declared that his Government fully understood the aspirations
of an important section of the Jewish people for the creation of
a State of their own, and appreciated that the experiences of the
Jewish people in the Second World War had intensified this.

This speech was made a year before Israel became an independent State. The Jewish Press all over the world welcomed
Mr Gromyko's reference to the suffering of the Jews during the
war for the contrast it afforded with the cool speeches made at
the same time by the Anglo-Saxon representative.[8] A year later
both Soviet delegates, Andrei Gromyko and Semyon K. Tsarap-
kin, voted for the establishment of a Jewish State. To the Jewish
people in Israel and elsewhere the Soviet vote came as a great
relief after their years of suffering.

The fact that Russia granted full recognition to Israel soon
after the United States, and that in Tel Aviv the Soviet and
American envoys lodged under the same roof in the Gat Rimmon
Hotel gave rise to a new hope that Israel might become a bridge

between East and West. With this hope the Government of Israel under Mr Ben Gurion's leadership adopted a policy of non-identification. Israel was anxious to develop good relations with both the United States and the Soviet Union. On 9 March 1949 the Knesset (the Israeli Parliament) approved, among the 'basic principles' of the Government's programme, that the basis of Israel's foreign policy was to adhere to the principles of the United Nations Charter and to maintain friendship with all free-dom-loving States, particularly the United States and the Soviet Union. Three months earlier Mr Ben Gurion had told the Ameri-can envoy in Israel, James G. McDonald, that he would 'never play politics with an issue of foreign policy'. Moshe Sharett, speaking in the Knesset after the outbreak of the Korean war, said that he believed in the principle of non-identification for Israel as the best means to world peace and security for herself.[9]

But while Israel was promoting good relations in accordance with this policy, changes in the Russian attitude became notice-able. While Israeli leaders and the Israeli Press were still con-gratulating themselves on Russia's support, *Pravda* published the article by Ilya Ehrenburg which re-stated official Soviet policy and condemned the Zionist concept of an affinity between Jews of all nationalities.[10] Not only did the article come as a severe blow to Russian Jews; it also seriously affected Israel's aspirations. No official explanation of the sudden change in the Soviet atti-tude has ever been offered. Only two months earlier Mr Gromyko had been heard denouncing the Arabs for their efforts to prevent the establishment of Israel. Addressing the Security Council (21 May and 14 July 1948), he had stated how surprised he had been to learn of the military forces sent by Arabs into Palestine in an attempt to suppress the national liberation movement. He had also expressed the opinion that the Arab States had no reason to consider the creation of an independent Jewish State in Pales-tine as a threat to themselves. Why then the abrupt reversal, the sudden warning through Ehrenburg against Zionism?

One reason suggested by many Jews in Moscow years later was that the Kremlin was surprised to find how deeply attached Russian Jews still were to Zion. Gromyko's assertion that not many

Russian Jews would want to go to Palestine was clearly contradicted by the overwhelmingly warm reception given to the Israeli envoy, and the thousands of applications for exit permits received from Russian Jews, most of whom wanted to go to Israel for good. The reaction was immediate. The MVD arrested most of the applicants. Zionist sympathizers were tried in secret and deported for 're-education'. At the same time Soviet propaganda fell back on the old Communist hostility to Zionism as a 'bourgeois nationalist ideology' which had to be eliminated, however ruthlessly. Simultaneously the Israeli Government was attacked as a 'tool of imperialism'.

The real reason for the shift of policy can only be that Russia had had a particular interest in supporting the creation of Israel at the United Nations. Partition of Palestine would increase friction between Arabs and Jews. For the Jews Great Britain's departure and abandonment of the mandate fulfilled a Biblical prophecy. For the Russians it left a political vacuum which gave them an unexpected opportunity to gain a foothold in the Middle East.

With the subsequent deterioration of Russia's relations with the USA, Great Britain, France and the free world generally, Stalin's suspicion of the Jews grew and relations with Israel worsened from day to day. Despite all the efforts made to isolate Russian Jews from the world outside, large numbers of them refused to break their ties, which had been strengthened by the rebirth of Israel, with relatives abroad. To Stalin and his régime the sympathy of the Jews in Russia for Israel was an indication of their sympathy for Jews in the capitalist countries generally. This branded them as an unreliable group and a possible source of danger in the ever-cooling cold war. Hence the significance of the 'Doctors' Plot'. For the doctors were accused of being not only American and British agents, but also Zionist spies.[11]

On 9 February 1953 a bomb exploded in the garden of the Soviet legation in Tel-Aviv. Moscow lodged a prompt protest and charged the Israeli Government with full responsibility. Three days later the Soviet Union severed diplomatic relations with Israel. It was not until July when Stalin was dead and Malenkov had denounced the 'Doctors' Plot' as provocation that diplomatic contact with the Jewish State was renewed. To mark the occasion the envoys in Tel-Aviv and Moscow were raised to the rank of Ambassador. On this amicable note the first phase of Soviet-Israeli relations ended.

In their early support for the establishment of an independent Jewish State in Palestine Kremlin leaders apparently hoped that it might become a base for expanding Russian influence. Jews had been among Lenin's trusted supporters. They had fought against Tsarist oppression. More recently they had joined with the Russians in the war against Hitler and Nazism. Both nations were still counting their losses—the Russians had lost over 20,000,000, the Jews over 6,000,000 when the United Nations met to decide on the creation of Israel.

Had Stalin followed up his support for an independent Jewish State by allowing some of the 3,000,000 Russian Jews to leave and settle in Israel, the Jewish State could have become a nucleus of Russian influence in the Middle East. Russian Jews had been among the first and most devoted settlers in Israel in Tsarist days. But they retained a warm sentiment for their old country. Freedom of emigration is not however a right of Soviet citizenship. Russian Jews were prevented from leaving, first by Stalin, then by his successors. Israel has had to rely for immigration and material support on Western countries. Western influence, combined with what the Israelis knew of the sufferings of Jews under Communism, led them to build the Jewish State on the pattern of Western parliamentary democracy. Such a development was likely to increase Russian hostility. In addition, the existence of Israel hinders the assimilation of the Russian Jew in so far as he can see his national identity preserved elsewhere. Today, Brezhnev and Kosygin must be aware, like those before them, that as long as there is an independent democratic Israel, it will focus the attention of all Jews, the Russians no less than any others.

With Khrushchev's accession to power the aim to spread Russian influence became more prominent. Addressing the 20th Party Congress in February 1956 Khrushchev spoke of the importance for Communism of the underdeveloped areas. 'More than 1,200 million people, or nearly half of the World's population', he said, 'have been freed from colonial or semi-colonial dependence' and this offered great opportunities for strengthening 'friendship and co-operation' between these areas and the Soviet Union.[12]

Few areas could have been more vulnerable than the Middle East. It had only recently emerged from colonial domination. Millions of its people were living below the standard of civilized existence. Anti-colonial in spirit, and anti-Western in political outlook, they were receptive to Communist propaganda and attracted by a programme of industrialization and mechanization. With Russia's hostility to the West growing, the opportunity to increase her influence in this direction was welcome. On the Arab side, conflict with Israel made them more willing to align with the Soviet Union.

The second phase in Soviet-Israeli relations began with the Suez conflict in 1956 when the Soviet Union declared itself unreservedly on the side of Egypt against Israel. On 26 July Nasser nationalized the Suez Canal. Firmly established as the head of the Egyptian people, he now aspired to become the head of a pan-Arab movement. Hostility to Israel was the pivot of his political ideology. The Soviet Union had encouraged him : the massive supply of arms to Egypt inaugurated by the Czechoslovak-Egyptian Agreement was supplemented by vast deliveries of Russian aircraft and tanks.

The growth of Egypt's military strength became an immediate threat to the security, the very existence, of Israel. On 29 October 1956, Israel took steps to counteract Egypt's preparations for war, and in a five-day campaign forced the Egyptian army out of Sinai and Gaza. In Moscow, Israel's action provoked an immediate response. The Soviet envoy in Tel-Aviv was recalled to Moscow in protest. All trade contacts were broken; the Soviet delivery of oil to Israel was stopped completely. Diplomatic relations were resumed in April 1957 but business contacts remained severed.

Israel's Sinai campaign was followed by British and French military action against Egypt, and by Russia's increased pressure against Israel. As Soviet support for Egypt and antagonism towards Israel increased, the leaders of the Jewish State were forced to lean more and more on Britain, France and the United States. But over the Sinai campaign Israel met with opposition from the United States. President Eisenhower stopped all economic aid to Israel, and voices in Washington even spoke of sanctions. At the same time Marshal Bulganin, the Russian Premier, sent a strongly worded note to the Israeli Government charging it with 'criminally playing with the destiny of its country and people' and said that Israel was 'sowing hatred towards the State of Israel from peoples of the East which cannot but have an influence on Israel's future and which raises the question of the whole existence of Israel as a State'.[13] Fearful of the possible effects of her policy on the fate of the Jews in Russia, Israel displayed great caution in her replies to Moscow. With the aim of remaining neutral in the East-West struggle for power, she continued to proclaim a foreign policy of non-identification.

Russia's diplomatic manœuvres with Britain and France between September 1956 and April 1957 were mainly concerned with the Suez Canal, but at the same time she expressed anxiety for peace in the Middle East as a whole. She proposed a four-powered declaration by which she, the United States, Britain and France would bind themselves to a policy of 'non-interference in the domestic affairs of the countries in the Middle East region'.[14] But such a proposal totally ignored Israel.

In 1963 Khrushchev entered into an agreement with Nasser to build the Aswan Dam, and supplement economic aid with large supplies of arms. Encouraged, Nasser took the next step against Britain and France, and completed the nationalization of the Suez Canal. Khrushchev was quick to take advantage of the opportunity this offered. In 1964 he paid an official visit to Cairo, which was followed by further supplies of modern Russian arms to Egypt.

It was in these post-Suez days that the third phase of Soviet-Israeli relations began. It was marked by what the late Moshe Sharett, a former Israeli Foreign Minister, described as a 'savage intensification of Russian hostility towards Israel'.[15] The Kremlin launched a propaganda campaign which lauded Arab nationalism as a 'progressive' movement and condemned Jewish nationalism as 'reactionary'. Nasser and the rulers of Syria, and even some of the monarchs of the Arab States, were all depicted as liberators struggling to free their people from colonialism. At the same time the members of the Government of Israel were denounced as 'puppets of imperialism'.

The main theme of the anti-Israeli campaign was that Israel was going to attack the Arabs, first in Syria. Soviet propaganda presented Israel as an aggressor, armed by America, Britain and France. They alleged that Israel was being used to create 'another Vietnam', threatening not only 'the peace-loving Arab neighbours' but humanity at large.

The propaganda campaign intensified in the days immediately preceding the June War. When Russian military supplies, details of which had been worked out during Kosygin's visit to Egypt in 1966, were complete, and the political arrangements had been finalized during Gromyko's visit to Nasser in May 1967, the Soviet Press released a stream of anti-Israel attacks. Within days of Gromyko's return from Cairo, *Pravda* and *Izvestia* began to publish alarming reports about the concentration of Israeli armies on the Arab frontiers. All over Eastern Europe the Press asserted that the American Sixth Fleet was lying off the coast of Egypt, and that naval divisions were being rushed to the area. The Soviet people were also told that Britain had made large shipments of military supplies to Israel.

On 17 May the Egyptian Chief of Staff, General Mahmoud Fawzy, addressed a letter to the United Nations Emergency Forces Commander in which Egypt demanded the withdrawal of the UNEF from the Gaza Strip and the Egyptian frontier. The next day *Pravda* printed the letter along with allegations that Israeli troops were 'massing for attack' on the Syrian border, and that Egypt was preparing to come to Syria's aid.[16] According to *Pravda* there had been meetings between Israeli diplomats and British and American officials. On the same day *Izvestia* described secret plottings by American, British and Israeli authorities, adding that Syria was now in the front rank of the 'fighters against imperialism and reaction'. The same report was broadcast by Moscow Radio.[17]

The broadcast coincided with an announcement from Damascus in which the Syrian Government pledged their 'implacable hostility to Israel' and asserted that the Israeli army was 'in a state of readiness for anything including an armed conflict'. The Syrian delegate at the United Nations was reported by Tass to have protested on the same day against 'Israel's preparations for armed aggression' against his country. To support this Moscow Radio quoted the Polish Press on the 'approach of armed conflict in the Middle East'. A day later Moscow Radio alleged that Israeli troops on the Syrian and Egyptian borders had been increased to twelve brigades, and that Israel was already mobilizing its reservists. Some days later *Pravda* quoted Nasser as saying that there were thirteen brigades.[18] Reporting the Syrian Foreign Minister's hurried visit to Cairo to confer with Nasser about 'Israeli provocateurs', Radio Moscow said that 'from now on both armies join in the Arab struggle against imperialism and its agents'.

On 22 May Levi Eshkol, the Israeli Prime Minister, greatly alarmed by the hasty withdrawal of the United Nations Emergency Force and Soviet propaganda about Israeli troop concentrations, made a statement in the Knesset calling on the Great Powers to use their influence to remove the danger of war in the Middle East. Referring to Egypt and Syria Mr Eshkol said 'we harbour no aggressive designs. We have no possible interest in violating either their security, or their territory, or their legitimate rights'. He appealed in particular to the Soviet Union, 'because of her responsibility as a Great Power and her close ties with Egypt and Syria.[19] But his appeal was ignored in the Russian Press. *Pravda* published instead another front-page article about the movements of American and British troops and their supposed co-operation with Israel. The Russian Press also failed to mention Eshkol's invitation to the Soviet Ambassador in Israel to visit the Syrian border in order to convince himself of the absence of Israeli troops. The Ambassador declined the invitation.

Two days later, on 24 May, the Security Council of the United

Nations held an urgent meeting, convened at the suggestion of Canada and Denmark, to discuss the situation in the Middle East. The American delegate, Mr Arthur Goldberg, declared that his Government was prepared to join with all the other great powers—the Soviet Union, the United Kingdom and France—in a common effort to restore and maintain peace in the Near East'.[20] This declaration was also not mentioned in the Russian newspapers.

The Soviet delegate at the United Nations Security Council said that he found no justification for any hasty action, and seemed unaware of the alarming reports in the Russian Press. He rejected the proposal for consultation between the major powers, thus making any joint action to prevent conflict impossible. A couple of days later *Pravda* reported on the Security Council's meeting and charged America with having made this proposal merely to prevent the Arabs from taking concerted measures against the aggressive actions of Israel and 'the imperialist forces backing Israel'.[21]

On 28 May the Egyptian War Minister, Badran, returned from a visit to Moscow where he had been in consultation with the Soviet Minister of Defence, Grechko, and members of the Soviet Government. On the same day Nasser declared that Egypt's main objective was the destruction of Israel. The Palestine Liberation Organization made similar threatening declarations against Israel. But no mention was ever made in the Soviet newspapers of these statements.

What happened later is well known. The Six Days' War ended in a cease-fire, a victory for Israel and defeat for Egypt, Jordan and Syria. After such a build-up the Russian people were amazed at Israel's rapid victory. Even the Kremlin leaders, who had placed great confidence in both the size of the Arab army and the Soviet arms supplied to Egypt, were surprised. They produced a three-fold explanation of the Arab defeat. Moscow Radio, on 11 June, maintained firstly that Israel had made a surprise attack, secondly that the United States and Great Britain had supplied arms immediately before the attack, and thirdly that Israel had massed aircraft and arms in the Sinai to start the attack.

The 'big lie', as Randolph Churchill called it, of Israel's aggression was spread both in the Soviet Union and in the Satellite countries. On 10 June the Soviet Union broke off diplomatic relations with Israel. Pressure was put on the satellites to do the same. Previously Russia had not compelled other Eastern European countries to follow her line of policy either towards their own Jews or towards Israel. But on 9 June, Polish, East German, Hungarian, Bulgarian and Czechoslovak leaders were summoned to the Kremlin and asked to unite on the anti-Israel front. Poland, Hungary, Bulgaria and Czechoslovakia broke off relations with Israel shortly afterwards. Yugoslavia, although describing herself as a neutral power, followed suit a day later. Only Rumania refused.

On the Arab side, President Nasser set about regaining his position after the defeat of the Six Days' War. This offered a fresh opportunity to the Soviet Union to further her expansionist aims. Soviet leaders were quick to take advantage of the situation. They agreed to replace the military equipment lost in the war, on the condition that preparations for its use should be supervised by Russian military experts. With the influx of Russian officers and men into Arab countries which followed, the Soviet Union provided herself with a military base of considerable importance. With Russian warships in the Mediterranean as well, the centuries-long Russian dream of a foothold in the Middle East was near realization.

Having replaced Arab military supplies, the USSR followed this up with as much political support as she could muster. She continues to identify herself with Arab aims. In the Security Council she has exercised her right of veto five times against Israel, and the knowledge that she would continue to do so has inhibited the Security Council's attempts to put any constructive plans into action.

In fact ever since the June War the Soviet Union has been exerting her efforts in and outside the United Nations, to profit politically from both Israel's victory and the Arab's defeat. Having armed Egypt and encouraged the Arabs up to the very brink of war Soviet leaders were quick to realize the new opportunities which existed to extend and consolidate their influence as a result of the Arab defeat in the Middle East. With this object in mind the Russian leaders assiduously set out to frustrate every effort made by Britain and the other Western powers to reach a settlement. Their activities in this sphere were largely prompted by the fear that a quick peace, or indeed peace of any kind, would be bound to weaken and ultimately even deprive Russia of the position she had managed to establish for herself in the area.

It was the Arab-Israeli conflict which ever since 1965 and Suez had given the Soviet Union the chance to enter the Middle East. The longer that conflict lasts, the more exacerbating it becomes, the more advantageous it will be for Russia. Instability gives Russia greater opportunity to strengthen her position and creates a favourable mental climate for the acceptance of her political and military presence. In this way she can constantly widen the effects of her incursion and increase her penetration and dominance over Egypt and the Arab world as a whole.

Overcome by a blind hatred towards Israel, and determined upon her destruction, President Nasser and most of the autocratic Arab rulers must out of sheer political necessity become pawns in the Soviet political game. In order to justify Russia's growing incursions to their own peoples President Nasser and the other Arab leaders have been hailing the Soviet Union as their only true friend and denouncing Britain, America and the democratic states as imperialists who cannot be trusted. This doctrine, which Russia's vast propaganda machine was quick to elaborate upon had a great emotional impact upon the Arabs making them deaf to every rational suggestion for a peace settlement with Israel.

NOTES

INTRODUCTION

1. As the secret police repeatedly changed its name and status the following summary may be useful. First, under Lenin, came the establishment of the Cheka. This was abolished in 1922 and its functions were carried out by the OGPU (Unified State Political Board). In 1934 Stalin incorporated the GPU into the NKVD (People's Commissariat for Internal Affairs) which also had sections dealing with such matters as crime, fire brigades and highways. In February 1941 the Administration for State Security became a separate Commissariat, the NKGB, and Beria co-ordinated the activities of both the NKGB and NKVD. In 1946 People's Commissariats were retitled ministries and they became the MGB and MVD respectively. After Stalin's death in 1953 they were combined again under Beria but in 1954 the MGB's functions were transferred to the KGB (Commission for State Security). The various designations used in the present volume correspond to whichever name is correct at any given period.

2. Anatoly Kuznetsov, *Babi Yar*, London and New York, 1967, p. 390.

3. Monthly Report No. 6 for the period 1-31 October, 1941, from the S.S. to Reinhard Heydrick.

4. *Die Goldene Keit*, No. 43, Tel Aviv, 1962. See also Albert Einstein, 'Why do They Hate the Jews?', *Ideas and Opinions*, London, 1956, New York, 1964.

5. Yakov Kantor, *Nationalnoye Stroitel'stvo Sredi Yevreyev SSSR* (The National Construction among Jews in the USSR), Moscow, 1934.

6. Lev Zinger, *Dos Banaite Folk* (The Rejuvenated People), Moscow, 1941.

7. Simon Dubnov, 'On Studying the History of Russian Jews', *Voskhod*, April-September, 1891.

8. Lozovsky was later Chairman of the Profintern Trade Union International. During the Second World War he was Deputy Chief of the Soviet Information Bureau and Vice-Minister of Foreign Affairs for the Far East under Molotov. He was

among the sponsors of the Jewish Anti-Fascist Committee. Arrested and charged with being a nationalist Zionist he was shot in August 1952 together with Fefer, Quitko, Halkin and others.

9. He later became Chairman of the Revolutionary Tribunal.

10. Slutsky, whose real name was Naftally Grigorevich, later became Premier of the Crimean Republic, and was shot by the Tartar anti-Bolshevik forces.

Chapter 1: THE BACKGROUND

1. By a decree of Catherine II in 1791 Jews were excluded from nine-tenths of the Russian Empire. They were confined to a 'Pale of Settlement' mainly in areas of Western Russia and Poland. By subsequent decrees certain groups of Jews, such as leading business men, professionals and certain classes of artisans were exempted. The rules were so strict that even Jewish soldiers serving in the Tsar's army stationed outside the 'Pale of Settlement' could not by the law of 1896 spend their leave in the places where they were serving.

2. Louis Greenberg, *The Jews in Russia*, London and New Haven, 1965, Vol. I, p. 51.

3. *Ibid*, Vol. II, p. 48.

4. S. L. Zitron, *Drei Literarishe Doroth* (Three Literary Generations), London and New Haven, 1965.

5. Louis Greenberg, *op. cit.*, Vol. I, p. 147-8.

6. *Ibid.*, Vol. I, p. 148.

7. *Ibid.*, Vol. I, p. 150.

8. N. Menes, 'Yeshivas in Russia', *Russian Jewry 1860-1917*, ed. Jacob Frumkin, New York, 1966.

9. Gregor Aronson, 'Jews in Russian Literary and Political Life', *Russian Jewry 1860-1917*.

10. Yevzel Ginsburg was the leading banker. The brothers Samuil, Yakov and Lazar Poliakov established a banking network in Petrograd, Rostov, Kiev and Oriol, which later became the United Banks of Russia. Another Banking House was Azov-Don Bankers of E. A. Kaminka. The Siberian Commercial Bank was established by M. Soloveychik and the Discount Bank of Petersburg by A. Y. Zak.

    Baron Alfred Ginsburg was a pioneer in gold-mining and became the director of the Lena Goldfields Company in 1913.

11. Ten large oil companies chiefly in the Baku region were

developed by Jews. Having been barred from direct exploitation of the Tsar's oil wells Russian Jews engaged in processing and transport. Dembo and Kagan were the Jewish pioneers who laid the first oil pipelines in Russia in 1870.

12. Article 762 of the Law of Personal Status. Code of Laws of the Russian Empire, Vol. IX, 1899.

13. Compendium of Laws and Ordinances of the Government, published by the Senate, No. 94, article 845, 1907.

14. Jacob Frumkin, 'The Dumas and Emancipation 1906-17', *Russian Jewry 1860-1917*, cit. at No. 8 above.

15. Itzchak Ben-Zvi, *Poale B Russia* (Labour Zionism in Russia), New York, 1916.

16. S. Agursky, *Di Yiddishe Commissariaten* (The Jewish Commissariats), Minsk, 1928. The fact that the members of the Zionist Party bought shekels is an indication of their devotion to the cause. This gave them the right to vote for the delegates to be sent to the Zionist Congress.

17. Alexander Chemerisky, *Tsionistishe Treiberayen* (Zionist Machinations), Moscow, 1926.

18. Simon Dubnov, *History of the Jews in Russia and Poland*, Philadelphia, 1916, Vol. II, p. 386ff.

19. Nikolai Berdyayev, *Christianity and Anti-Semitism*, Aldington, 1952.

20. Bruno Bauer, *Die Judenfrage*, Vienna, 1843.

21. Karl Marx, *A World Without Jews*, New York, 1959. The quotations cited in the text appear on pp. 37, 40-2, 45 of this edition.

22. Isaiah Berlin, *Karl Marx. His Life and Environment*, 3rd ed., London and New York, 1963, p. 98.

Chapter 2: LENIN AND STALIN : EARLY ATTITUDES

1. Vladimir Medem, *Fun Main Leben* (About My Life), 2 vols., New York, 1923.

2. *Iskra*, No. 56, 1 January, 1904.

3. Medem, who had been baptized in the Russian Orthodox Church, was the son of a high-ranking military surgeon in the Tsarist army. He broke with his family and devoted himself to the Jewish Workers' Movement, learned the Yiddish language and became one of the most devoted champions of the cause of the Jewish workers. After the Revolution he settled for a while in Poland but left for the USA where he died in 1923 aged 44.

4. It is interesting to note that three Communist Party Congresses took place in London : the 2nd in 1903, the 3rd in 1905, and the 5th in 1907.

5. *Iskra* was edited by Lenin from 37a Clerkenwell Green, London, and smuggled into Russia. Sixteen of the seventeen issues published in 1902-3 were set up by Jewish printers free of charge in sympathy with the revolutionary movement.

6. 'Rasse und Judentum', *Erganzungshefte*, Stuttgart, 1921; 'Das Massaker von Kischineff und die Judenfrage', *Die Neue Zeit*, 3 June 1903.

7. Vladimir Lenin, 'The Position of the Bund in the Party', *Collected Works*, Vol. VII, Moscow and London, 1961, pp. 99, 100, 101.

8. Nadezhda Krupskaya, *Reminiscences of Lenin*, Moscow and London, 1959, p. 239.

9. *Ibid.*, p. 245.

10. Vladimir Lenin, 'Critical Remarks on the National Question,' *Collected Works*, Vol. XX, Moscow and London, 1964, p. 26.

11. Josef Sieradzki, *Polskie Lata Lenina* (Lenin's Years in Poland), Warsaw, 1964.

12. The article which Stalin was writing was 'Marxism and the National Question', first published in *Prosveshcheniye*, March-May, 1913. It can be found in Josef Stalin, *Marxism and the National and Colonial Question*, London, 1936. Lenin's letter to Maxim Gorky is quoted in Bertram D. Wolfe's *Three Who Made a Revolution*, New York, 1948; London, 1956, p. 577.

13. See Bertram D. Wolfe, *Three Who Made a Revolution*, p. 578.

14. Josef Stalin, 'Marxism and the National Question,' *loc. cit.*, pp. 5, 10, 42, 58-9.

15. Leon Trotsky, *Stalin*, London and New York, 1946, p. 244.

Chapter 3: THE POST-REVOLUTIONARY DECADE

1. See Louis Greenberg, *The Jews in Russia*, London and New Haven, 1965, Vol. II, p. 51.

2. A. F. Kerensky, *The Kerensky Memoirs*, London, 1966; New York, 1965, p. 194.

3. Interview with the Jewish Telegraphic Agency, January 1931.

4. A. F. Kerensky, *op. cit.*, p. 210.

5. Leon Trotsky, *The History of the Russian Revolution*, London, 1965; Ann Arbor, 1957, p. 892.

6. M. Mysh, *Rukovodstvo k Russkim Zakonam o Yevreyakh*

(Handbook of Russian Laws Concerning the Jews), 4th ed., Petrograd, 1914.

7. Louis Greenberg, *op. cit.*, Vol. II, p. 158.

8. Isaac Deutscher, *The Prophet Armed*, London and New York, 1954, pp. 11-14.

9. Leon Trotsky, *Trotsky's Diary in Exile*, London and Cambridge, Mass., 1958.

10. S. Agursky, *Der Yiddisher Arbeter in der Komunistisher Bave gung* (The Jewish Worker in the Communist Movement), Minsk, 1925; and *Die Wahrheit*, 8 March 1918.

11. S. Agursky, *Di Yiddishe Commissariaten* (The Jewish Commissariats), Minsk, 1928.

12. Semen Dimanshtein, *Revolutsiya i Nat'ionalsnyi Vopros* (Revolution and the National Problem), Moscow, 1930.

13. Russian titles and details of publication of the books cited on pp. 68-9 of text as indications of anti-Semitism are given below:
S. K. Bezborodov, *Signaly. Ob antisemitizmie* (Signals. On Anti-Semitism), Moscow, 1929.
S. K. Bezborodov, *Yad. Ob antisemitizmie nashikh dney* (The Poison of Anti-Semitism in Our Time), Leningrad, 1930.
Leonid Radishchev, *Protiv antisemitizma* (Against Anti-Semitism), Moscow, 1929.
M. Y. Alexandrov, *Klasovyi vrag v maskie* (The Class Enemy Masked), Moscow, 1929.
M. Y. Alexandrov, *Otkuda byeriotsya vrazba k yevreryam i komu ona vygodna?* (Hatred of the Jews : Where Does it Come From? Whom Does it Benefit?), Moscow, 1929.
Anatoli Lunacharsky, *Ob antisemitizma* (On Anti-Semitism), Moscow, 1929.
G. L. Zhigalin, *Prokliatoye nasledie—Ob antisemitizmie* (The Accursed Heritage—On Anti-Semitism), Moscow, 1927.
N. Semashko, *Kto i pochemu travit yevreyev* (Who Persecutes the Jews and Why?), Moscow, 1926.
Y. Kochetkov, *Vragi li nam yevrei?* (Are the Jews our Enemies?), Moscow, 1927.
L. Liakov, *O vrazhbie k yevreyam* (On the Hatred of the Jews), Moscow, 1927.
M. Y. Maltsev, *Sud nad antisemitizmom* (Anti-Semitism on Trial), Leningrad, 1928.
Y. Sandomirsky, *Puti antisemitzma v Rossyi* (The Road of anti-Semitism in Russia), Leningrad, 1928.
G. Nagorny, *Na bor'bu s antisemitizmom* (To War against Anti-Semitism), Moscow, 1929.

M. Ryutin, 'Antisemitizm i partinaya rabota' (Anti-Semitism and Party Activities), *Pravda*, 13 August 1926.

Mikhail Kalinin, *Yevreyski vopros i pereseleniye yevreyev v krym* (The Jewish Question and the Resettlement of Jews in the Crimea), *Izvestia*, 11 July 1926.

A. Chemerisky, *Antisemitizm orudye kontrrevolyutsii* (Anti-Semitism, a Weapon of the Counter-Revolutionary), Moscow, 1929. Yury Larin, *Yevrei i antisemitizm v SSSR* (Jews and anti-Semitism in the USSR), Moscow, 1929.

14. Yury Larin, *op. cit.*

15. The appeal was issued by the Bolsheviks immediately after the Revolution and published in *Pravda*, October 1917.

Chapter 4: STALIN : ANTI-SEMITISM TO THE END OF THE WAR

1. For two years the Soviet Authorities kept absolute silence. It was not until the spring of 1943 that admission of the execution was made in a letter from Litvinov, the Soviet Ambassador in the USA, to W. Green, the chairman of the American Federation of Labour.

2. Stanislaw Kot, *Conversations with the Kremlin*, London and New York, 1963.

3. Ilya Ehrenburg, *Murder fun Felker* (Genocide), Moscow, 1944.

4. Leon Leneman, *In an Anderer Wolt* (In Another World), with a frontispiece by Marc Chagal, Paris, 1968.

5. Edward Mark, 'The Attitude of the Polish Workers' Party towards the Jewish Question during the Nazi Occupation', *Biuletyn Zydowskiego Instytutu Historycznego*, Warsaw, 1962.

6. Bernard Goldstein, *The Stars Bear Witness*, New York, 1947; London 1950.

7. Mark Dworzecki, *Yerushelaim d'Lite* (The Jerusalem of Lithuania), Paris, 1948.

8. Figures issued by the Jewish Anti-Fascist Committee in the USSR; reproduced in part in a pamphlet published in London at the time of Solomon Mikhoels' and Itzik Fefer's visit to the UK in 1943; and published in the Information Bulletin of the Soviet Embassy in Washington, 11 April 1944. These facts were never published in *Pravda* or *Izvestia*. The report together with other material was later to have been published as a separate volume but this was prevented by the Kremlin in 1945.

9. Mendel Mann gives a vivid portrait of a Polish officer in the Red Army who is distrusted simply because he is a Jew, in his

novel *At the Gates of Moscow* (New York, 1963; London, 1966).

10. Moshe Kaganovich, *Der Yidisher Unteil in ther Partizaner-Bevegung fun Soviet Russland* (Jewish Participation in the Partisan Movement in the Soviet Union), Rome, 1948.

11. D. Diamant at an international conference of historians of the Underground held in Warsaw in April 1962. *Biuletyn Zydowskiego Instytutu Historycznego*, No. 43-44, December 1962.

Chapter 5: STALIN : *1945-53*

1. Lavrentii Pavlovich Beria was the head of the Soviet secret police, (see Chapter 1, Note 1), from 1938-45. He was Deputy Prime Minister from 1945-53, arrested in June 1953 after Stalin's death, and shot as an 'Imperialist agent' in December 1953. Similar statements were made in answer to other foreign visitors. See for instance B. Z. Goldberg, *The Jewish Problem in the Soviet Union*, New York, 1961.

2. Maxim Litvinov, *Notes for a Journal*, London and New York, 1955, pp. 22-3, 46-7.

3. Svetlana Alliluyeva, *Letters to a Friend*, London and New York, 1967, pp. 193, 197.

4. 'On the Subject of a Letter', *Pravda*, 21 September 1948.

5. The incident is recorded in Walter Bedell Smith's *Moscow Mission 1946-1949*, London, 1950. The same book was published in Philadelphia, 1950 under the title *My Three Years in Moscow*.

6. Josef Stalin, '*Marxism and the National Question*', *loc. cit.*, pp. 8, 10.

7. The following is a list of those arrested :
Writers and Poets:
Abtshuk, A.; Altman, Moyshe; Arones, P.; Auslander, Nachum; Balyasne, Riva; Baumwol, Rochl; Beilis-Legis, Shloyme; Bergelson, David; Bielenky, M.; Bloshtein, H.; Boruchovich, J.; Briansky, Sh.; Broderson, Moshe; Buchbinder, Nachum; Chaimsky, M.; Chaykina, Dora; Cherniavsky, Eilya; Cherniavsky, Shloime; Chintchin, J.; Choral, Deborah; Chropkovsky; Dechtyer, M.; Dobin, Hirsh; Dobrushin, J.; Doljoplsky, Tsudik; Druker, A.; Dubilet, N.; Dvorkin, J.; Dvorkin, M.; Emyot, J.; Erkes, B.; Erngross, J.; Fefer, Itzik; Finkel, H.; Finkel, Yuri; Friedland, G.; Gildin, Chaim; Globstein, M.; Goldstein, J.; Gordon, Elli; Gordon, Shmuel; Greenberg, G.; Greenberg, J.; Greenberg, Zorach; Grubyan, M.; Halkin,

Shlomo; Helmond, R.; Helmond, Shmuel; Her, Meyer; Hochberg, D.; Holdes, A.; Holmstock, Chaim; Holmstock, L.; Joffe, Mordachy; Kadishevitsh, M.; Kagan, A.; Kagan, Abraham; Kagan, H.; Kagan, Isaak; Kamenetsky, Hirschl; Kamenstein, M.; Kantor, A.; Kantor, Jankel; Kegan, Abraham; Kegan, Ch.; Kegan, Isaac; Kemenetsky, Joseph; Kipnis, Itzik; Kipnis, Sjoma; Kipper, Motel; Kirshnitz, A.; Klitenaik, Shloime; Koblents, B.; Kolker; Kovnator, R.; Kruglyak, M.; Kurlyand, D.; Kvitko, Leylo; Kvitny, J.; Labovsky, B.; Latzman, J.; Lev, Abba; Levin, Jantel; Levin, N.; Levine, Gregory; Levine, Hanna; Levman, J. Sh.; Lipman Lipshitz, Mendel; Loitzker, H.; Lopatin, Sch.; Lozovsky, A.; Lumkin, I.; Lurie, H.; Lurie, Noa; Lurie, Nute; Maidansky, M.; Maidansky, Z.; Makagon, A.; Maltinsky, Chaim; Mariasine, S.; Markish, Perets; Marshak, Daniels; Margulies, A.; Medresh, B.; Meisl, H.; Melamed, H.; Mereshin, Abraham; Miller, B.; Minsky, P.; Mishritsai, M.; Mishkovsky, L.; Mittelman, J.; Monim, D.; Morevsky, Abraham; Naden, Hirschl; Nistor (Nyedomnyashtshi); Notovits, M.; Nusimnov, Jozchok; Palatnik, Sh.; Palikman, J.; Palkovich, B.; Pereomeisky, L.; Perlman, Yakov; Pintshevsky, Moris; Platner, Isak; Polyak, H.; Polyanker, Hirshl; Portnoi, E.; Poynitzay, D. N.; Prussman, L.; Pups, Meir; Rabin, J.; Rabinovich, Israel; Rattnes, M. B.; Ravalsky, M.; Rav, Rabe, J.; Ravin, Joseph; Resnick, Yasha; Resnik, Lipe; Rimini, J.; Rives, J.; Rives, Sh.; Rodak, J.; Roitman, David; Rosenblum, L.; Rosenblum, M.; Rosenhaus, J. L.; Roytman, Shloma; Rubin, Rifka; Rubinstein, Nahum; Rubinstein, R.; Ruskin, J.; Sabkekovsky, Ell; Saktzimer, Motel; Sanbverg, M.; Sarin, E.; Schectmann, Elli; Schectmann, J.; Schectmann, N.; Scheingold, M.; Scherniavsky, L.; Schitz (co-editor of Einigkeit); Serebryanii, J.; Shadur, M.; Shames, P.; Shatz, V.; Shatzke, N.; Shenier, Okun; Shiv, J.; Shmain, Nehemia; Shprach, Ephraim; Shrebman, Yechiel; Silbermann, Haim; Skuditsky, Z.; Slutsky, Ber.; Sokolov, Spivak, B.; Spivak, Elija; Stelmach, Hanna; Sternberg, J.; Strongin, L.; Strelitz, A.; Sturzman, M.; Sudarsky, J.; Taif, Moyshe; Taitsch, Jokob; Talalayevsky, M.; Telesin, Zyama; Tsard, L.; Udovin, M.; Velednitsky, Abraham; Vergeles, Aron; Vilenki, Lisa; Weiner, Prof, V.; Weinhaus, Nute; Weissman, Z.; Werit, S.; Witenson, Z.; Wolkenstein, D.; Wolobrinsky, A.; Wortman, L.; Wortman, M.; Yakubovich, J.; Yelin, Meir; Yoffe, Sh.; Zabore, Natan; Zaretsky, Prof. A.; Zuskin, B.

Actors:
Abraham, G.; Alesker, E.; Alperovich; Altman, M.; Aront-chik, U.; Ashkenazi, M.; Baslovsky, A.; Berkovskaya, E.; Bider; Blintchevskaya, A. J.; Brodkin, A.; Bursak; Chazak, T. O.; Davidson; Diamont, M.; Dreisina, A.; Eisenberg; Elia-sheva; Epstein, E.; Fabrikant, S.; Feldman, B.; Fingerov; Finkelkraut, Z.; Friedman, P. B.; German, J.; Gerstein, C.; Gertner, Ya.; Goldblatt, David; Goldburt, A.; Golman; Grien; Gulailo, M.; Horovitz, M. J.; Imenitova; Itzshovsky, Y. E.; Kagan, M.; Kaminsky, Z. M.; Kaplan, Esther; Kartshmer, E.; Koptshevskaya, E.; Korick, A.; Kotliareva, M. E.; Kreit-shman, B.; Kremer, Krugliansky, M.; Kulkin-Karnovsky; Kurtz, R.; Lauter, Ephraim; Lemberg, S.; Libert, E.; Liman, V.; Lukovsky, V.; Lurie, Masak, T.; Masur, A.; Melamet; Merenson, A. S.; Mindlin; Minkova, U. I.; Minsker, M.; Nadina; Nayin, M.; Ney, M.; Niger; Pasman; Patlach; Pikeltshik, E.; Pustelink, A.; Ragaler, J.; Rapalsky, M. P.; Rom, L. J.; Rosina, L. M.; Rotbaum, S.; Rivin, M.; Rosen-feld, J.; Rutstein, K.; Shapiro, J.; Shapiro; Sheinberg, M. G.; Shick, A.; Shidlo, A.; Shmayokek, A.; Sigalovsky; Silberblatt, S.; Sokol, M.; Sopz, A.; Steinman, M. D.; Suskin, B. L.; Tarlo, H.; Teiblina, E. S.; Tomback; Treistman, N.; Trepel, A.; Tshetshit, T.; Tshitshelmitsky; Tsibuledsky, Y. A.; Tsipkina, P. N.; Tzimerov, M.; Viniar; Vistotskaya, J.; Vitlin; Volpina, M.; Yampolsky, B.; Zucker.

Artists, painters and sculptors:
Aaronson, B.; Alexandrov, A.; Altman, Nathan; Apter, Jacob; Axelrod, M.; Birenbaum, M.; Blank, B.; Blank, M.; Borshch, A.; Chotinok, G.; Deich, Joseph; Dlugach, Michael; Eidelman, E.; Elman, J.; Epstein, M.; Fischer, G.; Frankel, Isaak; Fret-kin, M.; Fridkin, B.; Garvin; Goldman, Sh.; Golovotinsky, M.; Gerburg, A.; Gorshman, M.; Gripel, L.; Gutgin, A.; Hefter, A.; Heidelman, E.; Inger, G.; Kaganer, A.; Kaplan, L.; Katz, P.; Kipnis, D.; Kipnis, G.; Kotliarevsky, M.; Kovar-ska; Kroll, A.; Lapshin, N.; Larsh, M.; Lebedovo, T.; Leibo-vich, N.; Lipshitz, N.; Lishitsky, Eliezer; Litvinenko, M.; Lugansky; Marinov, A.; Marlkin, Michael, Y. O.; Marshalov, M.; Midikovsky; Mitzelmacher, M.; Perele; Pleshchinsky, J.; Pohoster, M.; Poliakov, M.; Ran, L.; Rashal, A.; Rautman, M.; Resnikov, H.; Rubinsky, M.; Rudniev, L.; Sandler, H.; Savim, V.; Segalovich, A.; Shabad, A. J.; Shalaver, Joseph; Shechter, A.; Shechtman, A.; Shechtman; Shifrin, N.; Shitnit-sky, M.; Shuvin, B.; Sokolovsky, D.; Soyfer, J.; Steinberg,

Edi; Tennenbaum, A. J.; Tishler, A.; Tselmer, V.; Tselniker; Tsheikov, Joseph; Vermus, J.; Vladimirsky, B.; Zaborov, A.; Zalmutsky, M.; Zevin, L.; Zmudznisky, G.
Musicians:
Beregovsky, Moyshe; Boyarska, Riva; Feintuch, Y. A.; Helmond, A.; Krein, A.; Kukles, Y. O. V.; Levin; Lichtenstein, O. G.; Limone, M.; Mendeles, A.; Milner; Polonsky, S.; Pulver, A.; Risking, B.; Sheinin, J. P.; Steinback, A.; Streicher, L.; Veprick, A.; Yamodsky, L.

8. Lena Solomouna Shtern, born in Lithuania in 1878, was the Director of the Soviet Institute of Physiology; she has been a member of the USSR Academy of Sciences since 1954.

9. *Unser Stimme,* Paris, May-December 1957.

10. See Roman Smal'-Stots'ky, *The Nationality Problem of the Soviet Union and Russian Communist Imperialism,* Milwaukee, 1952, pp. 105ff.

11. Khrushchev read her latest book of experiences which was to have been published under the title of *Tempest.* But he was deposed before it was published. Only a partly damaged proof copy reached France. It was translated and printed under the title of *Huragan* by the Polish Instytut Literacki in Paris in 1967.

12. While on a visit abroad Ehrenburg denied that he ever knew Fefer or Bergelson. See B. Z. Goldberg, *The Jewish Problem in the Soviet Union,* New York, 1961, p. 112.

13. Judd L. Teller, *The Kremlin,* London, 1957.

14. *Einikeit,* November 1948.

15. Tass Communiqué, *Pravda,* 13 January 1953.

16. An official communiqué of the Soviet Ministry of the Interior issued in April 1953 stated that the following twelve had been rehabilitated : Prof. M. F. Vovsi, Prof. V. H. Vinogradov, Prof. M. B. Kogan, Prof. V. V. Kogan, Prof. P. I. Yegorov, Prof. A. A. Feldman, Prof. I. S. Ettinger, Prof. V. Kh. Vassilengo, Prof. A. H. Greenstein, Prof. V. F. Zelenin, Prof. B. S. Preobrazhensky and Prof. N. A. Popova. There were two who died in prison as a result of torture.

17. In an interview with Prof. Hyman Levi of London University, a member of the British Communist Party, Suslov said that Jews no longer wanted to have any Jewish schools because the vast majority of them in Russia had been completely integrated into Russian life.

18. *Swiss Review of World Affairs,* Vol. VII, Zurich, November

1957, and Rabbi Morris Kertzev, *Evening Star*, Washington, 31 July 1956.

19. Lazar Moyseyevich Kaganovich, born in 1893, the son of a Jewish cobbler, was a member of the Central Committee from 1924, the People's Commissar of Transport, the First Deputy Premier 1947-57, and finally dismissed from the Party in June 1957.

20. A detailed account of the police interrogation and the 'confession' was given by Dr Evzen Loebel, a former high-ranking official in the Czech Ministry of Foreign Trade. He was arrested with the Slansky group, and imprisoned from 1949-60 having been sentenced for 'anti-State conspiratorial activities'. He published two articles, in *Reportér, Prague*, 15 May 1968, and *Literární Listy*, Prague, 25 April 1968.

21. Khrushchev made two speeches to the 20th Party Congress. The first on 14 February which was his presenation of the Report of the Central Committee to the Congress, and the second on 24 and 25 February before a closed session of the Congress. This second speech was leaked out of Russia and eventually reached the West. The text, from which my quotes are taken, is the one published by the *Manchester Guardian*, June 1956, under the title *The Dethronement of Stalin*.

Chapter 6: THE BEGINNINGS OF DE-STALINIZATION

1. Georgii Malenkov, b. 1902, became the Secretary of the Central Committee after Stalin's death. On 14 March 1953, he became the Premier. He resigned in February 1955, and was expelled from the Party in June 1957.

2. Harrison E. Salisbury, *To Moscow and Beyond*, New York and London, 1960, p. 72.

3. Martin Ebon, *Malenkov: Stalin's Successor*, New York and London, 1953, pp. 10-11.

4. 'Harvest of Half a Century of Bolshevik Rule', *Dziennik Polski*, London, 25 January 1968. See also Robert Conquest's *The Great Terror—Stalin's Purges of the Thirties*, London and New York, 1968; and Iverach McDonald's review in *The Times*, 19 September 1968.

5. A third prominent Jewish doctor arrested somewhat earlier who, according to reports which circulated in Moscow, also died under police torture, was Dr Shimelovich, a Pole. He was believed to have been charged with spreading Zionist propaganda.

6. Meilech Bakalczuk-Felin, *Zichronot fun an Yiddish en Partisaner* (Memoirs of a Jewish Partisan), Buenos Aires, 1958; Johannesburg, 1960.
7. See *The Dethronement of Stalin*, cited at Chapter 5, note 21, from which the relevant quotations from Khrushchev's speech are taken. See also Bertram D. Wolfe, *Khrushchev and Stalin's Ghost*, New York, 1957.

Chapter 7: KHRUSHCHEV AND ANTI-SEMITISM

1. The interview was reported and discussed in a series of articles by J. B. Salzberg in *Morgen Freiheit*, New York, November-December 1956.
2. The full text of Khrushchev's reply to the question on the Jewish problem put by the French Socialist Party delegation on 12 May 1956 is given in B. Z. Goldberg, *The Jewish Problem in the Soviet Union*, New York, 1961, pp. 234-5.
3. *National Guardian*, New York, September 1956.
4. The interview is quoted in 'Report of an International Socialist Study Group on the Situation of the Jews in the USSR', by Alvar Alstesdal (Sweden), John Clark (Great Britain), Prof. Morgens Pihl (Denmark), Dr P. J. Koets (Netherlands) and Dr John Sannes (Norway), Socialist International, London, April 1964.
5. *Le Figaro*, 9 April 1958.
6. Walter Kolarz, *The Peoples of the Soviet Far East*, London, 1954, p. 34.
7. Ben-Ami, *Between Hammer and Sickle*, Philadelphia, 1967, p. 241.
8. Solomon Rabinovich, *Jews in the Soviet Union*, Moscow, 1967, p. 29.
9. *Sovietish Heimland*, January 1968.

Chapter 8: THE JEWS UNDER KHRUSHCHEV AND HIS SUCCESSORS

1. Figures submitted to the Commission on Human Rights, Sub-Commission on the Prevention of Discrimination and the Protection of Minorities, United Nations, New York, 1959.
2. Nikita Struve, *Christians in Contemporary Russia*, London and New York, 1967, pp. 179, 300.
3. Emilien Yaroslavsky, *The Bible for Believers and Unbelievers*, Moscow, 1929.
4. A. Erichev, *Sektanstvo i ego sushchnost'* (The Sects and their Essence), Kiev, 1959.

5. *Krymskaya Pravda*, 7 September 1957.
6. For a full account of these sects see Nikita Struve, *op. cit.*, pp. 218-52.
7. Russian titles and details of publication of the books attacking Judaism cited on pp. 151-3 of text are given below :
   M. K. Kitchko, *Iudaism bez Prikas* (Judaism Unembellished), Moscow, 1963.
   M. U. Shakhnovich, *Reakcyonnaya Shushez nost Iudaisma* (The Reactionary Essence of Judaism), Moscow, 1960.
   Moshe Solomonovich Bielenky, *Krityka Iudeyskoy Religii* (Criticism of the Judaic Religion), Moscow, 1962; and *Chto Takoye Talmud?* (What is the Talmud?), Moscow, 1963.
   Paul Holbach, *Galeriya Sviatykh* (Gallery of Saints), Moscow, 1962.
8. K. Ivanov and Z. Sheinis, *Gosudarstvo Izrail* (The State of Israel), ed. by I. Dinerstein, Moscow, 1958.
9. Joseph Barzilai, *Zohar Bakhzot*, (Light at Midnight), Tel Aviv, 1963.
10. For a fuller account of the use of *Blat* see Edward Crankshaw, *Russia Without Stalin*, London, 1956, pp. 71-88.
11. *Sovietskaya Litva*, 4 April 1962.
12. *Pravda*, 11 February 1962.
13. *Lvovskaya Pravda*, 16 March 1962.
14. Benjamin Gulko also figured in another trial of the same nature in Odessa in June 1962 reported in *Pravda Ukrainy*, 12 June 1962.
15. *Sovietskaya Rossiya*, 19 August 1963.
16. *The Guardian*, 28 January 1964.
17. *Jewish Chronicle*, 6 April 1962.
18. Jewish Telegraphic Agency, Bulletin No. 101, 26 February 1963; and *Jewish Chronicle*, 1 March 1963.

Chapter 9: NATIONAL MINORITIES IN THE USSR I

1. His principal work is *History of the Jews in Russia and Poland*, 3 vols., Philadelphia, 1916.
2. Supplement to *Moscow News*, No. 26, 1 July 1967.
3. 'Great October Socialist Revolution of 1917', *The Soviet Union*, Moscow, July 1967.
4. 'Report of an International Socialist Study Group on the Situation of the Jews in the USSR', London, April 1964.
5. Official figures vary between 109 and 169.

6. I. P. Tsamerian and S. L. Ronin, *Equality of Rights between Races and Nationalities in the USSR*, Paris, 1962.

7. *Moscow News*, 8 August; 22 August; and 5 August 1967. The series of articles continued for eight months with contributions from about fifty representatives of national minorities large and small, but none from a Jew.

8. Walter Kolarz, *The Peoples of the Soviet Union*, London and New York, 1954, p. 149.

9. Solomon Schwarz, *The Jews in the Soviet Union*, Syracuse, New York, 1951, p. 138.

10. The world figure was 451. David Bergelson, *Three Centuries of Yiddish*, Vilna, 1926.

Chapter 10: NATIONAL MINORITIES IN THE USSR II

1. *Report of the Programme of the Communist Party delivered to the 22nd Party Congress*, Soviet Booklet No. 81, London, 1961.

2. *Izvestia*, 5 December 1961 and *Literatura i Zhizn'*, 2 March 1962.

3. *Voprosy Filosofii*, No. 4, 1963.

4. *Literaturnaya Gazeta*, 6 February 1962.

5. *Istoriya SSSR*, No. 3, 1962.

6. *Ibid.*, No. 1, 1963.

7. K. Ch. Chanazarov, *Zblizheniye natzii i natsional'nyie yazyki v SSSR* (The Integration of Nations and their Languages), Moscow, 1962.

8. *Kulturnoye Stroitel'stvo SSR 1959-1960* (Cultural Construction in the USSR), Moscow, 1961.

9. *Pravda*, September 1941.

10. *Ibid.*, August 1964.

11. *Neues Leben*, 11 January 1964.

12. *Ibid.*, 7 June 1967.

13. *Ibid.*, 1 January 1967.

14. In 1833 over 1,300 Jews were settled on land in Siberia as a group. More followed until a new decree in 1837 put a stop to the resettlement.

15. Aaron Vergelis (ed.), *Azoy Leben Mir* (How We Live), Moscow, 1964.

16. Solomon Rabinovich, *Jews in the Soviet Union*, Moscow, 1967, p. 52.

17. Interview with Goldberg in *Focus on Soviet Jewry*, London, September 1966.

18. Solomon Rabinovich, *op. cit.*, p. 45.
19. I. P. Tsamerian and S. L. Ronin, *Equality of Rights between Races and Nationalities in the USSR*, Paris, 1962.
20. Simon Dubnov, *History of the Jews in Russia and Poland*, Philadelphia, 1916, Vol. I, p. 348.
21. Solomon Rabinovich, *op. cit.*, p. 15.
22. *Ibid.*, p. 62.
23. Leonid Vladimirov, *The Russians*, London, 1968, p. 146.

Postscript: RUSSIA AND ISRAEL

1. *New York Tribune*, 19 April 1853.
2. Max Beloff, *The Foreign Policy of Soviet Russia*, London and New York, 1949, Vol. II, pp. 42-7.
3. V. I. Lenin, 'Critical Remarks on the National Question', *Collected Works*, Vol. XX, Moscow and London, 1964, p. 29.
4. Joseph B. Schechtman, *Zionism and Zionists in Soviet Russia*, New York, 1966.
5. S. Agursky, *Der Yiddisher Arbeter in der Kommunistisher Bavegung* (The Jewish Worker in the Communist Movement), Minsk, 1925.
6. Alexander Chemerisky, First Secretary of the Central Board of Jewish Sections, addressing White Russian Conference of Jewish Sections in Minsk, 15 October 1925.
7. Joseph B. Schechtman, *op. cit.*
8. *Ha'Aretz* and *New York Times*, 16 May 1947.
9. Walter Eytan, *The First Ten Years. Israel between East and West*, London and New York, 1958, p. 130 and James G. McDonald, *My Mission in Israel*, London and New York, 1951, p. 104.
10. *Pravda*, 21 September 1948. See Chapter 5, pp. 100-3
11. *Pravda* and *Izvestia*, 13 January 1953. See Chapter 5, pp. 108-9.
12. N. S. Khrushchev, *Report of the Central Committee to the 20th Congress, Soviet News Booklet* No. 4, 1956. See Chapter 5, Note 21.
13. Jewish Telegraphic Agency, Bulletin No. 47, 7 November 1956.
14. *The Soviet Union on the Middle East.* Statements by the Ministry of Foreign Affairs of the USSR, published in London as *Soviet News Booklet*, No. 8.
15. Moshe Sharett, *Jewry between East and West*, Vol. II, New York, 1962.

16. Jewish Telegraphic Agency, Bulletin No. 164, 18 May 1967; *Pravda*, 18 May 1967.
17. *Izvestia* and Moscow Radio, 18 May 1967.
18. *Pravda*, 24 May 1967.
19. Jewish Telegraphic Agency, Bulletin No. 167, 23 May 1967.
20. *The Times*, 25 May 1967.
21. *Pravda*, 26 May 1967.

SELECTED BIBLIOGRAPHY

ALEXANDROVA, VERA, *A History of Soviet Literature, 1917-1964*, Doubleday : New York, 1964.

ALLILUYEVA, SVETLANA, *Letters to a Friend*, Hutchinson : London; Harper : New York, 1967.

ALMEDINGEN, MARTHA EDITH VON, *The Romanovs*, Bodley Head : London; Holt, Rinehart : New York, 1966.

ARMSTRONG, JOHN A., *Ideology, Politics and Government in the Soviet Union*, Praeger : New York, 1967.

BAKALCZUK-FELIN, MEILECH, *Zichronot fun an Yidishen Partisaner* (Memoirs of a Jewish Partisan), Buenos Aires, 1958; Johannesberg, 1960.

BARON, SALO, *The Russian Jew Under Tsars and Soviets*, Collier-Macmillan : London; Macmillan : New York, 1964.

BELOFF, MAX, *The Foreign Policy of Soviet Russia,1929-1941*, 2 vols., Royal Institute of International Affairs : London; Oxford University Press : New York, 1947-9.

BEN-AMI, *Between Hammer and Sickle*, Jewish Publication Society of America : Philadelphia, 1967.

BEN-ZVI, Itzchak, *The Exiled and the Redeemed*, Vallentine, Mitchell : London, 1958.

BERDYAYEV, N. ALEXANDER, *Christianity and Anti-Semitism*, Hand & Flower : Aldington, 1952.

—— *The Origin of Russian Communism*, Bles : London, 1937.

BERLIN, ISAIAH, *Karl Marx. His Life and Environment*, 3rd ed., Oxford University Press : London and New York, 1963.

BORKENAU, FRANZ, *European Communism*, Faber : London; Harper : New York, 1953.

CARR, E. H., *The Bolshevik Revolution, 1917-23*, 3 vols., Macmillan : London and New York, 1950-53.

CHIROVSKY, L. NICOLAS, *An Introduction to Russian History*, Vision : London, 1967.

COLLARD, DUDLEY, *Soviet Justice and the Trial of Radek and Others*, Gollancz : London, 1937.

CONQUEST, ROBERT, *The Great Terror*, Macmillan : London, 1968.

CRANKSHAW, E., *Russia by Daylight*, Michael Joseph : London, 1951.

DALLIN, D. J., *Real Soviet Russia*, New Haven : Yale University Press, 1944.

DEUTSCHER, I., *Stalin. A Political Biography*, Oxford University Press : London and New York, 1949.

—— *Russia After Stalin*, Hamish Hamilton : London, 1953.

—— *The Phophet Armed: Trotsky, 1879-1921*, Oxford University Press, London and New York, 1954.

—— *The Prophet Unarmed: Trotsky, 1921-1929*, Oxford University Press : London and New York, 1959.

DUBNOV, SIMON, *History of the Jews in Russia and Poland*, 3 vols., Jewish publication Society of America : Philadelphia, 1916-20.

EHRENBURG, ILYA, *People and Life. Memoirs of 1891-1917*, Macgibbon & Kee : London; Knopf : New York, 1962.

EINSTEIN, ALBERT, *Ideas and Opinions*, Alvin Redman : London, 1956; Crown : New York, 1962.

ENGELS, FREDERICK, *Dialectics of Nature*, Lawrence & Wishart : London, 1940; International Publishers : New York, 1940.

EYTAN, WALTER, *The First Ten Years. Israel between East and West*, Weidenfeld & Nicholson : London; Simon & Schuster : New York, 1958.

FAINSOD, MERLE, *Smolensk Under Soviet Rule*, Macmillan : London, 1959; Harvard University Press : Cambridge, Mass, 1958.

FARBMAN, MICHAEL, *After Lenin. The New Phase in Russia*, Leonard Parsons : London, 1924.

FAST, HOWARD, *The Naked God*, Bodley Head : London, 1958; Praeger : New York, 1957.

FINKELSTEIN, LOUIS, *The Jews. Their History, Culture, and Religion*, 2 vols., Peter Owen : London, 1961; Harper : New York, 1960.

FISCHER, LOUIS, *The Life of Lenin*, Weidenfeld & Nicholson : London; Harper : New York, 1965.

FREUND, GERALD, *Unholy Alliance. Russian German Relations from the Treaty of Brest-Litovsk to the Treaty of Berlin*, Chatto & Windus : London, 1957.

GINZBURG, EVGENIA, S., *Krutoj maršrut* (Into the Whirlwind) Mondadori : Milan, 1967.

GLUCKSTEIN, YGAEL, *Stalin's Satellites in Europe*, Allen & Unwin, London, 1952.

GOLDBERG, B.Z., *The Jewish Problem in the Soviet Union*, Crown : New York, 1961.

GOLDHAGEN, ERICH, (ed.), *Ethnic Minorities in the Soviet Union*, Praeger : New York, 1968.

GRAHAM, STEPHEN, *Summing-up on Russia*, Benn : London, 1951.

GREENBERG, LOUIS, *The Jews in Russia*, Yale University Press : London and New Haven, 1965.

GUNTHER, JOHN, *Inside Russia Today*, Hamish Hamilton : London; Harper : New York, 1962.

HAZARD, JOHN N., *Law and Social Change in the USSR*, Stevens & Sons : London, 1953.

HUNT, R. N. C., *The Theory and Practice of Communism*, Bles : London; Macmillan : New York, 1957.

IVANOV, K., and SHEINIS, Z., *Gosudarstvo Izrail* (The State of Israel), ed. by I. Dinerstein, Moscow, 1958.

KAGANOVICH, MOSHE, *Der Yidisher Unteil in ther Partizaner-Bevegung fun Soviet Russland*, (Jewish Participation in the Partisan Movement in Soviet Russia), Rome, 1948.

—— *Di Milchume fun Yidishe Partisaner in Mizrech Europe* (The War of Jewish Partisans in Eastern Europe), Buenos Aires, 1956.

KERENSKY, ALEXANDER F., *The Kerensky Memoirs: Russia and History's Turning Point*, Cassell : London, 1966; Duell, Sloane : New York, 1965.

KHRUSHCHEV, NIKITA, *World Without Arms, World Without Wars*, 2 vols., Moscow, Foreign Languages Publishing House, 1959.

KOLARZ, WALTER, *The Peoples of the Soviet Union*, George Philip : London; Praeger : New York, 1954.

—— *Religion in the Soviet Union*, Macmillan : London, 1961; St Martins Press : New York, 1962.

—— *Russia and her Colonies*, George Philip : London, 1952; Shoe String Press : Hamden, Conn., 1967.

KOT, STANISLAW, *Conversations with the Kremlin and Dispatches from Russia*, Oxford University Press : London and New York, 1963.

KRAVCHENKO, V. A., *I Chose Freedom; the Personal and Political Life of a Soviet Official*, Robert Hale : London, 1947; Scribner's : New York, 1946.

KRUPSKAYA, NADEZHDA, *Reminiscences of Lenin*, Foreign Languages Publishing House : Moscow; Lawrence & Wishart, London, 1959.

KULSKI, W. W., *The Soviet Regime*, Syracuse University Press : Syracuse, New York, 1954.

KUZNETSOV, ANATOLY, *Babi Yar*, MacGibbon & Kee : London; Dial Press : New York, 1967.

LAWRENCE, JOHN W., *Russia in the Making*, Allen & Unwin : London, 1957.

LEVINE, IRVING R., *The Real Russia*, W. H. Allen : London, 1959. Published in America under the title *Main Street, USSR*, Doubleday : New York, 1959.

LENEMAN, LEON, *In an Anderer Wolt*, (In Another World), with a frontispiece by Marc Chagal, Paris, 1968.

—— *La Tragedie des Juifs en U.R.S.S.*, Paris 1959.

LENIN, VLADIMIR, *Collected Works*, Foreign Languages Publishing House : Moscow; Lawrence & Wishart; London, 1960—.

LEONHARD, WOLFGANG, *The Kremlin Since Stalin*, Oxford University Press : London; Praeger : New York, 1962.

LEVY, HYMAN, *Jews and the National Question*, Hillway Publishing Co : London, 1958.

LEWICKYI, BORIS, *Politika Narodowosciowa S.Z.S.R.* (Minorities Policy in the USSR), Paris, 1959.

LITVINOV, MAXIM, *Notes for a Journal*, André Deutsch : London; Morrow : New York, 1955.

MARX, KARL, *A World Without Jews*, Philosophical Library : New York, 1959.

MEIZEL, NACHMAN, *Dus Yidishe Shafen un Der Yidisher Shreiber in Sovetenfarband* (Jewish Creativity and the Jewish Writer in the Soviet Union), New York, 1959.

MEYER, PETER, et al., *The Jews in the Soviet Satellites*; Syracuse University Press; Syracuse, New York, 1953.

MIKHAILOV, N., *Discovering the Soviet Union*, Progress Publishers : Moscow, 1965.

MILLS, C. WRIGHT, *The Marxists*, Penguin Books : Harmondsworth; Dell Paperback : New York, 1967.

REITLINGER, GERALD, *The Final Solution. The Attempt to Exterminate the Jews of Europe, 1939-45*, Vallentine Mitchell : London, 1953; A. S. Barnes : Cranbury, N.J. : 1961.

RUNES, DAGOBERT D., *The Soviet Impact on Society. A Recollection*, Philosophical Library : New York 1953.

SALISBURY, HARRISON E., *Stalin's Russia and After*, Macmillan : London, 1955. Published in America under the title, *American in Russia*, Harper : New York, 1955.

SCHWARTZ, SOLOMON, *The Jews in the Soviet Union*, Syracuse University Press : Syracuse, N.Y., 1951.

SETON-WATSON, HUGH, *The Pattern of Communist Revolution*, Methuen : London, 1953; Published in America under the title, *From Lenin to Malenkov; the History of World Revolution*, Praeger : New York, 1953.

SHUB, DAVID, *Lenin (A Biography)*, Doubleday : New York, 1951.

SIERADZKI, JOSEF, *Polskie Lata Lenina*, (Lenin's Years in Poland), Warsaw, 1964.

SLONIM, MARK, *Soviet Russian Literature*, Oxford University Press : New York, 1964.

SMAL'-STOTS'KY, ROMAN, *The Nationality Problem of the Soviet*

Union and Russian Communist Imperialism, Bruce Publishing Co. : Milwaukee, 1952.

SMITH, WALTER BEDELL, *Moscow Mission, 1946-1949*, Heinemann : London, 1950. Published in America under the title, *My Three Years in Moscow*, Lippincott : Philadelphia, 1950.

SOBOLEV, P. N., Gimpelson, Y. G., Trukan, G. A., *History of the October Revolution*, Progress Publishers : Moscow, 1966.

STALIN, JOSEPH, 'Marxism and the National Question', *Marxism and the National and Colonial Question*, Lawrence & Wishart : London, 1936.

STRUVE, NIKITA, *Christians in Contemporary Russia*, Harvill : London; Scribner : New York, 1967.

STYPULKOWSKI, Z., *Invitation to Moscow*, Thames & Hudson : London, 1951; Walter & Co. : New York, 1962.

TELLER, JUDD L., *The Kremlin, the Jews and the Middle East*, Yoseloff : London, 1957.

TENEBAUM, JOSEPH, *Underground; the Story of a People*, Philosophical Library : New York, 1952.

—— *Race and Reich*, Twayne : New York, 1956.

TETENS, T. H., *Germany Plots with the Kremlin*, Schuman : New York, 1953.

TROTSKY, LEON, *The History of the Russian Revolution*, Allen & Unwin : London, 1965; University of Michigan Press : Ann Arbor, 1957.

—— *Stalin. An Appraisal of the Man and his Influence*, London, 1946; Harper : New York, 1946.

—— *Trotsky's Diary in Exile, 1935*, Faber, London, 1959; Harvard University Press : Cambridge, Mass., 1958.

—— *The Stalin School of Falsification*, Pioneer Publishers : New York, 1937.

TSAMERIAN, I. P., and RONIN, S. L., *Equality of Rights between Races and Nationalities in the USSR*, UNESCO : Paris, 1962.

VITVITSKY, N. P., *The Moscow Trial, April, 1933*, compiled by W. P. Coates, National Hands Off Russia Committee : London, 1933.

VLADIMIROV, LEONID, *The Russians*, Pall Mall : London, 1968.

WEBB, S. J., and B., *Soviet Communism: A New Civilisation?*, 2 vols., Longmans : London, 1935.

WEISSBERG, ALEX, *Conspiracy of Silence*, Hamish Hamilton : London, 1952. Published in America under the title *Accused*, Simon & Schuster : New York, 1951.

WERTH, ALEXANDER, *The Khrushchev Phase*, Robert Hale : London, 1961. Published in America under the title *Russia under Khrushchev*, Hill & Wang : New York, 1962.

WOLFE, BERTRAM D., *Three Who Made a Revolution*, Thames & Hudson : London, 1956; Dial Press : New York, 1948.

—— *Khrushchev and Stalin's Ghost; Text, Background and Meaning of Khrushchev's Secret Report to the 20th Party Congress on the Night of 24-25 February, 1956*, Praeger : New York, 1957.

WOLIN, SIMON, and SLUSSER, ROBERT, M., *The Soviet Secret Police*, Methuen : London; Praeger : New York, 1957.

ZINGER, L., *Dos Benaite Folk* (The Rejuvenated People), Moscow, 1941.

INDEX

DATE DUE
